Command and Creation

The Institute of Ismaili Studies

Ismaili Texts and Translations Series, 25

Editorial Board: Farhad Daftary (general editor), Wilferd Madelung (consulting editor), Orkhan Mir-Kasimov (series editor), Carmela Baffioni, Nader El-Bizri, Heinz Halm, Hermann Landolt, Mehdi Mohaghegh, Roy Mottahedeh, Azim Nanji, Ismail K. Poonawala, Ayman F. Sayyid, Paul E. Walker

Previously published titles:

1. Ibn al-Haytham. *The Advent of the Fatimids: A Contemporary Shi'i Witness*. An edition and English translation of Ibn al-Haytham's *Kitāb al-Munāẓarāt*, by Wilferd Madelung and Paul E. Walker (2000).
2. Muḥammad b. ʿAbd al-Karīm al-Shahrastānī. *Struggling with the Philosopher: A Refutation of Avicenna's Metaphysics*. A new Arabic edition and English translation of al-Shahrastānī's *Kitāb al-Muṣāraʿa*, by Wilferd Madelung and Toby Mayer (2001).
3. Jaʿfar b. Manṣūr al-Yaman. *The Master and the Disciple: An Early Islamic Spiritual Dialogue*. Arabic edition and English translation of Jaʿfar b. Manṣūr al-Yaman's *Kitāb al-ʿĀlim wa'l-ghulām*, by James W. Morris (2001).
4. Idrīs ʿImād al-Dīn. *The Fatimids and their Successors in Yaman: The History of an Islamic Community*. Arabic edition and English summary of Idrīs ʿImād al-Dīn's *ʿUyūn al-akhbār*, vol. 7, by Ayman Fuʾad Sayyid, in collaboration with Paul E. Walker and Maurice A. Pomerantz (2002).
5. Naṣīr al-Dīn Ṭūsī. *Paradise of Submission: A Medieval Treatise on Ismaili Thought*. A new Persian edition and English translation of Naṣīr al-Dīn Ṭūsī's *Rawḍa-yi taslīm*, by S. J. Badakhchani

with an introduction by Hermann Landolt and a philosophical commentary by Christian Jambet (2005).

6. al-Qāḍī al-Nuʿmān. *Founding the Fatimid State: The Rise of an Early Islamic Empire*. An annotated English translation of al-Qāḍī al-Nuʿmān's *Iftitāḥ al-daʿwa*, by Hamid Haji (2006).
7. Idrīs ʿImād al-Dīn. *ʿUyūn al-akhbār wa-funūn al-āthār*. Arabic critical edition in 7 volumes by Ahmad Chleilat, Mahmoud Fakhoury, Yousef S. Fattoum, Muhammad Kamal, Maʾmoun al-Sagherji and Ayman Fuʾad Sayyid (2007–2014).
8. Aḥmad b. Ibrāhīm al-Naysābūrī. *Degrees of Excellence: A Fatimid Treatise on Leadership in Islam*. A New Arabic Edition and English Translation of al-Naysābūrī's *Ithbāt al-imāma*, by Arzina Lalani (2009).
9. Ḥamīd al-Dīn Aḥmad b. ʿAbd Allāh al-Kirmānī. *Master of the Age: An Islamic Treatise on the Necessity of the Imamate*. A critical edition of the Arabic text and English translation of Ḥamīd al-Dīn Aḥmad b. ʿAbd Allāh al-Kirmānī's *al-Maṣābīḥ fī ithbāt al-imāma*, by Paul E. Walker (2007).
10. *Orations of the Fatimid Caliphs: Festival Sermons of the Ismaili Imams*. An edition of the Arabic texts and English translation of Fatimid *khuṭbas*, by Paul E. Walker (2009).
11. Taqī al-Dīn Aḥmad b. ʿAlī al-Maqrīzī. *Towards a Shiʿi Mediterranean Empire: Fatimid Egypt and the Founding of Cairo*. The reign of the Imam-caliph al-Muʿizz, from al-Maqrīzī's *Ittiʿāẓ al-ḥunafāʾ bi-akhbār al-aʾimma al-Fāṭimiyyīn al-khulafāʾ*, translated by Shainool Jiwa (2009).
12. Taqī al-Dīn Aḥmad b. ʿAlī al-Maqrīzī. *Ittiʿāẓ al-ḥunafāʾ bi-akhbār al-aʾimma al-Fāṭimiyyīn al-khulafāʾ*. Arabic critical edition in 4 volumes, with an introduction and notes by Ayman F. Sayyid (2010).
13. Naṣīr al-Dīn Ṭūsī. *Shiʿi Interpretations of Islam: Three Treatises on Theology and Eschatology*. A Persian edition and English

translation of Naṣīr al-Dīn Ṭūsī's *Tawallā wa tabarrā*, *Maṭlūb al-mu'minīn* and *Āghāz wa anjām*, by S. J. Badakhchani (2010).

14. al-Mu'ayyad al-Shīrāzī. *Mount of Knowledge, Sword of Eloquence: Collected Poems of an Ismaili Muslim Scholar in Fatimid Egypt*. A translation from the original Arabic of al-Mu'ayyad al-Shīrāzī's *Dīwān*, translated by Mohamed Adra (2011).
15. Aḥmad b. Ibrāhīm al-Naysābūrī. *A Code of Conduct: A Treatise on the Etiquette of the Fatimid Ismaili Mission*. A critical Arabic edition and English translation of Aḥmad b. Ibrāhīm al-Naysābūrī's *Risāla al-mūjaza al-kāfiya fī ādāb al-du'āt*, by Verena Klemm and Paul E. Walker with Susanne Karam (2011).
16. Manṣūr al-'Azīzī al-Jawdharī. *Inside the Immaculate Portal: A History from Early Fatimid Archives*. A new edition and English translation of Manṣūr al-'Azīzī al-Jawdharī's biography of al-Ustādh Jawdhar, the *Sīrat al-Ustādh Jawdhar*, edited and translated by Hamid Haji (2012).
17. Nāṣir-i Khusraw. *Between Reason and Revelation: Twin Wisdoms Reconciled*. An annotated English translation of Nāṣir-i Khusraw's *Kitāb-i Jāmi' al-ḥikmatayn*, translated by Eric Ormsby (2012).
18. al-Qāḍī al-Nu'mān. *The Early History of Ismaili Jurisprudence: Law and Society under the Fatimids*. An Arabic edition and English translation of al-Qāḍī al-Nu'mān's *Kitāb minhāj al-farā'id*, edited and translated by Agostino Cilardo (2012).
19. Ḥātim b. Ibrāhīm al-Ḥāmidī. *The Precious Gift of the Hearts and Good Cheer for Those in Distress. On the Organisation and History of the Yamanī Fatimid Da'wa*. A critical edition of the Arabic text and summary English translation of Ḥātim b. Ibrāhīm al-Ḥāmidī's *Tuḥfat al-qulūb wa furjat al-makrūb*, by Abbas Hamdani (2012).
20. Abū Ṭāhir Ismā'īl al-Manṣūr bi'llāh. *The Shi'i Imamate: A Fatimid Interpretation*. An Arabic edition and English translation

of al-Manṣūr's *Tathbīt al-imāma* attributed to Abū Ṭāhir Ismāʿīl al-Manṣūr bi'llāh, edited and translated by Sami Makarem (2013).

21. Idrīs ʿImād al-Dīn. *The Founder of Cairo: The Fatimid Imam-Caliph al-Muʿizz and his Era*. An English translation of the section on al-Muʿizz from Idrīs ʿImād al-Dīn's *ʿUyūn al-akhbār*, edited and translated by Shainool Jiwa (2013).
22. Ibn al-Walīd. *Avicenna's Allegory on the Soul: An Ismaili Interpretation*. An Arabic edition and English translation of Ibn al-Walīd's *al-Risāla al-mufīda*, edited by Wilferd Madelung and translated and introduced by Toby Mayer (2015).
23. Ḥasan-i Maḥmūd-i Kātib. *Spiritual Resurrection in Shiʿi Islam: An Early Ismaili Treatise on the Doctrine of* Qiyāmat. A new Persian edition and English translation of the *Haft bāb* by Ḥasan-i Maḥmūd-i Kātib, edited and translated by S. J. Badakhchani (2017).
24. Muḥammad Ḥasan al-Ḥusaynī, Aga Khan I. *The First Aga Khan: Memoirs of the 46th Ismaili Imam*. A Persian edition and English translation of the *ʿIbrat-afzā* of Muḥammad Ḥasan al-Ḥusaynī, also known as Ḥasan ʿAlī Shāh, edited and translated by Daniel Beben and Daryoush Mohammad Poor (2018).

Command and Creation
A Shiʿi Cosmological Treatise

A Persian edition and English translation of
Muḥammad al-Shahrastānī's *Majlis-i maktūb*

by

Daryoush Mohammad Poor

I.B.TAURIS
LONDON • NEW YORK • OXFORD • NEW DELHI • SYDNEY
in association with
THE INSTITUTE OF ISMAILI STUDIES
LONDON, 2021

I.B. TAURIS
Bloomsbury Publishing Plc
50 Bedford Square, London, WC1B 3DP, UK
1385 Broadway, New York, NY 10018, USA

In association with The Institute of Ismaili Studies
Aga Khan Centre, 10 Handyside Street, London N1C 4DN
www.iis.ac.uk

First published in Great Britain 2021

Cover design: Adriana Brioso

A catalogue record for this book is available from the British Library.

A catalog record for this book is available from the Library of Congress.

ISBN: HB: 978-0-7556-0296-4
PB: 978-0-7556-0297-1
ePDF: 978-0-7556-0298-8
eBook: 978-0-7556-0299-5

Series: Ismaili Texts and Translations Series

Typeset by RefineCatch Ltd, Bungay, Suffolk

The Institute of Ismaili Studies

The Institute of Ismaili Studies was established in 1977 with the object of promoting scholarship and learning on Islam, in the historical as well as contemporary contexts, and a better understanding of its relationship with other societies and faiths.

The Institute's programmes encourage a perspective which is not confined to the theological and religious heritage of Islam, but seeks to explore the relationship of religious ideas to broader dimensions of society and culture. The programmes thus encourage an interdisciplinary approach to the materials of Islamic history and thought. Particular attention is also given to issues of modernity that arise as Muslims seek to relate their heritage to the contemporary situation.

Within the Islamic tradition, the Institute's programmes promote research on those areas which have, to date, received relatively little attention from scholars. These include the intellectual and literary expressions of Shiʿism in general, and Ismailism in particular.

In the context of Islamic societies, the Institute's programmes are informed by the full range and diversity of cultures in which Islam is practised today, from the Middle East, South and Central Asia, and Africa to the industrialized societies of the West, thus taking into consideration the variety of contexts which shape the ideals, beliefs and practices of the faith.

These objectives are realised through concrete programmes and activities organized and implemented by various departments of the

Institute. The Institute also collaborates periodically, on a programme-specific basis, with other institutions of learning in the United Kingdom and abroad.

The Institute's academic publications fall into a number of inter-related categories:

1. Occasional papers or essays addressing broad themes of the relationship between religion and society, with special reference to Islam.
2. Monographs exploring specific aspects of Islamic faith and culture, or the contributions of individual Muslim thinkers or writers.
3. Editions or translations of significant primary or secondary texts.
4. Translations of poetic or literary texts which illustrate the rich heritage of spiritual, devotional and symbolic expressions in Muslim history.
5. Works on Ismaili history and thought, and the relationship of the Ismailis to other traditions, communities and schools of thought in Islam.
6. Proceedings of conferences and seminars sponsored by the Institute.
7. Bibliographical works and catalogues which document manuscripts, printed texts and other source materials.

This book falls into category three listed above.

In facilitating these and other publications, the Institute's sole aim is to encourage original research and analysis of relevant issues. While every effort is made to ensure that the publications are of a high academic standard, there is naturally bound to be a diversity of views, ideas and interpretations. As such, the opinions expressed in these publications must be understood as belonging to their authors alone.

To

my daughter Toranj

گر پیر مغان مرشد من شد چه تفاوت

در هیچ سری نیست که سری ز خدا نیست

And if the Elder of the Magi were to become my guide,
what difference would it make?
There is no head that is not party to God's mystery!
Ḥāfiẓ

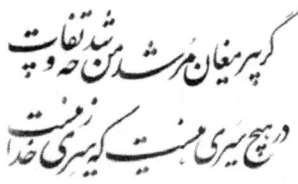

Contents

Preface xiv

Introduction 1

Majlis-i maktūb-i munʿaqid dar Khwārazm (English translation) 71

Select Bibliography 119
Index 123
Index of Qurʾanic citations 129

Index of Qurʾanic citations (Arabic)

Majlis-i maktūb-i munʿaqid dar Khwārazm (Persian edition)

Preface

My journey into the study of Ismaili theology and philosophy began in my very early years when I inherited a rather large corpus of Ismaili works from my father. But since I was only ten years old, my engagement with those texts was nothing but curious probing into an unknown territory. A few years later, I began reading more closely as many Persian and Arabic medieval Ismaili texts as I could get my hands on. Instrumental in all of this was Mr Gholamreza Mirshahi in Mashhad who always encouraged me and kindly made available to me materials I would otherwise have had difficulty obtaining. It was during this period, about twenty years ago, when I first encountered the text of the *Majlis-i maktūb*. I would like to express my gratitude to him here for originally drawing my attention to this text.

There are many other individuals to whom I owe thanks for their assistance in the process of preparing this publication. The inception, development and continuation of this work would not have been possible without the kind patronage of Dr Farhad Daftary who never wavered in supporting and encouraging me in the completion of this work. His patience and grace in allowing me the time and the space to further polish the text gave me the peace of mind I could hardly find elsewhere. He also generously reviewed the English introduction several times and made detailed comments and suggestions for improvement. For all of this, I am deeply grateful to him. I have repeatedly consulted Dr S. J. Badakhchani on textual references in other Nizārī Ismaili works, discussed a number of subtle points with him and received valuable feedback which has helped improve this edition. In the final stages of the preparation of this edition, he patiently sat with me on several occasions to do a thorough proof-reading of the Persian text, which proved to be extremely helpful in rectifying some oversights. His contributions, even beyond the scope of this text, are immeasurable for any study of Nizārī Ismaili texts and I am greatly indebted to his work and the opportunity to consult him frequently.

Among my colleagues at The Institute of Ismaili Studies in London, I have had exemplary interlocutors who were immensely helpful with disentangling the text of the *Majlis*. I am deeply grateful to Professor Hermann Landolt who offered recommendations for the reading of the text and to Professor Wilferd Madelung who made useful comments on the early drafts of the introduction. I am particularly grateful to Dr Toby Mayer, who is the forerunner in publishing and studying al-Shahrastānī's works in English. He kindly reviewed the English translation thoroughly and as a result we have a much more improved version. His review and comments on the English introduction were also a source of encouragement as I was completing the latest version of it. I should also like to thank Dr Karim Javan with whom I have often discussed delicate doctrinal and historical points about Ismaili philosophy in general and al-Shahrastānī in particular; he kindly went through the Persian text and suggested some revisions. I should also like to thank Dr Mohammad Rasekh whom I have often consulted regarding the translation and understanding of certain Arabic phrases and passages in the text.

I am also grateful to Dr Mohammad Reza Shafiee Kadkani with whom I consulted on reading some sections of the text. I should also like to thank Mr Alireza Kadivar in Iran, who kindly made available to me some of the books I needed in the course of this research. I am also grateful to Dr Sadra Sadeh for reviewing the first drafts of the introduction and making useful comments. The completion of this work would not have been possible without the meticulous and careful editing of my colleague, Dr Isabel Miller. I am deeply indebted to her for the exemplary work she has done in the final preparation of this work. I am also grateful to Mr Keramat Fathinia for kindly accepting to do the calligraphy in the dedication page and to Mr Nasir Allahdini for finalising the graphics of the image.

Last but not least, the completion of this work would not have been possible without the support and patience of my wife, Elahe Kianpoor. Her contribution to my scholarly work cannot be measured in words; she has been present in the spirit of my academic work for which I am infinitely grateful. The final revisions of this work were completed during the Covid-19 pandemic when we had to spend all our time under conditions of lockdown; it would have been inconceivable to finish this had it not been for the patience and cooperation of my family.

Any errors and shortcomings in the present work, whether in translation or in the edition of the Persian text are entirely mine.

Daryoush Mohammad Poor
London, June 2020

Introduction

Abu'l-Fatḥ Muḥammad b. Abu'l-Qāsim ʿAbd al-Karīm b. Abū Bakr Aḥmad al-Shahrastānī, commonly understood to be a Shāfiʿī, Ashʿarī, Persian scholar who also bore the honorifics Afḍal, Ḥujjat al-Ḥaqq and Tāj al-Dīn, is known through his numerous important writings, some twenty in all, and in particular his magnum opus, the heresiographical work, *al-Milal wa'l-niḥal.* He was born in 467/1074, 469/1076 or 479/1086, in Shahristāna in Khurāsān. Yāqūt al-Ḥamawī (d. 626/1225) gives the first of these dates in his *Muʿjam al-buldān*,[1] deriving it apparently from the *Taʾrīkh-i Khwārazm*[2] from which he translated the biography of al-Shahrastānī.

Most of the biographies of al-Shahrastānī are taken from the narratives of three of his contemporaries. The first is Ibn al-Samʿānī (d. 562/1166),[3] the second is Ẓahīr al-Dīn Bayhaqī[4] (d. 565/1169) and the third, Abū Muḥammad Maḥmūd b. Arsalān al-Khwārazmī (d. 568/1172), however, his *Taʾrīkh-i Khwārazm* is now lost and only fragments of it are quoted by Yāqūt.

As regards other source material, in his notes, Ibn Khallikān (d. 681/1282)[5] gives 467/1074 as the date of al-Shahrastānī's birth, although without quoting any source, and this date is accepted by

1 Yāqūt al-Ḥamawī, *Muʿjam al-buldān*, ed. F. Wustenfeld (Leipzig, 1866–1870), vol. 3, p. 339.
2 The place name Khwārazm is pronounced Khārazm.
3 For a biography of Ibn al-Samʿānī, see R. Sellheim, 'al-Samʿānī', *EI2*. Consulted online on 4 June 2020 http://dx.doi.org.iij.idm.oclc.org/10.1163/1573-3912_islam_COM_0994.
4 See D. M. Dunlop, 'al-Bayhaḳī', *EI2*. Consulted online on 4 June 2020 http://dx.doi.org.iij.idm.oclc.org/10.1163/1573-3912_islam_SIM_1316.
5 Aḥmād b. Muḥammad Ibn Khallikān, *Wafayāt al-aʿyān*, ed. Iḥsān ʿAbbās (Beirut, 1968–1972), vol. 4, p. 274.

Abu'l-Fidā' (d. 732/1331) in his *Ta'rīkh*.[6] However, Ibn al-Sam'ānī heard the third date from al-Shahrastānī himself and gave this date in his *Dhayl*[7] and then Ibn Khallikān and al-Subkī[8] reported it from him. Since there is no reason to choose either of the first two dates, the evidence of a contemporary trustworthy source reporting the date from al-Shahrastānī himself should be reliable. So, it can reasonably be said that al-Shahrastānī was born in 479/1086.

In the primary sources there are virtually no references to the family of al-Shahrastānī. However, judging from the *kunya*s given to his father and grandfather, one can infer that individuals from this family were scholars in Shahristāna.

Early life

Al-Shahrastānī received his early education in Shahristāna and Gurgānj (Jurjāniyya) studying with the scholars there, who were like those of any other town in the Islamic lands of that era. However, in the late fifth/eleventh century, Nīshābūr was the greatest centre of learning in the Islamic east, largely as a result of the establishment of the Nizamiyya madrasa and so al-Shahrastānī moved on to Nīshābūr in his quest for knowledge. The Nizamiyya was a centre of Ash'arī *kalām* and there he became a proponent of it. According to Ibn Arsalān al-Khwārazmī, in Nīshābūr al-Shahrastānī studied jurisprudence with Abu'l-Muẓaffar Aḥmad Khwāfī and Abū Naṣr Qushayrī, the principles of *kalām* with Abu'l-Qāsim Anṣārī and *ḥadīth* with Abu'l-Ḥasan

[6] The full title of his work is *Mukhtaṣar ta'rīkh al-bashar*. For a biography of Abu'l-Fidā', see H. A. R. Gibb, 'Abu'l-Fidā', *EI2*. Consulted online on 3 June 2020 http://dx.doi.org.iij.idm.oclc.org/10.1163/1573-3912_islam_SIM_0182.

[7] See Ibn Khallikān above.

[8] See 'Abd al-Wahhāb al-Subkī, *Ṭabaqāt al-Shāfi'iyya al-kubrā*, ed. 'Abd al-Fattāḥ Muḥammad al-Ḥulw and Maḥmūd Muḥammad al-Ṭanāḥī (Cairo, 1383/1964), vol. 6, pp. 128–130.

Madā'inī.[9] The Niẓāmiyya madrasas, founded across the eastern lands of the caliphate by the vizier of the Great Saljūqs, Niẓām al-Mulk, were the pre-eminent centres of Sunni learning and the lecturers there approached their fields of learning with sophistication and subtlety. Only the most talented students could attend their lectures and, one can be certain that al-Shahrastānī was more talented than most. His reputation as someone endowed with vast knowledge, a sharp memory, an enthralling eloquence including the use of rhyming language and a subtle use of vocabulary and terms, all accompanied by tolerance and moral courage, maturity of thought, a mastery of Persian and Arabic literature and philology, as well as his competence in traditional and philosophical fields of learning, brought him to prominence at the Niẓāmiyya. His knowledge was such that Ibn Arsalān al-Khwārazmī said of him, 'If he had not had corrupt beliefs and had not been inclined to heresy, he would have been an imam.'[10] At some point after this it appears that he moved to Khwārazm and lived there for a few years.

Scholarly activity

Al-Shahrastānī's preoccupation with the rational and philosophical sciences and his support of the philosophers and their beliefs, led the scholars of his time to call him someone engrossed in the 'darkness of philosophy' (*ẓulumāt-i falsafa*).[11] Individuals such as Ibn Arsalān al-Khwārazmī and Ibn al-Sam'ānī, were amazed that, given his profound

[9] See Yāqūt al-Ḥamawī, *Mu'jam al-buldān,* vol. 3, p. 339. All that Yāqūt says about al-Shahrastānī is taken from the lost work of Ibn Arsalān al-Khwārazmī. For a detailed account of al-Shahrastānī's teachers see, Toby Mayer, *Keys to the Arcana: Shahrastānī's Esoteric Commentary on the Qur'ān: A Translation of the Commentary on Sūrat al-Fātiḥa from Muḥammad b. 'Abd al-Karīm al-Shahrastānī's Mafātīḥ al-asrār wa maṣābīḥ al-abrār* (Oxford, 2009), pp. 3–5.

[10] Cited in Yāqūt al-Ḥamawī, *Mu'jam al-buldān,* vol. 3, p. 339.

[11] Ibid.

knowledge and maturity of intellect, he adhered to what the Ismailis were inclined to. In his *al-Taḥbīr*, al-Samʿānī says that 'he was suspected of being inclined to the people of innovation, meaning the Ismailis, and their misguidedness (*kān muttahaman bi al-mayl ilā ahl al-bidaʿ yaʿnī al-Ismāʿīliyya wa'l-daʿwat ilā ḍalālatihim*)'.[12]

So it appears that during his time in Khwārazm, which lasted ended in 510/1116, al-Shahrastānī was accused of having an inclination for the faith of the *taʿlīmiyya* or the *bāṭiniyya*, that is to say the Ismailis. What Ibn Arsalān Khwārazmī, as cited by Yāqūt, calls the 'affair' (*amr*) or 'thing', and implicitly attributes to him, is adherence to the doctrines of the *bāṭiniyya* and Shiʿism.[13]

At the time, even though Khwārazm had developed significantly under the rule of the Khwārazmshāhs, the city of Khwārazm could not have rivalled Marw and Nīshābūr, two of the great cities of Khurasān, or Baghdad, the ʿAbbasid capital in Iraq. Thus, at the time of al-Shahrastānī scholars seeking to advance their learning and their careers went to study at the colleges in Khurasān or in Baghdad.

According to al-Khwārazmī, al-Shahrastānī travelled to the Ḥijāz to perform the *ḥajj* in 510/1116 and afterwards he went to Baghdad. At the time, Asʿad Mīhanī (from the village of Mīhna) was a renowned teacher at the Niẓāmiyya college of Baghdad. Mīhanī was close to the court of the ʿAbbasid caliph, al-Mustaẓhir bi'llāh (d. 512/1118), to whom al-Ghazālī dedicated his famous anti-Ismaili work, the *Mustaẓhirī*. Mihanī encouraged al-Shahrastānī, whom he had known earlier in Khwārazm, to give lectures and sermons in the Niẓāmiyya.[14]

The power and eloquence of al-Shahrastānī's speech may be imagined given the eloquence of his writings, notably the *Majlis*, and his sermons became popular during the three years that he stayed in

[12] See ʿAbd al-Karīm b. Muḥammad al-Samʿāni, *al-Taḥbīr fi'l-muʿjam al-kabīr*, ed. Munīra Nājī Sālim (Baghdad, 1975), vol. 2, p. 161.

[13] Yāqūt al-Ḥamawī, *Muʿjam al-buldān*, vol. 3, p. 339.

[14] See Yāqūt, citing Ibn Arsalān, *Muʿjam al-buldān*, vol. 3, p. 339: '*wa kān baynahumā ṣuḥbatun sālifatun bi Khwārazm*'.

Baghdad. His lectures and sermons were attended by the scholars and senior figures of the ʿAbbasid capital, along with large numbers of ordinary people. However, in 514/1120 he left Baghdad and returned to the east, spending the rest of his life in the towns and cities of Khurāsān. He went first to Marw-i Shāh-i Jahān and was able to enter the service of Sulṭān Sanjar as opposed to remaining a marginal figure in the ʿAbbasid state. Through the patronage of Sanjar's vizier, Naṣīr al-Dīn Maḥmūd b. Muẓaffar al-Marwazī, who had been the chief tax accountant (*mustawfī*), al-Shahrastānī was appointed a *nāʾib-i dīwān*.[15] Installed in Marw, he began writing his scholarly works with the encouragement and sponsorship of Sanjar and his vizier, and later Majd al-Dīn ʿAlī b. Jaʿfar al-Mūsawī, the *naqīb* of the ʿAlids of Tirmidh.[16]

He lived in Marw for over twenty years, between 514/1120 and 536/1141. During this period two of his most important works were produced, namely *al-Milal wa'l-niḥal* and *Nihāyat al-aqdām fī ʿilm al-kalām*. The *Milal* is well known as al-Shahrastānī's heseriography which presents histories of different denominations and religions. There are several editions of this book in Arabic and translations of it in Persian and one partial translation in English. The *Nihāya* consists of a discussion of twenty philosophical problems or principles in the course of which he criticizes philosophers. This work was edited and partially translated by Alfred Guillaume as *The Summa Philosophiae of al-Shahrastānī* in 1934.

The years which al-Shahrastānī spent at Sulṭān Sanjar's court coincided with the beginning of the reign of the second lord of

15 See M. R. Jalalī Nāʾīnī, *Sharḥ-i aḥwāl wa āthār-i ḥujjat al-ḥaqq Muḥammad b. ʿAbd al-Karīm b. Aḥmad Shahrastānī* (Tehran, 1343 Sh./1964), p. 14; G. Monnot, 'al-Shahrastānī', *EI2*, vol. 9, pp. 220–222.

16 The details given so far about al-Shahrastānī's biography are mainly taken from the introduction to M. R. Jalālī Nāʾīnī, ed., *Du maktūb az Muḥammad b. ʿAbd al-Karīm Shahrastānī* (Tehran, 1369 Sh./1990), pp. 3–27.

Alamūt and leader of the Nizārī Ismaili community, Kiyā Buzurg-Umīd (518–532/1124–1138). And it was during these early years of the reign of Kiyā Buzurg-Umīd, in 520/1126, that Sanjar renewed his attacks against the Nizārīs after a haitus, possibly a truce, which had lasted for almost two decades.[17] Considering al-Shahrastānī's appointment by Sanjar as his confidant (*ṣāḥib-i sirr*), Muḥammad Taqī Dānishpazhūh has put forward the argument that the 'secret' in this title was probably a reference to Sanjar's conciliatory relationship with the Ismailis at the time, which is known about. What Dānishpazhūh seems to be suggesting is that there was some kind of rapprochement with the Ismailis on the part of Sanjar, in addition to any possible military agreement or truce.[18]

In 521/1127 al-Shahrastānī completed his *al-Milal*. However, he then fell out of favour with Sanjar.[19] And in 526/1132, al-Shahrastānī's patron, Naṣīr al-Dīn Maḥmūd was removed from office. There are ambiguous references in the *Muṣāra'a* to 'the trials of the time and the blows of misfortune' which may refer to these events.[20] If the date of Sanjar's renewed assaults on the Nizārīs is taken into account, these events at court could be seen as part of an anti-Nizārī policy, at a time when anyone perceived as a Nizārī infiltrator might well suffer ill-treatment, and al-Shahrastānī's remarks may be an allusion to such events.[21] This persecution could very well have included al-Shahrastānī given the rumours about his affiliations with the Nizārīs and be the explanation for his fall from grace at court.

[17] See F. Daftary, *The Ismā'īlīs, their History and Doctrines* (2nd ed., Cambridge, 2007), p. 345.

[18] See Muḥammad Taqī Dānishpazhūh, 'Dā'i al-du'āt Taj al-Dīn Shahrastāna', *Nāmah-yi āstān-i quds*, 26 and 27 (1967), pp. 71–80.

[19] See T. Mayer, *Keys to the Arcana*, p. 16.

[20] Ibid.

[21] Ibid. See here for references to the allegations and suspicions of al-Sam'ānī. Also, see Muḥammad Bahrāmī, 'Girāyish-i madhhabī-yi Shahrastānī, ṣāḥib-i tafsīr-i Mafātīḥ al-asrār', *'Ulūm-i Qur'ān wa Ḥadīth: Pazhūhishhāy-i Qur'ānī*, 21–22 (2000), pp. 358–359.

However, little else is known about al-Shahrastānī's life during his time in Marw. After this period of silence, the sources say that in the year 536/1141, when at the battle of the Qaṭwān steppe Sanjar was defeated by the Qarā Khitā'ī, a nomad polity in Central Asia, who then advanced on the capital and sacked it, al-Shahrastānī fled Marw and apparently went to Tirmidh.[22] It is likely that it was in Tirmidh that he wrote another important work, the *Muṣāraʿat al-falāsifa*, since it is dedicated to the *naqīb* of Tirmidh, Majd al-Dīn al-Mūsawī. In it al-Shahrastānī discusses seven issues in philosophy and *kalām* and criticizes much of Ibn Sīnā's philosophy.[23] An edition and English translation of the *Muṣāraʿa* was published by Wilferd Madelung and Toby Mayer in 2001. The *Mafātīḥ al-asrār wa masābīḥ al-abrār*, a Qur'anic commentary, now incomplete, should also be included among works written around this time, possibly in Tirmidh since the autograph copy of the first volume was written between 538 and 540/1143 and 1145.

Al-Shahrastānī then returned to his birthplace, Shahristana, and it was here that the *Majlis* was completed. The Ismaili tenor of al-Shahrastānī's writing was now far more explicit and unequivocal. Possibly because he was no longer in Sanjar's service, he felt could express himself with greater clarity than had been possible hitherto. For example, in the *Milal*, his account of the doctrines of Ḥasan-i Ṣabbāḥ contains criticism but in later works, as can be seen in the present edition,[24] he uses exactly the kind of arguments that it is known Ḥasan-i Ṣabbāḥ deployed. This indicates that he was practising *taqiyya* while he was in the employ of the Saljūqs and can be seen as corroboration of the argument that he was, very likely, a member of the Ismaili *daʿwa*.

22 See T. Mayer, *Keys to the Arcana*, p. 17.
23 To which al-Ṭūsī responded later in his *Maṣāriʿ al-muṣāriʿ*, see Naṣīr al-Dīn al-Ṭūsī, *Maṣāriʿ al-muṣāriʿ*, ed. Wilferd Madelung (Tehran, 2004).
24 See the present edition of the *Majlis*, paragraphs 69 and 78.

Al-Shahrastānī died in Shaʿbān 548/November 1153. Mayer cites Ādharshab's note in his introduction to his 1386 Sh./2008 edition of the *Mafātīḥ* regarding the possible site of al-Shahrastānī's tomb 'in the ruins of the old town of Shahrastāna' where a 'grave was found which locals simply refer to as "Mulla Muḥammad's grave"'.[25]

Posthumous connections with the Nizārī Ismailis

After his death al-Shahrastānī's writings became central to the intellectual direction that the Ismailis now took, as can be seen in almost every surviving text of the later Alamūt period, most notably al-Ṭūsī's *Rawḍa* and *Sayr wa sulūk*.

Al-Shahrastānī died in the middle of the reign of the third lord of Alamūt, Muḥammad b. Buzurg-Umīd (532–557/1138–1162). Ḥasan II, the fourth lord of Alamūt, who declared the *qiyāmat* or spiritual resurrection and subsequently claimed the Imamate, was born in 520/1126 which means that during the final years of al-Shahrastānī's life, Ḥasan II was in his early youth. It was in 559/1164, little over a decade after al-Shahrastānī's death that Ḥasan II declared the *qiyāmat*. The intellectual and doctrinal content of the *qiyāmat* is closely connected to the later works of al-Shahrastānī. In very simple terms, the era of spiritual resurrection is the era in which a few believers who have reached the stage of unity (*waḥdat*) and have gone beyond the stages of contrariety (*taḍādd*) and gradual hierarchy (*tarattub*) are no longer required to observe the physical rituals of worship. This is a point which is extensively discussed in the *Majlis*.[26] This narrative of the resurrection – specifically using the terms contrariety (*taḍādd*), hierarchy (*tarattub*) and unity (*waḥdat*) – seems to have been

[25] See T. Mayer, *Keys to the Arcana*, p. 17.
[26] See paragraphs 51, 79, 96 and 98.

deployed initially by al-Shahrastānī in his *Mafātīḥ* and *Majlis* and then greatly so in Ḥasan II's elaboration of his doctrine of *qiyāmat*.[27] Al-Shahrastānī's work can be seen as a prelude to and an earlier rendering of what became the declaration of *qiyāmat*. It is in this way that the impact of al-Shahrastānī's work on later Nizārī thought is evident.

The *Majlis-i Maktūb* and its significance for Ismaili studies

The relatively short work edited and translated here is a clear demonstration of al-Shahrastānī's direct role in the articulation and reorientation of Nizārī doctrine and what he himself called *al-daʿwa al-jadīda* or 'the new preaching' in his chapter on the *Taʿlīmī*s, that is to say the Ismailis, in the *Milal*.[28] The theme of the *Majlis* concerns the Divine command (*amr*), that is to say the *Kun* or 'Be' (the *kalima*), and creation (*khalq*). Al-Shahrastānī challenges the views of various theological schools as well as those of certain philosophers, such as Ibn Sīnā, and their engagement with the concept of God and His attributes. He mentions specifically the Ashʿarīs, the Muʿtazila and the Karrāmīs (who were quite active during his time)[29] in paragraph 54 of the present text. Given that in the past al-Shahrastānī has been described as an Ashʿarī *mutakallim*, his criticisms here – for instance saying their positions are in conflict with the Word of God – makes evident the fact that he did not in fact belong to any of these groups. Shortly after this paragraph, in paragraph 56, he invokes a saying of

27 Also, see the translation in T. Mayer, *Keys to the Arcana*, pp. 113–118 for use of the specific Nizārī Ismaili terms '*taḍādd*' and '*tarattub*'.

28 See al-Shahrastānī, *al-Milal wa'l-niḥal*, ed. Amīr ʿAlī Muhannā and ʿAlī Ḥasan Fāʿūr (Beirut, 1414/1993), p. 231.

29 See C. E. Bosworth, 'Karrāmiyya', *EI2*. Consulted online on 4 June 2020 http://dx.doi.org.iij.idm.oclc.org/10.1163/1573-3912_islam_COM_0452.

Jaʿfar al-Ṣādiq in contrast to the position of the *mutakallims* once again firmly demonstrating his Shiʿi position. Later in paragraph 76, he expands his criticism to the *Mushabbiha* while once again criticizing the three theological schools and then adds all philosophers to this category. This particular paragraph is a succinct summary of what we find in the writings of the Ismaili *dāʿīs* al-Sijistānī, particularly in the *Kashf al-maḥjūb,*[30] and Nāṣir-i Khusraw (both pre-dating al-Shahrastānī), and in the *Sayr wa sulūk* of al-Ṭūsī (who came after al-Shahrastānī). Based on al-Shahrastānī's judgements of the views of these groups, it can safely be argued that he is neither an Ashʿārī, nor a Muʿtazilī, a Karrāmī, a *Mushabbih,* nor yet a philosopher. Moreover, in this paragraph, al-Shahrastānī uses terms which incidentally he had attributed earlier to Ḥasan-i Ṣabbāḥ,[31] to show why these different groups have gone astray.[32]

It should be pointed out that while, as was noted earlier, some of al-Shahrastānī's contemporaries accused him of engaging in the study of philosophy, al-Shahrastānī was not a philosopher in the generic sense. What is clearly indicated in the accusation against al-Shahrastānī is his inclination for the Ismailis, who were known to favour the rational sciences. One must make a distinction between philosophy in the general sense of it and its use by the Ismaili *daʿwa.*[33]

30 See Abū Yaʿqūb al-Sijistānī, *Kashf al-maḥjūb*, ed. Henry Corbin (Paris and Tehran, 1327 Sh./1949).

31 See al-Shahrastānī, *al-Milal*, ed. Amīr ʿAlī Muhannā and ʿAlī Ḥasan Fāʿūr, p. 234: '*Inna ilāhunā ilāh Muḥammad*' and hence Ḥasan argues that they must not go into detailed discussions of God's qualities, as the theologians do.

32 See *Majlis*, footnotes to paragraph 78 of the Persian here making a comparison with the reference in the *Mafātīḥ*.

33 I have discussed this point in my chapter, 'Extra-Ismaili Sources and a Shift of Paradigm in Nizārī Ismailism', in Orkhan Mir-Kasimov, ed., *Intellectual Interactions in the Islamic World: The Ismaili Thread* (London, 2020), pp. 219–245.

The genre and content of the *Majlis*

The genre of the *Majlis* is that of a sermon (*waʿẓ*) and it can be compared with the *Majālis-i sabʿa* of Rūmī[34] or the *Majālis* of Saʿdī.[35] In the Ismaili context, it is comparable to the sermons or lectures found in al-Muʾayyad fi'l-Dīn al-Shīrāzī's *al-Majālis al-Muʾayyadiyya*.[36] The genre remained relatively unchanged in classical literature but the content of individual works differed of course, depending on the taste and disposition of the author, as can clearly be seen in the examples of *majālis* just given.

The *Majlis* begins with an explanation of the dyad of *amr* and *khalq*. Then al-Shahrastānī proceeds by adding yet further dyads as he expands his argument. The *Majlis* is a cosmological text. The author is setting out his interpretation of how this world came into existence. He does this by employing certain dyads which the Ismailis held in common with philosophers and Sufis (like the *ẓāhir* and the *bāṭin*), but then invokes further dyads which were used exclusively by the Nizārī Ismailis. These include *mafrūgh* vs. *mustaʾnaf* (accomplished vs. inchoate), *sharīʿat* vs. *qiyāmat* and *taklīf* vs. *taqdīr* (obligation vs. determination).[37] Al-Shahrastānī does not simply expand on these dyads or binaries; he continues to add further layers by using triads as well. In one sense, the text of the *Majlis* might seem to be a carefully crafted piece of art fashioned of the geometrical symmetries that al-Shahrastānī continually discovers in the Qurʾanic verses and

34 See Jalāl al-Dīn Rūmī, *Majālis-i sabʿa* (*Haft khiṭāba*), ed. Tawfīq Subḥānī (Tehran, 1986).

35 See Mūsliḥ b. ʿAbd Allāḥ Saʿdī, *Kulliyāt*, ed. Muḥammad ʿAlī Furūghī (Tehran, 1379 Sh./2000), pp. 927–946.

36 See al-Muʾayyad fi'l-Dīn al-Shīrāzī, *al-Majālis al-Muʾayyadiyya*, vols 1 (*al-miʾa al-ūlā*) and 3 (*al-miʾa al-thālitha*), ed. Muṣṭafā Ghālib (Beirut, [1974] and 1984); vols 1 and 2 (*al-miʾa al-thāniya*), ed. Ḥātim Ḥamīd al-Dīn (Mumbai, 1395/1975 and Oxford, 1417/1986; re-ed. Mumbai, 1422/2002); vol. 1, ed., Muḥammad ʿAbd al-Ghaffār (Cairo, 1994), p. 338.

37 See, for instance, paragraphs 43, 48, 60, 96, 98, 101 of this edition and translation for examples of al-Shahrastānī's use of these terms.

ḥadīths that he cites frequently in support of his argument. As he proceeds in his narrative of creation using this assembly of terms, he focuses on religious law and its ultimate evolution from the *sharī ʿat* to the *qiyāmat*, and includes his understanding of the role of a present living guide, who is the *qā ʾim* bringing to perfection the mission of all the prophets. Towards the end of the *Majlis*, paragraph 82 onwards in this edition, he turns his attention to the story of Mūsā and Khiḍr adding his commentary on verses from Surat al-Kahf. Al-Shahrastānī uses these verses, which are replete with allegorical themes, to demonstrate his earlier points about creation, command and the obligations of mankind in matters of faith. He explains the difference between the role of the Prophet (here Mūsā) and the Imam/*qā ʾim* (here Khiḍr) in how they guide mankind while neither of them makes the role and function of the other redundant or obsolete. Almost every theme considered here by al-Shahrastānī has parallels in his *Mafātīḥ* and in the notes to the text here comparisons between them are indicated. Reading the text of the *Majlis* and understanding it requires making comparative connections with al-Shahrastānī's other works and later Nizārī Ismaili texts, notably those of al-Ṭūsī.

The close parallel between al-Shahrastānī's narrative in the *Majlis* – and his criticism of the *mutakallims* – and al-Ṭūsī's discussion in *Sayr wa sulūk* written in the following century, should be seen in conjunction with Ḥasan-i Ṣabbāḥ's *Chahār Faṣl* (Four Chapters) written in the fifth/eleventh century,[38] for the dissemination of which to a wider audience al-Shahrastānī was responsible through his quotations of it in the *Milal*. The theme of *Sayr wa sulūk*, al-Ṭūsī's spiritual autobiography, is a discussion of different approaches to the issue of knowing God. The doctrine of *ta ʿlīm* suggested as the

[38] See S. J. Badakhchani, 'Shahrastānī's Account of Ḥasan-i Ṣabbāḥ's Doctrine of Ta ʿlīm', in Mohammad Ali Amir-Moezzi, ed., *Islam: Identité et Alterété: Hommage à Guy Monnot* (Turnhout, 2013), pp. 27–55.

preferred solution to this by the Nizārī Ismailis is closely connected to their ideas about cosmology and creation in which the Imam/*qāʾim* becomes the manifestation of God's command (*amr*). Thus, the discussion in *Sayr wa Sulūk* mirrors the argument presented in the *Majlis*.

Al-Shahrastānī provided a much more extensive and sophisticated Qurʾanic approach to these concepts in his *Mafātīḥ*, specifically on his understanding of the term *ḥanīfiyyat* as opposed to that of *ṣabwa*.[39] Indeed, an examination of al-Shahrastānī's works and all the Nizārī works of the Alamūt period available is required for tracing the evolution of Nizārī thought. Al-Shahrastānī's works, including his *Majlis*, are vital for the understanding of Nizārī doctrine generally and the doctrine of the *qiyāmat* in particular.[40] In the present edition of the *Majlis*, annotation giving some of these parallels has been added. There are numerous further examples but going into further comparative citation is beyond the scope of this introduction and these comparisons have been limited to instances that support the argument for al-Shahrastānī's Ismaili affiliations.

The question of al-Shahrastānī's Ismaili connections is not a particularly new one. As has been referred to and quoted earlier, there are references to his Ismaili leanings in the works of his contemporaries as well as in the writings of medieval scholars from later periods. The extent of al-Shahrastānī's Ismaili connections and whether he had indeed embraced Ismailism was an issue which fell into abeyance

[39] See footnotes to paragraph 62 of this edition for references to the *Mafātīḥ*.

[40] More comparative work is needed in this area. In particular, MSS 916 and 32 in the Ismaili Special Collections Unit at the Institute of Ismaili Studies are relevant. The first of these is dated 1095/1684 and the copyist was Maʿṣūm b. Farrukh Ḥusayn Qāʾinī. It is not easy to establish the exact time of the writing but comparing these fragments with what we know to be undoubtedly of the Alamūt period, we can safely say they are a reflection of the prevailing mood at the time of ʿAlāʾ al-Dīn Muḥammad III. And the content referring to the doctrine of *qiyāmat* in these manuscripts assists in establishing a closer connection between the works of al-Shahrastānī and the rest of the Nizārī literature.

after the fall of Alamūt in the sixth/thirteenth century and only really re-emerged[41] with the original publication of the present text by Sayyid Muḥammad Riḍā Jalālī Nāʾīnī in 1942, which was presented as an appendix to his edition of Afḍal al-Dīn Ṣadr Turka al-Iṣfahānī's (d. 850/1446) Persian translation of al-Shahrastānī's *al-Milal wa'l-niḥal.* Jalālī Nāʾīnī had access to only one manuscript of this work which was in the Library of the Majlis, the Iranian parliament in Tehran. This manuscript (Ms. no. 593) was also the one he used for a later and more detailed edition of the text in 1964, when he published it as an appendix to a longer monograph on the biography and works of al-Shahrastānī, entitled *Sharḥ-i ḥāl wa āthār-i ḥujjat al-ḥaqq Abu'l-Fatḥ Muḥammad b. ʿAbd al-Karīm b. Aḥmad Shahrastānī.* Then, in 1990, Jalālī Nāʾīnī published yet another version of the *Majlis* based on another manuscript acquired from Istanbul. By that time, another indication of al-Shahrastānī's Ismaili affiliation had come to light: his commentary on the Qurʾan called *Mafātīḥ al-asrār wa maṣābīḥ al-abrār.*[42] Even though in his introduction to a Persian translation of the *Milal* in 1956[43] and in his 1964 biography of al-Shahrastānī[44] Jalālī Nāʾīnī discussed briefly certain details of the *Mafātīḥ*, he did not probe deeply into the text which further remained unpublished for some twenty years. However, in 1982, P. Adhkāʾī examined the *Mafātīḥ* highlighting the prominent Ismaili themes in it.[45] One of the points specifically raised by Adhkāʾī is al-Shahrastānī's reference to the Ithnā ʿasharīs (*al-Shīʿa al-muntaẓira*) in the course of discussing the necessity of acknowledging the authority of a present living Imam,

41 As we move further away from the time of al-Shahrastānī, most probably because of lack of access to his Ismaili works, his affiliation with the Ismailis remains almost totally forgotten until contemporary times.

42 For a partial English translation, see T. Mayer, *Keys to the Arcana*.

43 See al-Shahrastānī, *al-Milal wa'l-niḥal*, tr. Afḍal al-Dīn Ṣadr Turka Iṣfahānī, ed. and intro. Jalālī Nāʾīnī (Tehran, 1335/1956).

44 Muḥammad Riḍā Jalālī Nāʾīnī, *Sharḥ-i ḥāl wa āthār-i ḥujjat al-ḥaqq Muḥammad b. ʿAbd al-Karīm b. Aḥmad al-Shahrastānī* (Tehran, 1343/1964).

45 Parvīz Adhkāʾī, 'Nukātī chand az tafsīr-i Shahrastānī', *Maʿārif*, 15 (1982), pp. 117–126.

and he concludes that 'this leaves no doubt as to the *ta'līmī* Ismaili affiliation of the author'.[46]

Nonetheless, it can be said that the unmistakeable use of terms that were exclusively Nizārī in both the *Majlis* and the *Mafātīḥ*, led Jalālī Nā'īnī to place al-Shahrastānī close to the Nizārī Ismailis. With the publication of the facsimile edition of the *Mafātīḥ* in 1989, which includes a brief but dense introduction by 'Abd al-Ḥusayn Ḥā'irī, the systematic study of the *Mafātīḥ* began. However, in the text of Ḥā'irī's introduction there is no explicit reference to his connection with the Ismailis; it is only in the footnotes that it is mentioned, and then only in very broad terms before it is dismissed.[47]

It is noteworthy that in contemporary Persian scholarship the first scholar who wrote an essay on the *Majlis* was 'Abd al-Ḥusayn Zarrīnkūb, in 1950.[48] This essay is a brief summary of all the integral pieces of information about al-Shahrastānī in both medieval and contemporary texts. Zarrīnkūb inevitably referred to sources that mentioned al-Shahrastānī's Ismaili connections. However, in this review, he was mainly concerned about the genre of sermons (*majālis*), that is to say, devotional and doctrinal preaching. It should also be noted that Zarrīnkūb wrote the essay about eight years after the first publication of the text of the *Majlis* but only speaks of its manuscript, ignoring Jalālī Nā'īnī's edition and he focused primarily on the literary value of al-Shahrastānī's prose in the treatise.

The work of Jalālī Nā'īnī contains some lacunae despite his remarkable findings. Working with a single manuscript entails certain risks. Moreover, in the third publication (second edition) of the text

46 Ibid., p. 122.

47 See al-Shahrastānī, *Mafātīḥ al-asrār wa maṣābīḥ al-abrar*, intro. 'Abd al-Ḥusayn Ḥā'irī (Tehran, 1409/1989).

48 'Abd al-Ḥusayn Zarrīnkūb, 'Shahrastānī wa hamnashīn-i Farsī-yi ū', *Nāmah-yi furūgh-i 'ilm*, 2 (1950), pp. 35–42. This reference was kindly brought to my attention by Dr Mohammad Reza Shafiee Kadkani.

(1964), he made extensive modifications in the organization of sentences and paragraphs, apart from putting many phrases and words in brackets and adding words to the text based on his own editorial judgement. The purpose was to make the text more readable but the difficulties with his edition were not simply textual, they also stemmed from the lack of access to Ismaili works. At this point most of them had not yet been published and scholarly study of those that had been was in its early stages. For example, when Wladimir Ivanow, the pioneer of modern Ismaili studies, published his edition of al-Ṭūsī's *Rawḍa-yi taslīm*, in 1950, it was based on the single manuscript available to him.[49] Even though some Nizārī Ismaili texts were already known to Jalālī Nāʾīnī, such as al-Ṭūsī's *Sayr wa sulūk*,[50] he did not engage in any detailed comparison between al-Shahrastānī's work and these later texts. This is perhaps why his references to al-Shahrastānī's strong Ismaili affiliation seem unqualified and require more cross-references.

Al-Shahrastānī's influence on Nizārī Ismaili doctrine[51]

On 17 Ramaḍān 559/15 August 1164, Ḥasan II, also known as Ḥasan *ʿalā dhikrihi al-salām*, the fourth ruler of the Nizārī Ismaili state who subsequently declared himself the Imam that the community had been awaiting, made a declaration which left a lasting impact on the doctrines of the Nizārī Ismailis, also changing the focus of their politics and the course of their history. He declared that day to be the day of resurrection: *alā qūmū faqad qāmat al-qiyāma*.[52] This was clearly an eschatological declaration, however, not to be taken in a

[49] Naṣīr al-Dīn al-Ṭūsī, *Rawḍat al-taslīm*, ed. and tr. W. Ivanow (Leiden, 1950).

[50] Naṣīr al-Dīn al-Ṭūsī, *Sayr wa sulūk*, ed. and tr. S. J. Badakhchani as *Contemplation and Action: The Spiritual Autobiography of a Muslim Scholar* (London, 1998).

[51] This section is a revised version of a paper presented at the Twelfth Biennial Iranian Studies Conference at the University of California, Irvine, on 15 August 2018.

[52] See Abū Isḥāq Quhistānī, *Haft bāb*, ed. and tr. W. Ivanow (Bombay, 1959), Persian text p. 40.

literal sense. The message was esoteric and spiritual and constituted yet one more exegetical engagement with the message of the revelation but one which was unprecedented in terms of impact, at least inside the Ismaili community. Other Muslims including prominent Sufi figures, had made similar declarations, specifically Sanāʾī Ghaznawī (*c.* 467–*c.* 525/1075–1131) and ʿAyn al-Quḍāt Hamadānī (492–526/1098–1131), both Sufi figures living during the early Alamūt era, before the declaration of *qiyāmat.*[53] They were drawing attention to the fact that being a Muslim was being reduced to the literalist practice of the rituals, marginalizing the ethical and spiritual message of the faith and its rituals.

For example, ʿAyn al-Quḍāt Hamadānī's fifth chapter in his *Tamhīdāt* is devoted to the esoteric interpretation of religious laws albeit it bears the title '*Sharḥ-i arkān panjgāna-yi Islam*', a somewhat inconspicuous introduction to content which is quite radical. The section on *namāz* is an incredibly similar narrative of prayer, almost as if a blueprint, to that in the doctrine of *qiyāmat* later promulgated by Ḥasan II after his initial declaration:

> Woe to you! What do you hear? 'So woe to the worshippers who are neglectful of their prayers' (107:5). So hear this from the Prophet when he said: 'A time will come for my community when they all gather in mosques and they pray but there is not a single Muslim among them.' These worshippers he speaks of are us! [True] prayer is the one that the Prophet Ibrāhīm seeks: 'My Lord, make me a performer of the prayer, and of my seed' (14:40) . . . Wait, O friend, until such time when the meaning of this *ḥadīth* becomes clear to you that: 'The Prophets pray in their tombs.' Then you will realize why 'the sound of the cockerel is his prayer' is the same as 'and [he] mentions the Name of his Lord, and prays' (87:15). And for God's sake, heed this point: one day, Shiblī rose to perform the *namāz*. He waited for a long time and then he performed

53 For specific examples, see my chapter, 'Extra-Ismaili Sources and a Shift of Paradigm in Nizārī Ismailism', in Orkhan Mir-Kasimov, ed., *Intellectual Interactions*, pp. 219–245.

> the prayer. Once he was done, he said: 'Woe to me! By God, if I pray, I will be in denial and if I do not prayer, I will become a disbeliever.' Do you imagine that Shiblī was not among the people who are described as those 'who are constant at their worship'?[54]

This is, of course, a Sufi approach to the subject, but there are themes in it which are clearly similar to Nizārī ones. Here is a further passage from the *Tamhīdāt*:

> Alas! I do not know what I am saying! At this stage, all directions perish! Whatever the soul turns, that will become its direction (the *qibla*). 'Wherever you turn, there is the face of God', will be there: there is neither night there nor day. How can one work out five times for prayer there? 'Near my Lord there is neither morning nor evening' refers to the same meaning. Alas! The bandits of the age, scholars filled with ignorance and immature children consider these to be incarnation (*ḥulūl*)! May my soul be sacrificed at the feet of such *ḥulūlī*s![55]

One can compare these sections with what is found in the *Majlis* in paragraph 51.[56] Historically, if we move further back, the fortress of Alamūt was seized on 6 Rajab 483/4 September 1090 by Ḥasan-i Ṣabbāḥ, the chief *dāʿī* of the Persian Ismailis and the founder of the Nizārī Ismaili state in Persia.

Upon the death of the Fatimid Imam-caliph al-Mustanṣir in 487/1094, the Persian *daʿwa* effectively separated from the Fatimid regime by supporting the right of his son and heir-designate Nizār (d. 488/1095) to succeed him. Ḥasan-i Ṣabbāḥ's reign as lord of Alamut lasted until 518/1124 when he was succeeded by Kiyā Buzurg-Umīd who ruled until 532/1138. It was in 510/1116 that al-Shahrastānī left Khwārazm with the intention of going to the Ḥijāz. He then spent three years in Baghdad where he taught at the Niẓāmiyya

54 ʿAyn al-Quḍāt Hamadānī, *Tamhīdāt*, ed. ʿAfīf ʿUsayrān (Tehran, 1962), pp. 81–82.
55 Ibid., p. 83. Translations are mine.
56 See also, al-Ṭūsī, *Rawḍa*, p. 110.

(511–514/1117–1120), during which time his teacher Abu'l-Qāsim Salmān b. Nāṣir b. ʿImrān al-Anṣārī died in 512/1118.[57]

Ḥasan-i Ṣabbāḥ (Ḥasan I) and al-Shahrastānī, are connected through the critical doctrinal treatise of the Nizārī Ismailis written by the former, called the *Chahār faṣl* (Four Chapters) which covers the key Ismaili doctrines on the knowledge of God and the necessity of believing in the Shiʿi Imams from the progeny of the Prophet through ʿAlī. Today, all that is extant of this work are the quotations from it, in Arabic, in al-Shahrastānī's *al-Milal wa'l-niḥal.*[58] Al-Shahrastānī translated these extracts into Arabic to give his readers a true rendering of the doctrine of the Nizārī Ismailis. In his article on al-Shahrastānī's writings, Adhkāʾī argues that the *Chahar faṣl* was a purely internal Nizārī document and the fact that al-Shahrastānī has had access to it suggests he had intimate interactions with Nizārī *daʿwa*.[59] What gives more weight to his argument is that al-Shahrastānī is the only source for this now lost treatise. This point was also noted by Fakhr al-Dīn al-Rāzī (d. 606/1209) in his *Munāẓarāt.*[60]

Given the date of *al-Milal*'s completion, it is possible that al-Shahrastānī and Ḥasan-i Ṣabbāḥ, who was born in the mid 440s/1050s, met at some point. It is also the case that *al-Milal* became quite popular among the Nizārī Ismailis, probably because, unlike other heresiographers, al-Shahrastānī did not denounce the Ismailis. Indeed, this popularity is demonstrated by the fact that a manuscript of a Persian translation of *al-Milal* made during the Alamūt era by the Nizārīs,[61] by far the oldest manuscript known, has been recovered[62]

57 We do not have much factual material on this figure but Mayer suggests that he might have been an Ismaili living under the guise of *taqiyya*. See T. Mayer, *Keys to the Arcana*, pp. 6–7.

58 Muḥammad b. ʿAbd al-Karīm al-Shahrastānī, *al-Milal*, ed. Muhannā and Fāʿur, pp. 232–234.

59 See Adhkāʾī, 'Nukātī chand az tafsīr-i Shahrastānī', p. 120.

60 See Fakhr al-Dīn al-Rāzī, *Munāẓarāt*, ed. Fatḥ Allāh Khalīf (Beirut, 1966), pp. 39–40.

61 Al-Shahrastānī, *Tarjuma-yi kitāb al-milal wa'l-niḥal*, intro. Muḥammad ʿImādī Ḥāʾirī, facsimile edition (Tehran, 1395 Sh./2016).

62 Ibid., ʿImādī Ḥāʾirī's introduction, pp. 31–32.

and as ʿImādī Ḥāʾirī suggests, judging by the style and language, the manuscript must date to the sixth/twelfth century. Details of the manuscript are discussed in ʿImādī Ḥāʾīrī's introduction to its facsimile edition published in Tehran in 2016. But the key point here is the popularity of al-Shahrastānī, which could not have been due to his quotations from the *Chahar faṣl*, since obviously at that time the Nizārīs had access to the full text itself. So there must have been other reasons for their interest in al-Shahrastānī. Contemporary scholars have already argued that it is very likely that al-Shahrastānī was a senior figure in the hierarchy of the Ismaili *daʿwa*. Guy Monnot's article in the *Encyclopaedia of Islam* is most important in this respect. Among contemporary Persian scholars who have worked on al-Shahrastānī, those who favour this position include Dānishpazhūh, Jalālī Nāʾīnī, Adhkāʾī and most recently ʿImādī Ḥāʾirī despite the fact that he retains his point about al-Shahrastānī's criticism of the Nizārīs in the *Milal*.

Other academics, such as Wilferd Madelung, have expressed reservations regarding the attribution of an adherence to Ismaili beliefs to al-Shahrastānī. But commenting on the use of specific terminology, notably the dyads[63] used almost exclusively by the Nizārīs, Monnot argues that the references to his Shiʿi and Ismaili affiliations are spread all across his works, saying that 'it is not only the *Madjlis* and the *Muṣāraʿa* which are impregnated with Ismāʿīlism, but the *Milal* and the *Nihāya* also bear subtle hints of it'.[64]

At the end of his article, Monnot cites the reference in al-Ṭūsī's *Sayr wa sulūk* to al-Shahrastānī being the *dāʿī al-duʿāt* with caution arguing that 'this title does not seem to have been employed by the Ismāʿīlīs of Persia' referring to F. Daftary's comprehensive survey of Ismaili history and thought.[65] But in the recent publication of the

[63] See notes above on the content of the *Majlis*.
[64] Monnot, 'al-Shahrastānī', *EI2*, vol. 9, p. 216.
[65] Citing Farhad Daftary, *The Ismāʿīlis*, pp. 227, 336 and 394.

Dīwān-i qāʾimiyyāt,[66] a compilation of poems by Nizārī Ismaili poets, the collection of which is attributed to Ḥasan-i Maḥmūd-i Kātib, there is evidence for the use of the title. In one of the *qaṣida*s the Sufi poet Sanāʾī Ghaznawī[67] is referred to as *dāʿī al-duʿāt*; so it appears that the Nizārīs may in fact have continued to use the title. There is probably no unequivocal documentary statement of al-Shahrastānī's Ismaili adherence to be found, but there is increasingly compelling evidence, above all educed from his writings, which can be seen to corroborate the view that al-Shahrastānī had become an Ismaili. Yet, there is another slightly different and more fundamental claim: that the ideas of people such as Sanāʾī and al-Shahrastānī, as found in their writings, are critical to the formulation and articulation of the doctrine of the *qiyāmat*.[68]

The intellectual and doctrinal content of the *qiyāmat* is closely connected to the later works of al-Shahrastānī. His work is a prelude to, an early blueprint for the declaration of *qiyāmat*. If we accept the conjecture presented here, it means that before Ḥasan II acceded to the Imamate, the Nizārī community had already been exposed to the ideas which were declared and promulgated with full force during the reign of Ḥasan II.[69]

As mentioned earlier,[70] the terminology in al-Shahrastānī's *Mafātīḥ* and the *Majlis* became an integral part of the language of Ḥasan II and that of every other piece of literature which came afterwards, not just up to the collapse of the Alamūt state in the mid-

[66] Ḥasan-i Maḥmūd-i Kātib, *Dīwān-i qāʾimiyyāt*, ed. S. J. Badakhchani (Tehran, 2011). See Badakhchani's introduction for further details.

[67] See my chapter, 'Extra-Ismaili Sources and a Shift of Paradigm in Nizārī Ismailism', pp. 219–245.

[68] Ibid.

[69] The words of Ḥasan II are found scattered throughout various texts, most notably in the *Rawḍa*. In this case, chapter 6 of the *Haft bāb of Abū Isḥāq* contains words from Ḥasan II using terms initially used by al-Shahrastānī such as *taḍādd* and *tarattub*. See Abū Isḥāq Quhistānī, *Haft bāb*, pp. 46–48.

[70] See note 28 above.

seventh/thirteenth century but even works produced in later centuries. Terms such as contrariety (*taḍādd*), hierarchy (*tarattub*) and unity (*waḥdat*) which are used to define people's relationship to the Imams[71] in the era of *qiyāmat* and the dyads of the accomplished (*mafrūgh*) and the inchoative (*musta ʾnaf*) which are used both in al-Shahrastānī's works[72] and in Nizārī writings expanding on Ḥasan II's discourse of *qiyāmat*, are just a few examples of this phenomenon.[73] We do not, however, have a complete extant version of the works of Ḥasan II which were known as the *Fuṣūl-i mubārak* (the text that al-Ṭūsī refers to in his autobiography).[74] Nonetheless, in every other existing Nizārī work, the doctrine and its terminology is extensively discussed and explained.[75]

Following the collapse of the Nizārī Ismaili state in 654/1256 as a result of the campaign against it led by the Mongol Hūlāgū Khān, the library of Alamūt, presumably the central repository of Ismaili literature, was destroyed, although individual items from it may have been saved. One prominent figure involved in this destruction was the historian ʿAṭā Malik Juwaynī, the author of the *Taʾrīkh-i Jahān-gushā*. It was only in the twentieth century, with the revival of modern Ismaili studies that some of the writings from the Alamūt period were recovered and published by Ivanow. Critical editions of some of the works first published by Ivanow, have been produced in the past two

71 See also Christian Jambet, 'A Philosophical Commentary', in J. S. Badakhchani, ed and tr., *Paradise of Submission: A Medieval Treatise on Ismaili Thought*. Edition and English translation of al-Ṭūsī, *Rawḍa-yi taslīm* (London, 2005), pp. 190, 206, and text, p. 92.

72 See T. Mayer, *Keys to the Arcana*, pp. 113–118.

73 These specific terms are also used in the works of al-Ṭūsī, *Āghāz wa anjām* and *Tawllā wa tabarrā*, ed. and tr. J. Badakhchani as *Shiʿi Interpretations of Islam* (London, 2010). More specifically, see pp. 28 and 64.

74 See al-Ṭūsī, *Sayr wa sulūk*, p. 31.

75 See, for example, Ḥasan-i Maḥmūd-i Kātib, *Haft bāb*, ed. and tr. S. J. Badakhchani as *Spiritual Resurrection in Shiʿi Islam: An Early Ismaili Treatise on the Doctrine of Qiyāmat* (London, 2017) and al-Ṭūsī, *Rawḍa-yi taslīm*, ed and tr. S. J. Badakhchani as *Paradise of Submission* (London, 2005).

decades by Jalal Badakhchani, who has developed and improved on Ivanow's pioneering work. Most of these are by Naṣīr al-Dīn al-Ṭūsī. The issue, now, is the reconstruction of the texts and the literature of the time of Ḥasan II from the scattered fragments in these works by al-Ṭūsī,[76] and in the verses of the *Dīwān-i qāʾimiyyāt*. The post-*qiyāmat* Nizārī writings consist of interpretations and elaborations on this event as well as hermeneutical engagement with it. But as far as earlier writings produced before the reign of Ḥasan II are concerned, similar themes and terminology are only to be found in the works of al-Shahrastānī, including his *Milal* but more importantly the *Mafātīḥ* and the *Majlis*.[77] In tracing the literature of the *qiyāmat* discourse and how it was articulated, there seems to be a missing link because of the gap between the time of Ḥasan II and the writings of al-Ṭūsī which requires a comparative study of the literature *before* and *after* the time of Ḥasan II. Al-Shahrastānī is the most eligible figure and point of reference in terms of literature written before the time of Ḥasan II. However, there are two other figures whose works are also useful in this regard: Sanāʾī Ghaznawī whose poetry is quoted when the doctrine of *qiyāmat* is discussed in literature written after the reign of Ḥasan II (apart from him being referred to with the title *dāʿī al-duʿāt*),[78] and ʿAyn al-Quḍāt al-Hamadānī whose writings were known to the Nizārī Ismailis, and who was also familiar with Ismaili ideas and used them in his writings.[79]

76 These include *Rawḍa-yi taslīm*, *Sayr wa sulūk*, *Maṭlūb al-muʾminīn*, *Tawallā wa tabarrā* and *Āghāz wa anjām*.
77 See examples in earlier footnotes but also the text of the *Majlis* in English and Persian.
78 Ḥasan-i Maḥmūd-i Kātib, *Diwān-i qāʾimiyyāt*, p. 287.
79 I have discussed these in my 'Extra-Ismaili Sources and a Shift of Paradigm in Nizārī Ismailism', pp. 219–245.

The Nizārī doctrine of *qiyāmat*[80]

The commonly held non-Ismaili narrative of what happened in the course of the declaration of *qiyāmat* in Alamūt points to a single claim: that the Ismailis abrogated the *sharī'at* after Ḥasan II declared the *qiyāmat* and no longer observed the canonical laws and rituals of the Muslim faith. This categorical statement squarely places the Nizārīs among the antinomians but new evidence shows that this claim is fundamentally flawed.[81] So the questions we need to ask are: What actually happened? Why did it happen? What did it mean? What were its implications?

The initial phase of the doctrinal reorientation of the Nizārī Ismailis happened with the formulation of the doctrine of *ta'līm* by Ḥasan-i Ṣabbāḥ. The briefest account of this formulation of an old Shi'i doctrine is that human reason is not sufficient by itself for knowing God; and it, therefore, requires the assistance and perfection of a truthful teacher, a unique individual, and that unique individual is the Ismaili Imam of the age.

The doctrine of *ta'līm* was developed not just as a theological doctrine on its own but in conjunction with or in response to a cosmological question: how does God create the world? The Ismaili response moved away from the familiar philosophical narrative

[80] This section is an extended version of a paper originally presented at the Eleventh Biennial Iranian Studies Conference at the University of Vienna on 5 August 2016.

[81] In a fragment of manuscript held in the Ismaili Special Collections Unit at the Institute of Ismaili studies (MS. 916), there is passage attributed to an Ismaili Imam (most probably Muḥammad III). It reads, 'Out of your own opinion and analogy, you have some imaginings and it is to your corrupt imagination that God is generous [and all forgiving for you]. Yes, God is generous, but his generosity is for the generous ones. And some of you have made interventions for your own pleasure and convenience and out of your hellish whims. You do not pay heed to the good and the evil and you observe nothing. You will have to account for these before God and you have no shame in you. You do not adhere to the laws of any nation, be they Zoroastrians, Jews or Christians. So, you belong to none of these. What should one call you? For your sake, I feel embarrassed as you have confused and conflated the decree of resurrection (*qiyāmat*) with antinomian behaviour (*ibāḥat*).'

(God being the first cause and intellect being the first effect) and built upon certain features from Ismaili thought in the Fatimid period, as articulated by the *dāʿīs* of the Fatimid era such as Abū Yaʿqūb al-Sijistānī (d. after 361/971), but this time presented in straightforward language free from the sophisticated terminology and concepts of the earlier Ismailis. Moreover, the Imam was now placed at the centre of creation. Creation happens through the Divine command. The Divine command itself has a physical manifestation in this world. That manifestation is the Imam. Therefore, God is utterly inaccessible except through knowledge of the Imam of the Time. Thus, it is only through the Imam of the Time, who is the manifestation of God's command that people can find a way to this knowledge.

The formula was now straightforward. Knowledge of (and practice of faith in) the One true God (*tawḥīd*) relies exclusively on knowledge of (and submission to) the Imam; in short, *tawḥīd* is incomplete without knowledge of the Imam of the Time; true and pure *tawḥīd* is the one which is subject to the instruction and guidance of the Imam of the Time. The next stage would be a return to the origin (*maʿād*) and this would be the function of the resurrector (*qāʾim*),[82] who would (allegorically) revive the believers and take them through stages of perfection in faith: from contrariety (*taḍādd*) to hierarchy (*tarattub*) to unity (*waḥdat*).[83] The first stage of this process of perfection occurred between the reign of Ḥasan-i Ṣabbāḥ

[82] In Ismaili terminology, every Imam is a *qāʾim* too, but it is exclusively used to refer to those Imams who make amendments to practice of rituals. See al-Ṭūsī, *Rawḍa*, p. 127: 'The meaning of the terms "*imām*" and "*qāʾim*" (Resurrector) are the same, but people use the name Qāʾim to refer to the Imam who introduces some great change in the religious laws (*sharīʿat*).'

[83] See earlier footnotes, but put simply, those who are among the people of contrariety are the ones who do not recognize the Imam of their the time (basically anyone who is not an Ismaili). The people of gradation are the members of the Ismaili community (inclusive of everyone) and these are the people who observe the ritual laws. The third group are the people of unity who are in union with the Imam of the Time and with God; for these people observing the ritual laws is not required according to the doctrine of the *qiyāmat*.

and that of Muḥammad b. Kiyā Buzurg-Umīd (the chief *dā ʿīs* with no claim to the Imamate).[84] The second stage began with the declaration of the *qiyāmat* by Ḥasan II.

The fundamental claim of Ḥasan II, according to all the sources,[85] in his declaration of the *qiyāmat* was that in relation to knowledge of the Imam, ordinary members of the community belong to the realm of gradation (*ahl-i tarattub*) and only the elite of the faithful who fully recognize the spiritual reality of the Imam belong to the realm of unity (*ahl-i waḥdat*). And whoever, of the people of unity, was considered to know the Imam and to have surrendered to him would no longer be required to observe the commandments and prohibitions of the *sharī ʿat*. The statement seems quite categorical because Ḥasan II himself spoke about a new era which had now arrived.[86] Apparently, he did not set any conditions. But there was a caveat in the Sermon of the Resurrection.[87] This is about addressing people already in the realm of unicity (*waḥdat*). The context and implicit message suggest that this lifting of the veil of *sharī ʿat* was not intended for those in the lower ranks (including ordinary Ismailis in the realm of *tarattub*). This is also suggested in the final sections of the *Maṭlūb al-mu ʾminīn.*[88]

Al-Shahrastānī's statements and terminology in the *Majlis-i maktūb*, presented here, and also in the *Mafātīḥ al-asrār,* make it quite clear that Ḥasan II's ideas built upon an existing way of interpreting faith, because apart from later Nizārī writings, no one but al-Shahrastānī used these terms. Moreover, eschatological ideas can be found throughout all Muslim communities and so belief in the

84 See, al-Ṭūsī, *Rawḍa*, p. 159. Here, these two stages are indicated in the interpretation of the first and second blast of the trumpet (*nafkh-i ṣūr*).

85 See, Marshall G. S. Hodgson, *The Order of Assassins, The Struggle of the Early Nizari Ismailis Against the Islamic World* (The Hague, 1955), pp. 148–157.

86 See, Abū Iṣḥāq Quhistānī, *Haft bāb*, pp. 35–44.

87 See, Hodgson, pp. 148–157 and *Ḥaft bāb*, pp. 35–44. The complete text of the *Khuṭba-yi qiyāmat* is not available.

88 See, al-Ṭūsī, '*Maṭlūb al-mu ʾminīn*', in *Shi ʿi Interpretations*, pp. 42–43.

appearance of a *qāʾim* was neither strange nor outrageous. For instance, the Ithnāʿasharīs believed the last Imam of their line, al-Mahdī, would return as the *qāʾim* and continue to do so.[89] Indeed, the actions and functions of the *qāʾim* are described in earlier Ismaili sources.

Ḥasan II's actions and policies are alleged by the adversaries of the Ismailis, to have brought them into the ranks of the antinomians (*ibāḥī*s) and heretics (*malāḥida*).[90] This was more in the nature of a slander rather than a factually accurate claim since the Ismailis had been labelled with such misnomers long before Ḥasan II's era, even during the time of the Fatimid Imam-caliphs, who were known to be rather particular in their observation of the *sharīʿa*. The larger context of such disputes and name-calling was the contentious area of religious authority, rather than the details of how various communities practised their faith. Be that as it may, at this point a closer examination of what the declaration implied is required.

Al-Shahrastānī's nuanced narrative of tripartite stages and contexts (hierarchy and contrarity, *taḍādd*, *tarattub* etc.), are crucial here, because his articulation of them is the same as is found in later Nizārī works. The era of *qiyāmat* was meant for the select few people of unity, called by al-Ṭūsī '*akhaṣṣ-i khāṣṣ*', the super-elite. The people of unity seek and require no direction, no time and no space. If they did, their practice of faith would be meaningless, as though they sought to restrict knowledge and faith to one particular language, geographical location or a certain specified set of rigid rituals never subject to change.

[89] See, Daryoush Mohammad Poor, *Authority without Territory* (New York, 2014), pp. 111–115.

[90] See, Hodgson, *Order*, p. 151 citing the work of the late Il Khanid historian, Rashīd al-Dīn.

The debate over al-Shahrastānī's faith

Given the growth in the evidence about al-Shahrastānī's religious affiliations, we are now in a better position to consider the various theories about it. Scholars and commentators who have dealt with the question have proposed the following:

1. Al-Shahrastānī was a Sunni Muslim, a Shāfiʿī in his jurisprudential training and an Ashʿarī in *kalām* but he also had a taste for the esoteric exegesis of the Qurʾan and for philosophy which made him appear close to the Ismailis.
2. Al-Shahrastānī was a non-Ismaili Shiʿi Muslim most probably an Akhbārī Imāmī one.
3. Al-Shahrastānī was not only a Nizārī Ismaili but a prominent and senior *dāʿī* in their *daʿwa* system who contributed significantly to the reorientation of Nizārī doctrines.

Here, it has been argued so far, based on textual evidence from his work compared with later Nizārī works, that the third position is the correct one. In order to corroborate this further, we can demonstrate that the first two positions are not only improbable but also inconsistent with the explicit references found in al-Shahrastānī's works, including his *Majlis*, leaving only the third option. There has only been one hypothesis, found in what Ādharshab writes, arguing that al-Shahrastānī was unrestrained in examining the ideas held by various communities in order to develop his own thought. Ādharshab argues that al-Shahrastānī studied the creeds of all communities and then developed his own system of thought independently of all of them. This is a highly idealistic and phenomenological narrative which does not fit well with the explicit wording and terminology in al-Shahrastānī's writings.[91] The inconsistency of al-Shahrastānī's

[91] See, Ādharshab's introduction to his edition of the *Mafātīḥ*, pp. 33–34.

views with (at least some) earlier Ismaili doctrines seems to be one reason why contemporary authors have rejected the possibility of an Ismaili affiliation. But writers during his lifetime and shortly after who thought that al-Shahrastānī had Ismaili affiliations did not see anything particularly contrary to Ismaili doctrines in his writings. Apart from the early contemporaries of al-Shahrastānī, another person who held this position was Ibn Taymiyya (661–728/1263–1328). Referring to the *Milal*, he held that the *naqīb* of Tirmidh, to whom the *Milal* is dedicated, was an Ismaili.[92] Also, in his *Dir᾿ ta῾āruḍ al-῾aql wa'l-naql* there is a passage in which Ibn Taymiyya explicitly called al-Shahrastānī an Ismaili because of the style of his commentary on Sūra Yūsuf, and he also considered the *Nihāya* an Ismaili text.[93] The second theory holds that al-Shahrastānī's ideas do not reflect 'Ismaili', that is to say Neoplatonic, thought, as in earlier Ismaili writings, and therefore he could not have been an Ismaili. It is this argument that is presented in Farmānīyān's article on al-Shahrastānī (see below). The provenance of this latter view is quite modern.

Another important consideration is the re-examination of the *Nihāya*'s Ash῾arī attribution. Apart from the sources mentioned earlier, ῾Imādī Ḥā᾿irī argued in his introduction to a newly published facsimile edition of the *Nihāya* that this is also one of al-Shahrastānī's crypto-Ismaili works.[94] Theologically and doctrinally, al-Shahrastānī stands so much aligned to Shi῾i doctrines of a distinct colour[95] that we would either have to invent a new version of Sunnism for his time to

92 See, Ibn Taymiyya, *Minhāj al-sunna al-nabawiyya*, ed. Muḥammad Rashād Sālim (Riyadh, 1986), vol. 6, pp. 305–307. Here, Ibn Taymiyya is adamant that al-Shahrastānī was either an Ismaili or had pretended to be an Ismaili.

93 See, Ibn Taymiyya, *Minhāj al-sunna al-nabawiyya*, ed. Muḥammad Rashād Sālim (rpr., Riyadh, 1991), vol. 5, pp. 172–173.

94 See, al-Shahrastānī, *Nihāyat al-aqdām fī ῾ilm al-kalām*, facsimile ed., intro., Muḥammad ῾Imādī Ḥā᾿irī (Tehran, 1391 Sh./2012).

95 As noted by Jalālī Nā᾿īnī, Adhkā᾿ī, Dānishpazhūh and Imādī Ḥā᾿irī in the above-mentioned works. See also, T. Mayer's introduction to *Keys to the Arcana* in which he discusses al-Shahrastānī's Ismaili adherence and the evidence for it found throughout his works.

accommodate him or explain the seemingly Sunni terminology and approaches in his works in a different light. The integral point in the writings of al-Shahrastānī is that he argues that the interpretation of the Qurʾan requires the authority of the *ahl al-bayt* and the *ulū'l-amr.*[96] These terms are used explicitly in the *Mafātīḥ* and the *Majlis* but also in the *Nihāya* when he refers to the *ḥunafaʾ*.[97]

The particular case that Mustafa Öztürk presents regarding whether or not al-Shahrastānī belonged to the Imāmī community, as shall be demonstrated further below, is extremely weak. For a start, in contrast to al-Ṭūsī's *Sayr wa sulūk*, a Nizārī Ismaili source which explicitly claims that he is a *dāʿī al-duʿāt*, there is not a single reference in any Imāmī source placing al-Shahrastānī among their co-religionists. Indeed, as noted by Farmānīyān, al-Ḥillī (d. 726/1325), who was a prominent Imāmī scholar, also a student of al-Ṭūsī, regarded him as opposed to the Imāmīs.[98]

As noted above, Öztürk's article offers an entirely different interpretation:

> . . . the utilization of concepts such as *khalq-amr*, *taḍādd-tarattub*, and the divine word in parallel with the Ismāʿīlī terminology should not be taken as an indication that he was a Bāṭinī-Ismāʿīlī. Rather, he only used Ismāʿīlī terms as an instrument to introduce a philosophical depth to the thought of the Akhbārī school of the Imāmiyya, as the identity put forth by al-Shahrastānī in *Mafātīḥ al-asrār* is an Akhbārī Imāmī Shiʿi identity rather than a Bāṭinī-Ismāʿīlī one.[99]

96 See, for instance, Mayer, *Keys to the Arcana*, tr. pp. 64–65.

97 See, ʿImādī Ḥāʾirī's introduction in his edition of the *Nihāya*, p. 13.

98 See, Mahdī Farmānīyān, 'Shahrastānī: sunnī-yi Ashʿarī yā Shiʿi-yi bāṭinī', *Haft-āsimān*, 7 (2000), pp. 135–182. For a biography of al-Ḥillī, see S. H. M. Jafri, 'al-Ḥillī', *EI2*. Consulted online on 5 June 2020 http://dx.doi.org.iij.idm.oclc.org/10.1163/1573-3912_islam_SIM_2867.

99 Mustafa Öztürk, 'The Different Stances of al-Shahrastānī: A Study of the Sectarian Identity of Abū l-Fatḥ al-Shahrastānī in Relation to his Qurʾānic Commentary, Mafātīḥ al-asrār', *Ilahiyat Studies*, 1/2 (2010), p. 233.

What Öztürk identifies as Ismaili terminology is the opposite of what Farmānīyān identifies as such. Farmānīyān has argued that since he used terms which were not used by the Fatimid Ismailis, he cannot have been an Ismaili. Öztürk acknowledges that al-Shahrastānī indeed used terms used by the Nizārī Ismailis but this should be interpreted otherwise. Both authors have assumed that Ismaili philosophy and doctrine were uniform and singularly articulated throughout different periods. The Ismailis rearticulated not only terminology but also aspects of doctrine in different periods, often even changing their terminology.[100] In the explanation Öztürk provides for rejecting al-Shahrastānī's Ismaili identity, he does not take into account the possibility that it may have been al-Shahrastānī himself who first used these terms which then became a part of Ismaili terminology. Were one to adopt Öztürk's line of argument, one would inevitably have to label most of the Nizārī works from the Alamūt period as 'Akhbārī Imāmī Shiʿi', which would be absurd. Finally, it should be pointed out that he has ignored al-Shahrastānī's criticisms of the Imāmiyya in his *Mafātīḥ*, which surely must indicate that he is not of their persuasion. Al-Shahrastānī writes:

> Just as Iblīs did not acknowledge the present, living, current imam, the commonalty are the same as that, while the expectant Shīʿa only acknowledge the awaited, hidden imam. And God has blessed servants on earth who do not get ahead of Him in speaking and they act on His Command, servants who are the purified servants of God, over whom Satan has no authority.[101]

Following a citation of this passage, we have a curious explanation of this passage by Ādharshab. He argues that it does not mean the rejection of the Shiʿi communities who await the reappearance of the Mahdī but that it suggests that in the absence of the Mahdī, the

[100] See, my 'Extra-Ismaili Sources', pp. 219–245.
[101] T. Mayer, *Keys to the Arcana*, p. 18.

believers must submit to the authority of the jurists and he spells this out as the *walāyat al-faqīh.*[102] The theory of the governance of the jurist has a history but it did not exist either under this name or with such articulation until the early Qājār period; it certainly was not there at the time of al-Shahrastānī some seven hundred years earlier.

A little further down in the *Mafātīḥ*, al-Shahrastānī argues that prostration before Adam is indeed prostration before God and without this prostration, there is no prostration before God.[103] He also argues that all submission to the present living Imam is equivalent to submission to God. This is a purely Ismaili idea that is often interpreted as extremist and attributed to the *ghulāt*. In his *Sayr wa sulūk*, al-Ṭūsī responds to the accusation of *ghuluww* made against the Nizārīs by a *faqīh* from Jājarm in respect of this idea.[104] These evidently Ismaili opinions presented here by al-Shahrastānī have been a source of concern in the past. A case in point is the comments made by Ādharshab on these passages in his introduction to the *Mafātīḥ*. He writes,

> And in his earlier sentence he even goes beyond this mentions that the earth will never be devoid of pure servants of God who are chosen by Him and have been brought near and close to him and about them he says that prostrating before them is like prostrating before God. And there is no choice but to undertake an esoteric exegesis of this in order to make it consistent with al-Shahrastānī's approach to purity in the worship of God.[105]

He then continues by offering a correction of these statements in line with an Imāmī interpretation. It is evident that Ādharshab's discomfort with these claims have led him to assume that such opinions are not in line with purity in the worship of God (this is the same kind of

[102] See, Ādharshab intro., *Mafātīḥ*, p. 33.
[103] See, al-Shahrastānī, *Mafātīḥ*, ed. M. ʿA. Ādharshab p. 280.
[104] See, al-Ṭūsī, *Sayr wa sulūk*, pp. 38–39.
[105] See, Ādharshab, intro., *Mafātīḥ*, p. 31.

attitude displayed by the *faqīh* in Jājarm whom al-Ṭūsī talks about, as mentioned above). But if we compare these same passages from the *Mafātīḥ* with similar passages in the *Rawḍa*, it becomes clear that these are purely Nizārī Ismaili doctrines about the Imamate.[106]

Thus, given al-Shahrastānī's rejection of the idea of an Imam in occultation he cannot be regarded as any kind of Imāmī, be it Akhbārī or Uṣūlī. Indeed, in his article on al-Shahrastānī's religious adherence, Bahrāmī is quite adamant that his ideas are not only Shiʿi but they are also specifically Ismaili, as the following quotation makes clear:

> All throughout his works, particularly in his *tafsīr* which had been produced in a rather safe environment free from the terror and fear of the Sunnis and shows far fewer signs of *taqiyya* compared to his other works, there are signs of the affiliation and attachment of the author of the *Mafātīḥ* to the Ismailis, the *Bāṭiniyya*, the *Taʿlīmiyya* and the *Malāḥida*.[107]

Bahrāmī then proceeds to assess some of al-Shahrastānī's key doctrines, arguing that only the Ismailis believed in these; these include al-Shahrastānī's position on knowledge of God, on the Imamate, on the interpretation of the Qurʾan and the necessity of *taʾwīl* and various other concepts, beside the use of specific terms, such as *dawr* and *adwār* (eras or cycles) or *mustawdaʿ* and *mustaqarr* (temporary and permanent) with reference to the concept of the Imamate.[108] But Bahrāmī does not examine later Nizārī works, like the *Rawḍa* or *Sayr wa sulūk* to determine if there are any parallels between them and al-Shahrastānī's writings.

[106] See, al-Ṭūsī, *Rawḍa*, pp. 120–121.

[107] Muḥammad Bahrāmī, 'Girāyish-i madhhabī-yi Shahrastānī, ṣāḥib-i tafsīr-i Mafātīḥ al-asrār', p. 371.

[108] Bahrāmī, 'Girāyish-i madhhabī-yi Shahrastānī', pp. 371–380. He cites the reference to *mustawdaʿ* and *mustaqarr* from the *Mafātīḥ*, ed. M. A. Ādharshab, p. 956, where al-Shahrastānī speaks about Dāʾūd and Ṭālūt (David and Saul). See R. Firestone, 'Ṭālūt', *EI2*, and I. Hasson, 'David', *Encyclopaedia of the Qurʾān*, ed. J. Dammen MacAuliffe, (Leiden, 2001–2006), for further on Dāʾūd and Ṭālūt in Islamic tradition generally.

There is a similarly interesting work by Muḥammad b. Nāṣir al-Suḥaybānī.[109] The author closely examines most of al-Shahrastānī's works particularly his *Mafātīḥ*, meticulously drawing parallels between it and the *Milal*. He then concludes that al-Shahrastānī was an Ismaili throughout his life but at the end regretted this belief and was an Ashʿarī Sunni when he embarked on writing the *Nihāya*. These contemporary examples are particularly relevant because the authors have probed deeply into the texts providing concrete examples which, when compared with later Nizārī literature, can help us put together different pieces of evidence corroborating the argument that al-Shahrastānī was indeed an Ismaili *dāʿī*.

It is clear that one cannot easily establish al-Shahrastānī's Ismaili identity by simply comparing his writings with earlier Ismaili works, particularly the Fatimid ones, even though one may find certain connections there too. For example, one particular *ḥadīth* that al-Shahrastānī uses in both the *Majlis* and the *Mafātīḥ* which he attributes to Jaʿfar al-Ṣādiq is only used by the Ismailis, both before as well as after him.[110] But the terminology which appears in his works and was used later by other Nizārī writers is not found in earlier Ismaili works. It is the typical mistake of some who endeavour to deal with the question of his religious identity and reject his connection with the Ismailis simply on the grounds of terminology. A good example of this can be seen in Farmānīyān's article, for instance in the following paragraph:

> I have investigated all relevant books in this regard including dictionaries of philosophy, *kalām* and *taṣawwuf*. Discussions about contradiction[111] (*taḍādd*) could be found in . . . philosophy and *kalām* but there is not a single topic on contrariety (*taḍādd*) and gradation

[109] Muḥammad b. Nāṣir b. Ṣāliḥ al-Suḥaybānī, *Manhaj al-Shahrastānī fī kitābih al-Milal wa'l-niḥal* (Riyadh, 1997).

[110] See, paragraph 52 of the *Majlis* in the present edition.

[111] Here the author uses the term *taḍādd* in a different sense from the way it is used by the Ismailis. In the next lines, he is using it in context. Hence, the difference in translation.

> (*tarattub*) as a relevant topic. I never found any term such as *tarattub* in *kalām*, philosophy, *taṣawwuf* or Ismaili books. These terms do not exist in Ismaili works such as the *Rasā'il Ikhwān al-ṣafā'*, *Rāḥāt al-ʿaql* and *Kitāb al-riyāḍ* by Ḥamīd al-Dīn al-Kirmānī, *Wajh-i dīn* and *Jāmiʿ al-ḥikmatayn* by Nāṣir-i Khusraw, *al-Iṣlāḥ* by Abū Ḥātim al-Rāzī.[112]

Farmānīyān highlights a valuable but puzzling point even though he is questioning al-Shahrastānī's Ismaili affiliation. Although his argument that these terms are not Ismaili because they are not found in works by Fatimid *dāʿīs* must be rejected, he is absolutely correct about all the works he cites because first of all they actually enter Nizārī doctrine after al-Shahrastānī; al-Shahrastānī is the source, the one who originally introduced the use of these terms. Secondly, except in matters concerning the Imamate,[113] Ismaili philosophy and doctrine were not uniform or consistent at all times, but went through a process of shifting and adaptation, hence the promulgation of *al-daʿwa al-jadīda* by Ḥasan-i Ṣabbāḥ. For instance, in Fatimid Ismaili doctrine there were certain terms which were not used before Ḥamīd al-Dīn al-Kirmānī (d. after 411/1020), a *dāʿī* and theologian writing in the reign of the Imam-caliph al-Ḥākim, but through his influence they were employed in the *daʿwa* literature afterwards.[114] One should also consider the fact that there were differences of opinion among senior figures of the *daʿwa* both before and during the Fatimid period. In his article in an earlier footnote, Farmānīyān says:

> It is quite surprising for someone to be a *dāʿī al-duʿāt*, having the second or third rank in the hierarchy of the Ismaili *daʿwa* and to have full authority over everything after the Imam and the *ḥujjat* and yet no Ismaili accepts him as an Ismaili.[115]

112 See, M. Farmānīyān, 'Shahrastānī: Sunnī-yi Ashʿarī yā Shiʿi-yi bāṭinī', pp. 166–167.
113 For further elaboration of this point, see my chapter, 'Extra-Ismaili sources', pp. 219–245.
114 These are primarily found in Mustaʿlian literature; al-Kirmānī is hardly referenced in Nizārī literature.
115 Mahdī Farmānīyān, 'Shahrastānī: sunnī-yi Ashʿarī yā Shiʿi-yi bāṭinī', p. 150, fn. 1.

Then he concludes: 'Therefore, I cannot at all accept al-Ṭūsī's words that al-Shahrastānī was the Ismaili *dāʿī al-duʿāt* of Khurāsān. This has to be interpreted differently'.[116] Farmānīyān seems to have been relying on early (and now almost outdated) editions of Arabic Ismaili sources and has underestimated the importance of the Nizārī sources and even of the works of al-Ṭūsī such as *Āghāz wa anjām*. Apart from al-Ṭūsī's reference to al-Shahrastānī being a *dāʿī*, more recent discoveries including the Persian translation of his *Milal* by the Nizārīs bring Farmānīyān's argument seriously into question. In the present edition of the *Majlis*, references to similarities and parallels with various Nizārī texts after the time of al-Shahrastānī and before the fall of Alamūt are provided. However, it is clear from various studies, including Farmānīyān's article, that there is no evidence to show that these terms were in use by the Nizārīs, or indeed other Ismaili groups, before al-Shahrastānī.

Bahrāmī[117] examines various passages in the *Mafātīḥ* and also references to al-Shahrastānī in historical sources. The examples that he considers present a very strong case for al-Shahrastānī having been an Ismaili though he falls short of stating this explicitly. Nonetheless, this is probably the only article in Persian which places al-Shahrastānī in the ranks of the Ismailis. He also makes an interesting observation about Naṣīr al-Dīn Maḥmūd, the vizier of Sanjar, and the *naqīb* of Tirmidh, arguing that these two were possibly 'infiltrators' in Sanjar's court who were instrumental in bringing al-Shahrastānī close to Sanjar (and he cites Ibn Taymiyya too). He also considers the possibility that their imprisonment was due to the discovery of their Ismaili connections.[118] Thus, for Bahrāmī, it is not merely the textual and doctrinal indications in his works and those of later writers which place al-Shahrastānī among the Ismailis.

[116] Ibid.
[117] See, Bahrāmī, 'Girāyish-i madhhabī-yi Shahrastānī, ṣāḥib-i tafsīr-i Mafātīḥ al-asrār'.
[118] Bahrāmī, 'Girāyish-i madhhabī-yi Shahrastānī, ṣāḥib-i tafsīr-i Mafātīḥ al-asrār', p. 359.

Al-Shahrastānī's criticisms of the Imāmiyya in the *Mafātīḥ* is a point raised by Jalālī Nāʾīnī in his biography of al-Shahrastānī when he discusses the negative comments about al-Shahrastānī made by the contemporary Iranian Imāmī author, Amīnī (d. 1970),[119] and considers his observations to be 'unfair and unfounded'.[120] Amīnī rejected any possibility of al-Shahrastānī being affiliated with the Shiʿi communities by which he clearly meant the Ithnāʿasharīs but he was also implicitly rejecting any other Shiʿi affiliation as well. Jalālī Nāʾīnī goes into the details of Amīnī's objections to al-Shahrastānī and responds to all of his points.[121] Jalālī Nāʾīnī argues that Amīnī's judgement was hasty because he had not closely studied the *Majlis* and the *Mafātīḥ* and that his rejection of al-Shahrastānī was due to a prejudice against someone who did not share his beliefs.[122]

For Amīnī, being an Ismaili (worse still a Nizārī Ismaili) was not Shiʿi enough. Öztürk (and Farmānīyān) seem to have accepted al-Shahrastānī's use of Ismaili terms, the only problem being that it appeared to be anachronistic: these terms were never used in Fatimid Ismaili sources and specifically they were not used by the Fatimids to articulate the doctrine of the *qiyāma* in the way that the Nizārīs later used them. The answer to this problem would be to compare al-Shahrastānī's works with all the available Ismaili literature.

Inter-textuality: parallels between al-Shahrastānī and later Nizārī sources

Al-Shahrastānī made extensive use of terminology, ideas and expressions which are otherwise almost exclusively employed by the Nizārī Ismailis in the Alamūt period of their history. These expressions

119 ʿAbd al-Ḥusayn Amīnī, *al-Ghadīr fī al-kitāb wa'l-sunna wa'l-adab* (Qumm, 1416/1995).
120 Jalālī Nāʾīnī, *Sharḥ-i ḥāl wa āthār-i ḥujjat al-ḥaqq*, p. 69.
121 Ibid., pp. 69–72.
122 Ibid., pp. 71–72.

cover the areas of cosmology, prophecy and the Imamate, all with considerable use of an esoteric vocabulary which includes a wide range of dyads (discussed earlier in this introduction), such as *amr* and *khalq*, *mafrūgh* and *mustaʾnaf*, and so on. The only possible explanation for al-Shahrastānī's use of unprecedented terminology, employed extensively by the later Nizārīs, is that either al-Shahrastānī himself introduced these terms and made them part of the Nizārī *daʿwa* literature, or that someone before him (and after Ḥasan-i Ṣabbāḥ) or one of his Ismaili contemporaries invented the terms and brought them into currency. One can consider either of these scenarios but there are allusions in al-Shahrastānī's works to an enigmatic figure, notably in the *Mafātīḥ*. In his foreword to *Keys to the Arcana*, Landolt notes:

> ... The anonymous teacher in the Qurʾānic arcana, to whom al-Shahrastānī alludes in the autobiographical part, presenting him in the role of the no less mysterious 'servant of God' of Q. 18:65, or Khiḍr, may well have been no one else than Ḥasan-i Ṣabbāḥ himself.[123]

If we accept the Ismaili provenance of the *Mafātīḥ* and the *Majlis*, given the fact that Ḥasan-i Ṣabbāḥ is also referred to in messianic terms in later Ismaili literature such as the *Rawḍa*, we can gradually put the pieces of the puzzle together and come up with a much sharper and more focused picture of the discourse propagated later by Ḥasan II. In the *Rawḍa*, this is how Ḥasan-i Ṣabbāḥ is described by al-Ṭūsī:

> Sayyidnā, our master [Ḥasan-i Ṣabbāḥ] – may God sanctify his soul – who was the supreme *ḥujjat* of our lord the Resurrector of the Resurrection (*qāʾim-i qiyāmat*), the messiah of the Cycle of Resurrection, the one who blew the first blast of the trumpet of Resurrection (*nāfikh-i ṣūr-i awwal*), made his appearance in the year 500 after *Hijra*. He set out in search of this pure and unique religion,

[123] Mayer, *Keys to the Arcana*, p. xv.

> betaking himself to the sacred presence of our lord Mustanṣir – may salutations ensue upon mention of him – and was specially favoured with a vision of the lights of divine assistance (*anwār-i taʾyīd*). By the command of the latter, he came forth and proclaimed openly the rightly-guided mission (*daʿwat-i hādiya*) – may God so confirm it! Upon the first blast of the trumpet of the holy mission, he announced the call, asking if knowledge of God is to be attained with or without the guidance of a person. He asked, 'Does reason suffice [as a guide to God] or not?' Thus, he who replied that 'reason is sufficient' assumed that with such a reply he would claim victory, because he saw that the whole world had made the intellect their ruler; however, if he replied, 'No, reason is not sufficient', he would himself have testified that there is a need for a ruler.[124]

As we can see, the arguments about Ḥasan-i Ṣabbāḥ are intermingled with an esoteric hermeneutical narrative in which he is connected to an articulation of the *qiyāmat* as later declared by Ḥasan II, here referred to as the messiah of the Cycle of Resurrection (*Masīḥ-i dawr-i qiyāmat*).[125] And this is how Ḥasan-i Ṣabbāḥ is mentioned in *Haft bāb-i Abū Isḥāq*:

> At the time of Jesus, Mawlānā was called Maʿadd, and at the time of Muṣṭafā, ʿAlī. And when Jesus said that he was going to return and take up the task of the Qiyāmat showing God to people, he referred to Sayyidnā. All signs have become manifested in him, from that date and until his, Sayyidnā's appearance. And Muṣṭafā said that ʿAlī ibn Abī Ṭālib – may God beautify his countenance! – on the day of Resurrection will raise the banner of the Qiyāmat single-handed.[126]

Al-Shahrastānī uses similar terms and references in his commentary, regarding the Prophet and the Imams being agents of revival (*iḥyāʾ*) and the esoteric exegesis of Q 2:244 in the *Mafātīḥ*:

[124] S. J. Badakhchani *The Paradise of Submission*, pp. 157–158.
[125] See also, Abū Isḥāq Quhistānī, *Haft bāb*, p. 40.
[126] Ibid.

> The people who learned from the examples of the stories of their predecessors said: in the story of the people, there is a decree and lessons to be learned that wariness of *al-qadar* (destiny) is useful (*al-ḥadhar min al-qadar nāfiʿ*), and it became clear to them that seeking this [knowledge] is not useful and it is most appropriate for their condition that they follow the command of their Prophet – peace be upon him – and whoever accompanied someone other than himself would be delivered (*fa huwa al-nājī*) and whoever followed his own reason would perish (*fa huwa al-hālik*). And among these lessons is that the revival of the dead had been realized for them before their eyes (*qad taḥaqqaqa lahum ʿayānan*); so the people who died and were revived would perceive this in their own selves.
>
> And the people who looked at them with the purpose of learning from their example so benefited from this that they acknowledged the resurrection (*al-maʿād*); and among these lessons is that the Prophet had achieved the noble condition of reviving the dead. This is a degree of perfection when God Almighty appoints a mere human to revive the dead in the same manner as he appointed Isrāfīl to blow the trumpet and revive the dead; and this is within the realm of possibility for God. And among these lessons is the summons of the prophets when they revive the souls from the death of ignorance (*tuḥyī al-nufūs ʿan mawt al-jahl*), as God Almighty said, '*Answer God and His Prophet when He summons you to that which gives you life*' (Q. 8: 24). And this is rationally possible, that their souls and their conditions may become the revivers of the bodies for the life of dead souls is far greater than the life of bodies, just as the death of souls is greater than the death of bodies. And Jesus – peace be upon him – said, 'I revived the dead with God's permission but I have been thwarted by the fool.'[127]

In the *Rawḍa* in a section on the topic of resurrection, al-Ṭūsī writes:

> The resurrection of such people will be the resurrection of their souls which have died the death of ignorance, [as has been said]: 'They lie fast asleep, entombed in their bodies, darkened by infernal passions

[127] Al-Shahrastānī, *Mafātīḥ*, ed. M. A. Ādharshab, p. 931.

> and desires'. Then, when the Trumpet of the [Day of] Resurrection (*ṣūr-i qiyāmat*) is blown, that is, when the call of the summons of the Resurrector (*daʿwat-i qāʾim*) is given – may salutations ensue upon mention of him – they will be resurrected from the tomb of the flesh, that is, they will be roused and revived by the spirit of faith: '*Answer God and His Prophet when He summons you to that which gives you life*' (8:24).[128]

These references and the parallels reinforce the argument that al-Shahrastānī was a critical example for the later Nizārīs in the articulation of their esoteric doctrines, distanced from the typical Neoplatonic style and language of Fatimid times. The idea that this resurrection is an intellectual revival and the resurrected will reach the life of knowledge is the common thread here (in al-Shahrastānī's words: *tuḥyī al-nufūs ʿan mawt al-jahl*). Both of these texts suggest a contrasting narrative opposed to the concept of physical resurrection and they highlight the role of the Imam/*qāʾim* in this spiritual and intellectual revival.

Similarities in terms and ideas between the works of al-Shahrastānī and those clearly by Nizārī authors are too many to list here.[129] But from what is presented here it is evident that al-Shahrastānī's works are vital for decoding and reconstructing the doctrine of *qiyāmat* as understood by the Nizārī Ismailis and for our understanding of it.

Al-Shahrastānī's Ismaili affiliation is not revealed simply through his *Majlis* and the *Mafātīḥ* or his references in the *Milal*. His *Muṣāraʿa* is also another indicator. In his foreword to *Keys to the Arcana*, Landolt draws attention to this point, quoting Gimaret: 'it is undeniable that certain aspects of Shahrastānī's personal doctrine as expressed in the *Muṣāraʿa*, the *Majlis,* and indeed the *Milal* itself, manifestly evoke major themes of Ismāʿīlism',[130] but draws attention to the absence of

[128] Al-Ṭūsī, *Rawḍa,* p. 92.
[129] For an extensive list of these terms, see Appendix I.
[130] Mayer, *Keys to the Arcana*, p. xiv.

the commentary in this statement. In this citation, Landolt mentions Madelung's opinion that the *Nihāya* is a classical defence of Ashʿarism and it is in this context that he cites Gimaret who believes otherwise.

Madelung is more specific in the following passage in his discussion of the *Muṣāraʿa*:

> In his Qurʾan commentary the breadth of his concept expressed itself in an eclectic use of Sunni and Shiʿi sources and a range of varying avenues of exegesis. In his *Majlis* and the *Muṣāraʿa* his Ismāʿīlī thought prevails more consistently. Al-Shahrastānī can thus be described as Sunni socially and communally, but as Shiʿi and Ismāʿīlī in some of his core beliefs and religious thought.[131]

Surely, anyone who has been practising *taqiyya* would have to be socially considered as something other than an Ismaili, otherwise the entire idea of *taqiyya* would become totally irrelevant. Madelung's earlier point about the eclectic use of Sunni and Shiʿi sources is valid though, because in the *Mafātīḥ* there is a clear distinction between different headings of *al-naẓm*, *al-maʿānī*, *al-tafsīr* and *al-asrār* (translated by Mayer as lexicography, semantics, exegesis and arcana). All the specifically Ismaili content of the *Mafātīḥ* is to be found in the arcana sections of the book. This is the context of what Madelung argues. Nonetheless, the presence of all the more general Sunni sources does not discount the Ismaili content which is critical to our study.

Steigerwald, who translated the text of the *Majlis* into French, says: 'This short treatise [i.e. the *Majlis*] is in the form of talk in Persian delivered in a mosque, most probably in front of a Twelver Shiʿi audience and it was written during the mature period of his life'.[132] But

[131] Al-Shahrastānī, *Muṣāraʿat al-falāsifa*, ed. and tr. Wilferd Madelung and Toby Mayer as *Struggling with the Philosopher: a Refutation of Avicenna's Metaphysics* (London, 2001), p. 4.

[132] Diane Steigerwald, 'Al-Shahrastānī's Contribution to Medieval Islamic Thought', in Todd Lawson, ed., *Reason and Inspiration in Islam: Theology, Philosophy and Mysticism in Muslim Thought: Essays in Honour of Hermann Landolt* (London, 2005), p. 264.

she does not provide any evidence as to why she thinks the audience was a Twelver one; indeed, there are no references in her article as to what her sources are for this. The text of the *Majlis* does not say anything about its delivery in a mosque either. Perhaps she regarded the *naqīb* of Tirmidh as a Twelver and as such assumed the *Majlis* must have been presented in a mosque and for a Twelver audience. Whatever the case, we have no evidence to this effect. However, continuing, Steigerwald gives further details regarding Monnot's views in favour of al-Shahrastānī's Ismaili affiliation and how he arrived at them:

> In 1983, Guy Monnot embarked on a detailed analysis of the *Mafātīḥ al-asrār* and year after year he discovered more and more Ismaili elements in it. In 1986–1987, Monnot was surprised to discover that al-Shahrastānī believed in an imam present in the world in the Shiʿi sense of the term. The only group which believed in a living imam at that time were the Nizārī Ismailis. Later on, in 1987–1988, he became convinced that al-Shahrastānī was in fact an Ismaili because, in the *Mafātīḥ al-asrār*, he attributes the expression 'Our God is the God of Muḥammad' to the true believers. This same expression is used in the Nizārī section of the *Milal*.[133]

In the *Mafātīḥ*, the nature of al-Shahrastānī's criticism of the Twelvers leaves no doubt about his Ismaili tendencies. Most importantly, as has been alluded to earlier, he criticizes the Twelvers for not following a present living Imam (*al-imām al-ḥāḍir al-ḥayy al-qāʾim*).[134] Regarding the expression of 'Our God is the God of Muhammad',[135] given in the *Mafātīḥ*, al-Shahrastānī employs similar phrases in the *Majlis*: 'We are the people of "thus said God" and "thus said the Messenger of God"'.[136]

[133] Ibid., p. 265.
[134] Al-Shahrastānī, *Mafātīḥ*, ed. M. A. Ādharshab, p. 280.
[135] Ibid., p. 655: 'And our God is the God of Muhammad; therefore, adherence to *tawḥīd* is only accepted as *tawḥīd* once it is accompanied with the *nubuwwa* [of Muhammad].'
[136] Al-Shahrastānī, *Mafātīḥ*, ed. M. A. Ādharshab, p. 655, compared with paragraph 78 of the *Majlis*.

As mentioned above, this is a reiteration of the position of Ḥasan-i Ṣabbāḥ in the doctrine of *ta ʿlīm* reported by al-Shahrastānī himself in the *Milal*. It is, incidentally, also in this section that he criticizes the Nizārīs, although in the *Majlis* and in the *Mafātīḥ* he follows the same logic and argument that he had previously criticized.

Al-Shahrastānī's phrase which makes belief in *tawḥīd* dependent on accepting the *nubuwwa* of Muhammad is remarkably similar to the Ismaili Imam ʿAlāʾ al-Dīn Muḥammad's[137] response to a question asked through al-Ṭūsī:

> This Muḥammad, the Chosen, has been set aside by the one who has given the judgement that the recognition of God depends solely on rational investigation and there is no need for Muḥammad, the Chosen, and the great Qurʾan which [God] has given him. For if he and the other prophets had not come, people would have recognized God by their own thinking and in this sense, there is absolutely no need for them to convey a message. Now, there are only two alternatives: either this Muḥammad-i Muṣṭafā is the messenger of that God according to whose command it is obligatory to accept the word: 'There is no God except Allah', and 'say that God is One', and to uphold his instruction in [the matter of God's] unity. This is religion but whose doctrine is it? Or else he is the messenger of that God whose name, in their judgement, it is not obligatory to pronounce and to confess to His unity and accept this message from him [i.e., Muḥammad], then, whose prophet is he and what is the reason for this message? Now, let them see whether they have set aside this Muḥammad, the Chosen, and his prophethood, or this community.[138]

This paragraph and the phraseology used by al-Shahrastānī are a reiteration of the doctrine of *tawḥīd* through the mediation of the

137 Muḥammad III, also known as ʿAlāʾ al-Dīn Muḥammad, was the seventh lord of Alamūt.

138 S. J. Badakhchani, 'The paradise of submission: a critical edition and study of Rawzeh-i Taslim commonly known as Tasawwurat by Khwajeh Nasir al-Din-i Tusi 1201–1275' (PhD University of Oxford, 1989), p. 239. This paragraph is not available in the published version of the *Rawḍa* and only available in the PhD dissertation of Badakhchani. This is the text of the questions that al-Ṭūsī presented verbally to the Ismaili Imam.

ta ʿlīm of the Imam (as the Truthful Teacher). Here, the argument is that *tawḥīd* relies entirely on the *ta ʿlīm* of the Imam. Once these two are established a new articulation of the Imamate is introduced, leading to a refined doctrine of *qiyāmat*. In the era of *qiyāmat*, responding to the call of the *qā ʾim* for spiritual and intellectual revival is critical for attaining the stage of *waḥdat*. The terms *waḥdat* and *tawḥīd* are different here but closely connected. The first is a spiritual stage and the second is a doctrine but true knowledge of the doctrine of *tawḥīd* is reserved only for the people of *waḥdat* in the doctrine of *qiyāmat*. This is closely connected to the idea of the personification of the Truth in the Imam. In the *Haft bāb-i Ḥasan-i Maḥmūd-i Kātib*, this passage is cited from Ḥasan II:

> Since in the *qiyāmat* God is known and manifest, what else remains to be unknown or hidden? But in the realm of the *sharī ʿat*, which is imaginary and fanciful, what else remains there which is not imaginary or fanciful? In other words, the commandment of God's reality is never imaginary or fanciful, but in the realm of the *sharī ʿat* people find it imaginary.[139]

In the above passage, the phrases 'known and manifest' are translations for '*mushakhkhaṣ wa mu ʿayyan*' which I maintain should be translated differently. It is the idea of personification which is key here. Thus, Ivanow translated the same terms as 'visible and personified'.[140] But whatever choice of words is adopted in a translation, the important idea is that the path to God is through receiving the instruction of the Imam (*ta ʿlīm*) and, further, reaching the stage of *waḥdat* to be unified with the Imam and the idea of God being '*mushakhkhaṣ wa mu ʿayyan*' is particularly important and relevant because al-Shahrastānī writes extensively about this under the category of having a pristine faith (*ḥanīfiyyat*). He describes this *ḥanīfiyyat* as accepting the deputyship

[139] See, Ḥasan-i Maḥmūd-i Kātib, *Haft bāb*, ed. and tr. S. J. Badakhchani, p. 76.
[140] See, Abū Isḥāq Quhistānī, *Haft bāb*, p. 46.

of a man (*niyābat al-rijāl*).[141] The similarities in these texts is remarkable and point to the key argument of al-Shahrastānī's impact on the later formation of Ismaili thought.

Wilferd Madelung deals cautiously the title al-Ṭūsī applied to al-Shahrastānī:

> The title of *dāʿī al-duʿāt* here is, no doubt, to be understood as merely honorary. While al-Shahrastānī was not a member of the Ismāʿīlī *daʿwa,* the passage indicates that his teaching and his works spread Ismāʿīlī thought and encouraged al-Ṭūsī to join the Nizārī community.[142]

Madelung's position does not seem quite congruous with later Nizārī doctrine, which is heavily under the influence of al-Shahrastānī, unless we concede that the Nizārīs freely borrowed ideas and terms from just about anyone. The question that remains is this: why only al-Shahrastānī? Why would they make extensive use of his system of thought and no one else's? While our only explicit source for this title is al-Ṭūsī in *Sayr wa sulūk*, we do not have any reason or source for refuting it either. If we take into account the practice of *taqiyya*, we may find one explanation for some of al-Shahrastānī's seemingly un-Ismaili ideas. However, arriving at an understanding of Ismaili doctrines is a delicate task since they have always been subject to the authority of the living Ismaili Imam and the contingencies of the *daʿwa* system itself. One might therefore argue that if the doctrines that al-Shahrastānī presented and argued for came to be accepted and endorsed by an Ismaili Imam or the *daʿwa,* either during his life or later, there is no reason why this title should be considered purely honorary.

[141] See, paragraph 61 of the *Majlis* and compare with the direct quotes from Ḥasan II in the *Rawḍa*, pp. 123–124. Similarly compare paragraphs 62 and 63 in the *Majlis* with *Rawḍa*, p. 137.

[142] Madelung and Mayer, *Struggling with the Philosopher*, pp. 5–6.

Before the above paragraph, Madelung also recounts al-Shahrastānī's critique of Ḥasan-i Ṣabbāḥ in the *Milal*:

> Al-Shahrastānī then complains that the followers of al-Ḥasan [*sic*] al-Ṣabbāḥ, whenever he sought to engage in theological discussion with any of them, would confine themselves to al-Ḥasan's statement 'Our God is the God of Muḥammad', and tell him that they had no need of him and could learn nothing from him. Al-Shahrastānī responded, conceding the need for an authoritative teacher and asking them where that teacher was, what he would impress on him in theology and what he would prescribe for him in rational matters. A teacher, he suggested, is to be sought not for himself, but for his teaching. In his view, they had thus closed the door of knowledge and opened that of submission and blind imitation *(taqlīd).* No person of sound mind would agree to adopt a doctrine without clear understanding or follow a path without evidence.[143]

He then concludes that this is evidence of al-Shahrastānī's disapproval of Ḥasan-i Ṣabbāḥ's policies and doctrinal positions. With regard to doctrinal positions, there are explanations of these, which al-Shahrastānī now defended in the *Majlis* and the *Mafātīḥ*.[144] Indeed, al-Shahrastānī himself provides an answer. He speaks with confidence about a present living Imam which leaves no doubt that he actually had an answer to the doubts raised by his earlier criticism. He draws a parallel between the Imam in occultation and *imām al-waqt* and *imām al-ḥāḍir al-ḥayy al-qāʾim* which are specific Ismaili terms.[145] This present, living and accessible Imam he talks about is not a figment of imagination for him. In his writings he does not give a name or a location, like Ḥasan-i Ṣabbāḥ who also would not do this, because this was a period of concealment (*satr*) but not of occultation (*ghayba*). In

[143] Madelung and Mayer, *Struggling with the Philosopher*, pp. 4–5.

[144] See, al-Shahrastānī, *Mafātīḥ*, ed. M. A. Ādharshab, p. 655; also see *Majlis*, paragraph 77 and paragraph 68 where he invokes the terms *baṣīrat* and *taqlīd* in a surprisingly similar manner, as if he is responding to his own criticism.

[145] See, al-Shahrastānī, *Mafātīḥ*, ed. M. A. Ādharshab, p. 280.

the *Mafātīḥ*, stating his attitude clearly, he uses particular phraseology in reference to the Imams: 'they are poles and saints, in the physical bodies of men, not in fanciful imagination' (*hum al-aqṭāb wa'l-abdāl fi'l-wujūd al-rijāl, lā fi'l-wahm wa'l-khayāl*).[146]

Regarding political matters, there is some evidence to suggest that an Ismaili could be critical of a peer's or superior figure's activities or ideas. The most prominent examples are the intellectual and theological disputes between the *dāʿīs* Abū Yaʿqūb al-Sijistānī, Abū Ḥātim al-Rāzī and Ḥamīd al-Dīn al-Kirmānī in the Fatimid *daʿwa*. So none of these objections automatically places al-Shahrastānī outside the ranks of the Ismailis. Madelung also makes an assumption which requires further evidence: 'The temporary absence of the Imam, moreover, in his view could not justify the suspension of the religious teaching and reasoning based on the guidance of the past Imams.'[147] Again, this statement is based entirely on the *Milal* and al-Shahrastānī's brief comments there. The context of Ḥasan-i Ṣabbāḥ's teaching concerns the knowledge of God not simply any religious teaching.

One of the other, probably the most interesting, inter-textual links between the works of al-Shahrastānī and later Nizārī works concerns the command (*amr*) being the originator of the Active Intellect (*ʿaql*). This is the major theme in al-Ṭūsī's discussion of command and creation in his *Sayr wa Sulūk*, which is incidentally where he gives al-Shahrastānī the title *dāʿī al-duʿāt*. Al-Ṭūsī's argument revolves around a critique of the position of the philosophers on creation, the role of the first intellect and the primary cause (*ʿillat-i ūlā*). In short, the philosophical argument maintains that there is no intermediary between the primary cause (God, the *wājib al-wujūd*) and the first effect (*maʿlūl-i awwal*).[148] In contrast, al-Ṭūsī maintains that the act of

[146] Ibid., p. 655.
[147] Madelung and Mayer, *Struggling with the Philosopher*, pp. 4–5.
[148] Al-Ṭūsī, *Sayr wa sulūk*, Persian, pp. 8–11; English, pp. 33–38.

creation cannot be directly attributed to God himself as He is above and beyond such attributions. Therefore, all such acts must be attributed to God's command rather than to God Himself. After reconstructing and critiquing the position of the philosophers, al-Ṭūsī concludes that the only community that maintains this position of attributing creation to His command is the Taʿlīmīs:

> There is no doubt that no one maintains such pure unity (*tawḥīd-i ṣirf*), such unconditioned absoluteness (*tanzīh-i maḥḍ*) [of God], except the Taʿlīmiyān; and none of the adherents of [the other] sects, nor any of their leaders, except the instructor of this group, has been able to go to the extent of unveiling this secret. This is because others talk about possibilities (*na shāyad buwad wa shāyad buwad*), whereas he speaks from the position of 'I recognize You through You, and You are my Guide to Yourself'.[149]

The idea of placing the Divine command as the intermediary between God and the active intellect had already been introduced by al-Shahrastānī in his critique of the philosophers (and the argument is the same as is found in al-Ṭūsī's writings). In the *Mafātīḥ*, al-Shahrastānī writes:

> And the philosophers slipped in their judgment when they moved forward in secondary causes (*al-asbāb*) and reached the active intellect (*ʿaql al-faʿʿāl*) giving the verdict that the active intellect was issued forth from the essence of God and not from the command of God. And they concluded the oneness of the active intellect from the oneness of God and not from the oneness of the command of God.[150]

The same kind of argument against the philosophers was also used by al-Ṭūsī in the opening chapters of the *Rawḍa*.[151] In the *Majlis*,

[149] Ibid., pp. 37–38.
[150] Al-Shahrastānī, *Mafātīḥ*, ed. M. A. Ādharshab, pp. 276–277.
[151] See, al-Ṭūsī, *Rawḍa*, pp. 16–30.

al-Shahrastānī does not use the same language but his critique of the philosophers on the issue of the Divine command remains as strong:[152]

> The Anthropomorphists (*mushabbiha*) held there was an essence and a face for God; and their proof was [the tradition] which says: And He created Adam in the image of God.[153] The Karrāmīs maintained there is a corporeal source and a direction for God or [considered Him] subsisting in an essence or a primordial attribute. Their proof was: 'He is Omnipotent over His servants' (6:18). The Ashʿarīs, an essence and eight pre-eternal attributes. Their proof: 'Nor shall they compass aught of His knowledge except as He willeth' (2:255). The Muʿtazilīs, an essence [for God] and attributional characteristics (*aḥkām-i ṣifātī*). Their proof: 'The Living, the Self-subsisting' (2:255). The philosophers, an essence and negative and relative attributes. Their proof: intellect.[154] And at the root of each denomination an anthropomorphism is implied and a negation is necessitated.

For al-Shahrastānī, as for Ḥasan-i Ṣabbāḥ, this intellect is not sufficient for knowing God and this is different from saying that the intellect is redundant. Similarly, we find the same arguments in *Sayr wa sulūk*.

The position of the Nizārī Ismailis on the cosmological question of creation and the role of the active intellect was connected to their articulation of the doctrine of *taʿlīm,* since the Imam was seen as the manifestation of the Divine command in an elevated position: the Imam has an aspect in the realm of creation (*wajh-i khalqī* or *wajh-i iḍāfī*) and an aspect which is of the realm of the command (*wajh-i amrī*). This aspect, or face, of the Imam is the one which became fully integrated into Nizārī doctrine with the Imam becoming the manifestation of God's command. This was a critical doctrine for the

[152] See the current edition, paragraph 76.
[153] See Khalīl Maʾmūn Shayḥā, *Mawsūʿat al-Muʿjam* (Beirut, 2013), vol. 9, p. 346.
[154] This can also be found in al-Ṭūsī's *Sayr wa sulūk*. See *Contemplation and Action*, pp. 34–44.

Nizārīs and the only source from the earlier generations of their community that they could refer to as a basis for this articulation was al-Shahrastānī's writings. These inter-textual links corroborate the claim that al-Shahrastānī did indeed have a senior position in the *daʿwa* system and this claim is not only based on a later comment by al-Ṭūsī or other Ismaili sources; it is supported by the writings of al-Shahrastānī himself as described above. These similarities, like those mentioned so far, are too numerous to be discounted as pure coincidence given that no other Muslim community at that time held such views.

Finally, in the *Milal*, there is an odd phrase found at the end of paragraph 61 of the current edition (in all the other Persian editions the last sentence is recorded incorrectly). The phrase describes *ḥanīfiyyat* as accepting the deputyship of men (meaning specific men, i.e. the Imams) and the *Ḥunafāʾ* are the ones who accept the authority of these men. These ideas are considered in the second volume of the *Milal* where al-Shahrastānī discusses the opinions of the *Ṣābiʾa* and the *Ḥunafāʾ*, presenting a debate between the two groups. In a paragraph which is a response to and rebuttal of the *Ṣābiʾa* by the *Ḥunafāʾ*, al-Shahrastānī writes, 'Most sages (*ḥukamāʾ*) tend to argue in favour of the eternal people (*unās sarmadiyyūn*), that is, people who are ever present.'[155] A parallel to this can be found in al-Shahrastānī's sharp critique of the Imāmiyya in the *Mafātīḥ* mentioned earlier.

The phrase '*unās sarmadiyyūn*' was later used solely by the Nizārī Ismailis to refer to their present, living Imams. There are two instances where the Nizārīs used this phrase in connection with the Imamate. They are both found in works written by al-Ṭūsī. The first one is from his *Rawḍa* where the author quotes Ḥasan II on the doctrine of the Imamate, in a lengthy passage which is apparently from the *Fuṣūl-i*

[155] Al-Shahrastānī, *al-Milal*, ed. Muhannā and Fāʿur, p. 318.

mubarak but in all likelihood part of the sermon of *qiyāmat*[156] given by Ḥasan II:

> If mankind knew what the Imamate is, no one would have entertained doubts such as these. If only they had realized that mutability cannot exist without some immutable [central] point, just as the circumference [cannot exist] without the centre point. For everything that rotates or moves requires a cause for its rotation and movement, and the moving force in relation to the object which rotates or moves must be stable and perfect, in order to be able to spin or move it. This is why it has been said [in the Gospels]: 'Heaven and earth will change, but the commandment of the Sabbath will never be altered'. This means that while the Prophets and the *ḥujjats* may change – at one time this one, at another time that one, at one time in this community, at another time in that – the Imam will never change: 'We are the people of eternity'.[157]

This same phrase appears in al-Ṭūsī's *Akhlāq-i muḥtashamī*[158] under traditions cited from the Imams:

> I am the Sabbath of Sabbaths. I am the aeon of aeons. We are eternal people and our Shiʿa belong to us (*ana sabt al-subūt wa ana dahr al-duhūr. Naḥnu unās sarmadiyyūn wa shīʿatunā minnā*).[159]

[156] See, Abū Isḥāq Quhistānī, *Haft bāb*, p. 42 where Ḥasan II is reported to have started by saying, '*Naḥnu al-ḥādhirūn al-mawjūdūn*' and also al-Ṭūsī, *Rawḍa*, p. 121 where the exact phrase is cited as the words of Ḥasan II. Similarly, it is also cited in al-Ṭūsī, *Akhlāq-i Muḥtashamī*, ed. M. T. Dānishpazhūh (Tehran, 1982), p. 19. For years I have remembered these phrases together as '*naḥnu al-ḥādhirūn al-mawjūdūn wa naḥnu unās sarmadiyyūn*'; Alas, I cannot recall or find where I have seen this phrase in this form.

[157] Al-Ṭūsī, *Rawḍa*, p. 123. The saying given here seems to be a recasting of verses from the Sermon on the Mount, see Matthew 5:18, notable also for its reference to fulfilment; or perhaps draws on Exodus 31:16 where observing the Sabbath is called a 'perpetual covenant', and Isaiah 40:8, 'The grass withereth, the flower fadeth but the Word of the Lord stands forever.'

[158] This is a work by al-Ṭūsī in forty chapters on doctrines of faith putting together in each chapter the relevant Qur'anic verse, *ḥadīth*s from the Prophet and the Imams, sayings of Ismaili *dāʿī*s and citations from philosophers and poets. For this quotation, see also Leviticus 16:31, 23:24, 41 and Exodus, 16:23 for references to the 'Sabbath of Sabbaths', and the Sabbath set in perpetuity, etc., all of which demonstrates al-Ṭūsī's range of learning.

[159] Al-Ṭūsī, *Akhlāq-i Muḥtashamī*, p. 19.

In a footnote to the English translation of the *Rawḍa* regarding the quoted speech of Ḥasan *ʿalā dhikrihi al-salām*, Badakhchani says this may be a saying by Imam Jaʿfar al-Ṣādiq and then refers to al-Kulaynī's *al-Kāfī* for similar sayings.[160] However, the particular phrase *unās sarmadiyyūn* cannot be found in al-Kulaynī's work. I have compared in more detail the similarity of terms and phrases used in the *Majlis* and the *Mafātīḥ* in several footnotes of the Persian text of the *Majlis*. So here, we have at least five texts (if we do not include the *Haft bāb-i Abū Isḥāq*) to compare: the *Majlis*, *al-Milal* and the *Mafātīḥ* by al-Shahrastānī with al-Ṭūsī's *Akhlāq-i Muḥtashamī* and *Rawḍa*. The outcome of this comparison and the reconstruction of the bigger picture gives us a better understanding of the *Majlis*.

The section of the *Milal* where this phrase appears is, as mentioned above, a description of a (supposed) debate, a dialectical conversation between the *Ṣābʾia* and the *Ḥunafāʾ*. Al-Shahrastānī's delineation of the position of the *Ḥunafāʾ* is very much a description of the Nizārī Ismailis and their doctrine of Imamate (emphasizing the centrality of a present living Imam in each era). This is further emphasized when these passages are placed alongside his references to the *ḥanīfiyyāt* in the *Majlis* referred to above. Intertextual comparison of references in the works of al-Shahrastānī and those in acknowledged seminal doctrinal Nizārī works produces a clear image of him. The fact that this terminology is an integral part of both al-Shahrastānī's thought and that of Nizārī Ismaili doctrine leaves little doubt that they belong to one and the same tradition. It would be a very rare, almost akin to an impossible, coincidence for a non-Ismaili author to be even tempted to speak in this language particularly at a time when a mere indication of being an Ismaili posed an immediate risk to life. Finally, it must be reiterated that the fact that *al-Milal* was translated into Persian by the Nizārīs in the Alamūt period (which is the oldest

[160] Badakhchani, ed. and tr., *Paradise of Submission*, pp. 123, 259 fn. 112.

known, accurate translation of this work into Persian) demonstrates that al-Shahrastānī was a very important figure for them. His ideas, his writings, the terminology he had invented (deploying the dyads of *mafrūgh* and *musta'naf, taḍādd* and *tarattub*, etc.), the way in which he articulated the Imamate, all became an inseparable part of Nizārī doctrine.

Fatimid precedents or a shifting narrative?

In trying to connect al-Shahrastānī with the Ismailis, Steigerwald tends to look back and compare him with the figures of the Fatimid period, including the *dā'īs* al-Qāḍī al-Nuʿmān and Abū Ḥātim al-Rāzī. She finds parallels between al-Shahrastānī's narrative of the encounter between Mūsā and Khiḍr in the *Majlis* and that of al-Qāḍī al-Nuʿmān in his *Risāla al-mudhhiba*. She also compares the story of Ibrāhīm's spiritual progress as narrated by al-Shahrastānī in the *Majlis* with Abū Ḥātim al-Rāzī's narrative in the *Kitāb al-iṣlāḥ* and al-Qāḍī al-Nuʿmān's in his *Asās al-ta'wīl*. Khiḍr is represented as the deputy of the Resurrection and ʿAlī as the *qā'im*. She summarizes these points as follows:

> In the *Majlis*, al-Shahrastānī clearly distinguishes different spiritual ranks: Moses as the judge of *sharī'a*, Khiḍr as the Deputy (*nā'ib*) of the Judge of the Resurrection (*qiyāma*) and ʿAlī as the Riser (*qā'im*). Two forms of light were inherited from Abraham: a visible light (*nūr-ī ẓāhir*) and a hidden one (*nūr-ī mastūr*). These two lights recall the Shiʿi concepts of the *nūr al-nubuwwa* (the light of prophecy) and the *nūr al-imāma* (the light of the *imāma*).[161]

[161] Diane Steigerwald, 'Al-Shahrastānī's Contribution to Medieval Islamic Thought', in Todd Lawson, ed., *Reason and Inspiration in Islam: Theology, Philosophy and Mysticism in Muslim Thought: Essays in Honour of Hermann Landolt* (London, 2005), p. 269. See also this edition, paras 59–63.

Steigerwald's parallels are interesting to follow, certainly suggesting that al-Shahrastānī was following an earlier template provided by previous figures in the Ismaili *daʿwa*. But al-Shahrastānī also develops a narrative that introduces new elements to Nizārī doctrine. In particular, we need to look at how Ḥasan II introduced himself first as the deputy of the Imam (*nāʾib*) when he declared the *qiyāmat*, only claiming the Imamate at a later point. One possibility is that when Muḥammad b. Buzurg-Umīd, the second ruler of Alamūt, died, the father to whom Ḥasan II supposedly traced his lineage may still have been alive. Hence, Ḥasan II might have been conveying a message from the Imam (these are his own words).[162] Be that as it may, we need to consider the point that after al-Shahrastānī, Nizārī doctrines were rearticulated and reoriented. The legacy of al-Kirmānī moved to a different branch of the Ismailis and the Nizārīs tended to articulate their beliefs using a different approach from the dominant Neoplatonism of earlier generations. Al-Shahrastānī, himself opposed to this Neoplatonism, had a fundamental role in this development.

Ashʿarism modified?

Ashʿarism, as a theological school, emerged in the early centuries of Islam and one of its central themes related to discussions around good and evil. The key question which led to their disagreement with the Muʿtazila was whether human beings can independently, without reference to revelation, decide on good and evil purely by relying solely on their autonomous human minds. Details of theological discussions between the Ashʿarīs and the Muʿtazilīs (and the differences in their subgroups) are beyond the scope of this discussion.

[162] See, Hodgson, *The Order*, pp. 148–157.

What I will be discussing here revolves around the question of objectivity of good and evil only.[163]

Hitherto, al-Shahrastānī has been widely known as an Ashʿarī *mutakallim*. For this reason, his connection with the Ismailis has frequently been summarily dismissed, not least because it would appear intuitively correct to declare that Ashʿarism is in conflict with Ismaili doctrines. In this section, the idea that al-Shahrastānī's Ashʿarī background does not preclude his being an Ismaili will be discussed. When speaking about al-Shahrastānī's faith, a coherent understanding of what constitutes Ismailism in the early Alamūt period is essential. It is often argued that Ismailism concerns a Neoplatonist cosmology. This is a correct description but only in a particular sense and in a particular era, that is to say as interpreted under the Fatimid caliphate. The same applies to how the Ismailis throughout the centuries have seen esotericism – *taʾwīl* – in regard to scripture. The list of items which fall under the category of what constitutes being an Ismaili is not infinitely long. There is more or less an agreement on what the Ismailis have believed in but yet again, 'being an Ismaili' is often reduced to singular abstract ideas rather than the multiple, fluid and concrete contingencies of different eras. For example, belief in a present living Imam is a key and integral part of being an Ismaili. But resorting to *taʾwīl* by employing a Neoplatonist form of language is not. This is demonstrated by the different genres of *taʾwīl* used by the Ismailis in different eras, examples of which can be found in al-Qāḍī al-Nuʿmān's *Asās al-taʾwīl* and al-Ṭūsī's *Āghāz wa anjām*, besides, of course, al-Shahrastānī's *Mafātīḥ*. These are all examples of different genres of *taʾwīl* and none of them could be considered 'non-Ismaili'.

The case of al-Shahrastānī's writings is no exception to this. In order to come up with a working definition which is neither too broad

[163] For an extensive discussion of the ideas of the Ashāʿira, see George Hourani, *Reason and Tradition in Islamic Ethics* (Cambridge, 1985).

nor too exclusivist, it would be fair to argue that being an Ismaili is defined by adherence to the authority of the Ismaili Imams. Depending on the Imam or the line of Ismaili Imams, the particular version of being an Ismaili immediately becomes clear. The claim here is that al-Shahrastānī, at the very least during the last two decades of his life, was a Nizārī Ismaili and this falls in a period of Ismaili history later known as one of concealment for the Imams between Nizār b. al-Mustanṣir and Ḥasan II. If it can be demonstrated that he acknowledged this particular line of Imams, we may safely argue that he was a Nizārī Ismaili. Within this context, it does not matter whether his *kalāmī* ideas were closer to those of the Ashʿarīs or those of the Muʿtazilīs. Indeed, the different and varying doctrinal positions of the Ismailis show that as long as they viewed themselves committed to their belief in a present and living Imam, they were happy to revise and reformulate their doctrinal beliefs within the wider parameters of how they viewed themselves as Shiʿi Ismaili Muslims. The most prominent examples of works that demonstrate this, apart from the works named above, are those produced in the post-Alamūt era such as *Pandīyāt Jawānmardī* attributed to the Ismaili Imam Mustanṣir bi'llāh II (d. 885/1480), and Shihāb al-Dīn Shah's (d. 1302/1884) *Risāla dar ḥaqīqat-i dīn*. Both of these works contain an esoteric interpretation, yet each presents a different genre of *taʾwīl*; but their Shiʿi Ismaili Muslim identity is beyond doubt. An overview of the evolution of Ismaili doctrine clearly demonstrates that apart from the actual doctrine of Imamate and adherence to the necessity of the existence of a present and living Imam, all other elements have been modified and revised depending on circumstances and in response to the problems that were faced. For instance, the mingling of the Nizārī Ismailis with the Sufis in the post-Alamūt era clearly shows how, over several centuries, their doctrines were influenced by various approaches found in the Sufism of Khurāsān, and the Sufism of the Niʿmatullāhī order that developed in the post-Mongol era.

Nonetheless, the fundamental doctrine of the Imamate has remained intact in practice through being always determined by way of the *naṣṣ* (designation) and the continuous line of Imams succeeding each other, one after another.[164] This can also be seen in earlier periods, including that in which al-Shahrastānī lived: succession by way of the *naṣṣ* remained as it were the spinal cord whatever the doctrinal variations.

One can clearly identify certain Ashʿarī tendencies in al-Shahrastānī's writings. Indeed, his *Nihāyat al-aqdām fī ʿilm al-kalām* is generally considered to be an Ashʿarī work.[165] What has received little attention is whether or not the Ismailis could bring their doctrines closer to Ashʿarī attitudes thereby moving further away from rationalist Muʿtazilī positions. The case of al-Shahrastānī is indeed one example of how the Ismailis were able to operate beyond the clear boundaries and differing identities of other Muslim communities. In the case of al-Shahrastānī, the present text is an eloquent proof of this point: in particular, the section on the encounter between Mūsā and Khiḍr is a discussion regarding the objectivity of good and evil. Mūsa's fundamental question is: how can one punish someone for an act which has not yet happened? This is the classical debate between the Ashāʿira and the Muʿtazila. Therefore, it constitutes an interaction or dialogue between an Ismaili doctrine or philosophy, to which the doctrine of Imamate is central and critical, and Ashʿarī theology presented by someone who, it should be said, was trained in the Shāfiʿī school of jurisprudence. Two prominent theological themes – which have their own share of rational substance – converge here: the traditional Ashʿarī ethical voluntarism – that is 'the only standard of value for God and man was the will of God; whatever

[164] See also Daryoush Mohammad Poor, *Authority without Territory*, p. 14.

[165] In his introduction to the facsimile edition of the *Nihāya*, ʿImādī Ḥāʾirī makes the argument that al-Sharastānī retained an Ashʿārī structure for his arguments but the content was Ismaili, pp. 11–15.

He wills is good by definition'[166] – and the classical Ismaili-Shiʿi elevation of the status of the Imam (which Öztürk, incidentally, attributes exclusively to Akhbārī Imamism). The resulting product is a new doctrine which is both an evolution of Ashʿarism (which al-Shahrastānī was generally held to have subscribed to) and of Ismaili thought. So, we are presented with multiple evolutions or perfections of doctrine (to use al-Shahrastānī's explanation of the development (*ikmāl*) of religion).[167]

Theistic subjectivism or ethical voluntarism: Ashʿarism evolved

In order to shed more light on what may constitute the central aspect of this evolution, we need to look a little closer at the way the question of ethics was approached among the Ashʿarīs in al-Shahrastānī's time.[168] For the Ashʿarīs, an act could ethical only if God said so. George Hourani provides a summation of this position:

> The only standard of value for God and man was the will of God; whatever He wills is good by definition. This is ethical voluntarism, which after the jurist Shāfiʿī (d. 820) became the first principle of Islamic law in most schools. By adopting it traditionalist theologians could claim that God's will suffers no ethical limits. Thus, even if He punishes sinners whose acts He has predestined He cannot be called 'unjust', for justice means nothing but obedience to divine laws, and God is not subject to any laws.[169]

[166] George Hourani, *Reason and Tradition in Islamic Ethics*, p. 8.

[167] It is important to note what is meant by terms such as development, perfection or evolution. In many cases, what al-Shahrastānī has in mind is the analogy of the development of a foetus in the womb and he applies the same analogy to religious laws. See *Majlis*, paragraph 29.

[168] Ashʿarī and Muʿtazilī thought came in various versions throughout their history. What is referred to here is what was current in al-Shahrastānī's time.

[169] George Hourani, *Reason and Tradition*, p. 8.

A comparison can be made between this approach and the section on the encounter of Mūsā and Khiḍr in the *Majlis*, paragraph 82 onwards.

The descriptive term of ethical voluntarism is broadly applicable to the Ismailis in the sense that ethical conduct is ultimately determined by the Imam. This proposition has a caveat of course. Were we to present this argument to al-Shahrastānī, he would immediately ask about the context: is this the context of contrariety or is it the context of hierarchy? Or is this supposed to be applicable in the realm of *tawḥīd*? In the words of al-Shahrastānī himself in the *Majlis* (paragraph 96):

> Your error is that you only know of one decree! Almighty God has two decrees for verdicts as they happen. One is the accomplished (*mafrūgh*) and the other is the inchoative (*musta ʾnaf*). One is already processed and other is being processed. One is the determination (*taqdīr*) and the other is the obligation (*taklīf*).

This is, of course, fundamentally different from Ashʿarism, because here there are *two* decrees and that is different from the categorical voluntarism of Ashʿarīs. Needless to say, this is a far more complicated issue and simply saying Nizārī Ismaili thought was close to Ashʿarī thought will not suffice. In explaining the context of the theological debates of the Ashʿarīs, Hourani adds:

> Following up the line of thought started by Shāfiʿī and Ibn Ḥanbal, theologians before al-Ashʿarī as well as al-Ashʿarī himself formulated these reactions, although still in rather brief statements. The main objection they raised against rationalistic ethics was that independent human reason implies a limit on the power of God; for if man could judge what is right and wrong he could rule on what God could rightly prescribe for man, and this would be presumptuous and blasphemous. They further objected that the judgements of reason were arbitrary, based only on desires; that such judgements in fact always contradicted each other; and lastly that they arrogated the function of revelation and rendered it useless. The doctrine of this school on ethics

> corresponded with that of Shāfiʿī on legal justice; in brief, that right action is that which is commanded by God. In fact we can find an even closer relation than one of correspondence, for such a view merges right ethical action with legal justice. I call this view (of both jurists and theologians) 'theistic subjectivism'.[170]

One can find many allusions in Shiʿi traditions and theology to similar arguments regarding how reason could approach the question of what is good or ethical, such as the famous rule which says 'whatever is decreed by reason is also decreed by religious law and vice versa'.[171] The key here is the independence and autonomy of human reason, rather than interdependence: can human reason discover or decide the goodness or evilness of something on its own, without the assistance of revelation? In the case of the Ismailis, this is what broadly leads to the genesis and development of the doctrine of *taʿlīm*; at least, this is what the Nizārī Ismailis and the Ashʿarīs share: human beings cannot determine good and evil independently of the authority of the Imam of the Time (or, the case of the Ashāʿira, God without any intermediary or guide). The Ismailis were not on particularly good terms with the rationalist Muʿtazila. We have at least one specific critique of the Muʿtazila by Ḥamīd al-Dīn al-Kirmānī in his *Rāḥat al-ʿaql*, but Ismaili objections do not necessarily suggest a hostile and aggressive position against reason or intellect as such.[172] The Ismailis employed human reason widely in matters of faith and evidence of this abounds.[173] Just to add one reference, one can look at the opening

[170] Hourani, *Reason and Tradition*, p. 17.

[171] See, Murtaḍā al-Anṣārī, *Farāʾid al-uṣūl*, ed. Ḥasan al-Marāghī (Qumm, 1384 Sh./2005), p. 598.

[172] See, Ḥamīd al-Dīn al-Kirmānī, *Rāḥat al-ʿaql*, ed. Muḥammad Kāmil Ḥusayn and Muḥammad Muṣṭafā Ḥilmī (Cairo, 1953), p. 53.

[173] This is contrary to al-Ghazālī's polemic in his *al-Munqidh* where he claims that the Ismailis had abandoned reason altogether. See Muḥammad al-Ghazālī, *al-Munqidh min al-ḍalāl*, ed. Jamīl Ṣalībā and Kāmil ʿAyyād (Beirut, 1967), pp. 91–99. See also Farouk Mitha, *Al-Ghazālī and the Ismailis: A Debate on Reason and Authority in Medieval Islam* (London, 2001).

chapter of al-Mu'ayyad fi'l-Dīn al-Shīrāzī's *al-Majālis al-Mu'ayyadiyya* in which he discusses whether a believer can question the Prophet or not regarding the decrees of the *sharī'a*. In this chapter, his main thesis is that all rules and decrees of the *sharī'a* are founded on reason. His response is that if ever the Prophet had failed to provide a reasonable answer as to why a particular rule is ordained in the *sharī'a* (such as in rituals of worship) or had requested the believers simply to accept a rule as it is, then they would have had a right to leave the faith.[174]

In the discussion on Ash'ārism and Ismailism however, we are not talking about whether the *sharī'a* is founded on reason or not; the key area of contention has to do with the concept of *tawḥīd*. Here, at least in form, the Nizārī Ismailis are notably closer to the Ash'arīs. Explaining his reason for using the phrase 'theistic subjectivism', Hourani continues:

> It is subjectivist because it relates values to the view of a judge who *decides* them, denying anything objective in the character of acts themselves that would make them right or wrong independently of anyone's decision or opinion. And the view is theistic because the decider of values is taken to be God. A more usual name is 'ethical voluntarism'.[175]

In the Ismaili context, the one who decides on values is taken to be the Imam, because in Ismaili doctrine knowledge of God is only possible through the instruction of a truthful teacher and indeed *tawḥīd* becomes obsolete without trust in this teacher.[176] In the first instance the teacher is the Prophet – to whose name a key testimony is linked[177]

[174] See, Hermann Landolt, Samira Sheikh and Kutub Kassam, ed., *An Anthology of Ismaili Literature* (London, 2008), pp. 131–134.
[175] Hourani, *Reason and Tradition*, p. 17.
[176] See, al-Ṭūsī, *Sayr wa sulūk*, p. 30.
[177] See, *Majlis*, paragraph 57, where al-Shahrastānī explains that without accepting the authority of Muhammad the *tawḥīd* itself remains incomplete.

and then this *ta ʿlīm* becomes the function of the Imams or *qā ʾims* who are responsible for the protection and perfection of the faith. In the words of al-Shahrastānī, if anyone were to describe the question of ethics in plain Ashʿarī terms, it would look like Mūsā's objections to Khiḍr's actions. But to see what would be the Nizārī Ismaili position that is closest to an Ashʿarī one in the matter of ethics, one can examine one of the seminal Nizārī texts, the *Rawḍa-yi taslīm* of Naṣīr al-Dīn al-Ṭūsī. It contains a chapter on the refinement of character (*tahdhīb-i akhlāq*), which is a juxtaposition of a radical Nizārī Ismaili imamology[178] and passages from the liturgical text of *al-Ṣaḥīfa al-Sajjādiyya*, the collection of psalms or supplications attributed to Imam Zayn al-ʿĀbidīn ʿAlī b. al-Ḥusayn b. ʿAlī.[179] The opening of the chapter contains the following passage:

> In every epoch, all ethical values (*akhlāq*) and social conduct (*mu ʿāmalāt*) are deemed good once they are attached to the command of the truthful master of the age (*amr-i muḥiqq-i waqt*) – may salutations be upon the mention of his name – and are deemed evil once severed from his command. Therefore, the foundation of refinement of character (*tahdhīb-i akhlāq*) is to obey the command of the truthful of the age and submit to him in sincerity.[180] For one cannot know, in effect, what type of morality every truthful master in each particular epoch prescribes, ordains and considers as appropriate for the people [of his time]. For this reason, if one persists in observing ethical codes and manners permitted and sanctioned by a truthful master, but when another truthful master [of a later epoch] perceives that moral prosperity lies in following a different course which he indicates to be licit, and if one hesitates to follow that [second] command and is troubled with confusion, thus generating objections

[178] The chapter extensively cites supplications of Imam Zayn al-ʿĀbidīn in *al-Ṣaḥifa Sajjādiyya* and argues that he composed these in order to teach his disciples how to respect the position of the Imams, which was above and beyond that of ordinary human beings. See *Rawḍa*, p. 94.

[179] See the footnote for paragraph 93 of the *Majlis* in this edition.

[180] This section is a revised translation. From here onwards, it is that by Badakhchani.

> and scruples within one, such objections will result in the impossibility [of all faith] – may God protect us from that![181]

Hourani no doubt would have seen nothing but ethical voluntarism in this! But, as explained earlier, there is a caveat here. Al-Ṭūsī proceeds to explain the reason for providing passages from the *Ṣaḥifa al-Sajjādiyya* in the context of the refinement of character:

> In order that devotees may learn how they may avoid falling into error, how they should fear their Lord, how they should submit to Him, how they should know themselves, and what they should ask for themselves, [the Imams] have given expression to sacred utterances. And out of extreme mercy towards [their] followers and for the sake of admonishing them, they have taken it upon themselves ... so that the obedient servants will understand that the Imams themselves are free [of such expressions] and exalted above such [matters].[182]

His explanation is not just an elevation of the status of the Imam but articulates a key Nizārī Ismaili argument which is at the heart of the doctrine of *taʿlīm*: the Imam is in truth and in reality above and free from anything worldly and from any flaw or defect. Therefore, these words are simply provided to *teach* the believers how they should respect their Lord and be fearful of him and also to know that the Imam himself is not subject to these human attributes. However, what keeps the Nizārī Ismailis from giving an absolute Divine attribute to the Imam is the theological articulation of the relationship between command and creation, the subject of al-Shahrastānī's *Majlis*: the Imam is the manifestation of God's command. Thus, the Imam is neither God nor is he the command of God. He is a manifestation of God's command. The point of the similarity in form between the Ashʿarī position on ethics (and morality) and the Nizārī Ismaili

[181] Al-Ṭūsī, *Rawḍa*, p. 93.
[182] Ibid., p. 94.

viewpoint is that the Nizārīs had taken the matter to a whole new level. To the Ashʿarīs, it was a theological debate which was dependent on the literal wording of the Qurʾan and the *ḥadīth*. To the Ismailis, it involved the esoteric truth and required a hermeneutical exegesis of the Divine word which placed the figure of the Imam at the centre of faith. The most significant event during the Alamūt period in terms of doctrine was clearly the declaration of *qiyāmat*. And the wording of various passages in the *Rawḍā*, including the opening of the chapter on the refinement of character cited above, indicates this. There were people who were uncomfortable with changes in the decrees of different Imams (from the time of Ḥasan II to the time of Ḥasan III and then Muḥammad III). The faithful were always required to look to the Imam of their Time for advice not to an earlier Imam. So, in the above statement God is only textually replaced by the Imam not literally and substantially. The Imam does not become God; the highest level of the Imamate is the manifestation of God's command.

The above comparisons help to clarify an earlier point. However, a further possibility can be presented concerning Ashʿarism. Ḥasan-i Ṣabbāḥ had declared political and doctrinal independence from the Fatimid caliphate in Cairo, reformulating Ismaili doctrine. If Ashʿarism were to meet or intersect with Ismaili doctrine then, in the process of a reformulation, the end result would have resembled something to which both al-Shahrastānī with his Ashʿarī background (he was, after all, educated in an Ashʿarī environment) and the cryptic figure,[183] the encounter with whom he refers to in the *Mafātīḥ*, could have contributed.[184]

What we find in the *Rawḍa* is a refined and polished version of what is already articulated in the *Majlis* and in the *Mafātīḥ* on questions

[183] See, T. Mayer, *Keys to the Arcana*, pp. 6–8.

[184] This is pure speculation for which I have no evidence or reference. This cryptic figure could very well have been the Ismaili Imam from the descendants of Nizār, as according to Ismaili tradition, living in concealment around Alamūt. Could this have been the Imam, who according to the Nizārīs, is the true father of Ḥasan II?

of ethics. This is, however, not limited to the *Rawḍa*. As pointed out in the footnotes to the edited Persian text and the English translation, the parallels between al-Shahrastānī's works and every known Nizārī text of the Alamūt period produced after him are so numerous that it leaves no doubt today that the Nizārīs almost always looked to the works of al-Shahrastānī when articulating their doctrine. No doubt they produced further refinements or amendments,[185] either in terms or in formulations (and this is the subject of future studies), but the content is sometimes fascinatingly similar – often the verbatim reproduction of texts and passages by al-Shahrastānī, which results in what Mayer has described as 'the lattice of complementarities'.[186]

The present edition of the *Majlis*

There are several reasons for preparing a new Persian edition and English translation of the *Majlis*. First of all, there is no complete English translation of the text available. In December 1983, Mumtaz Virani translated the text of the *Majlis* into English for her dissertation as part of her graduate studies at The Institute of Ismaili Studies. The text, which is based on Jalālī Nāʾīnī's edition, remains unpublished. Steigerwald's French translation is also based on Jalālī Nāʾīnī's edition.[187] She also reproduces the later version (1369 Sh./1990) of Jalālī Nāʾīnī's Persian edition which takes into account the manuscript from Istanbul.[188] The *Majlis* was also translated into Arabic and published in an appendix to the edition of the *Mafātīḥ* produced by Muḥammad ʿAlī Ādharshab in 2008.

[185] Examples of these differences can be found in al-Ṭūsī's *Rawḍa* and *Āghāz wa anjām*.
[186] Mayer, *Keys to the Arcana*, p. 6.
[187] Diane Steigerwald, *Majlis: Discours sur l'Ordre et la création* (Saint-Nicolas, Québec, 1998).
[188] H. Landolt's foreword in Mayer, *Keys to the Arcana*, p. 54, note 69.

The purpose of the current edition is, first of all, to provide a readable Persian text of the *Majlis*. The first Persian edition of the text by Jalālī Nā᾽īnī appears as an appendix to the Persian translation of the *Milal* by Afḍal al-Dīn Ṣadr Turka al-Isfāhānī (1956). This text of the *Majlis* is a long block quote and the entire text is printed as one paragraph only. The second Persian edition of the text by Jalālī Nā᾽īnī, which appeared in the *Sharḥ-i hāl wa āthār* (1964) is replete with interventions and insertions by the editor, either in terms of the phrases or in terms of parentheses and quotation marks added to make the text more readable. The ordering of the paragraphs is also based on the way he has read the text. There are several errors to be found in these editions which I have endeavoured to resolve in the present edition. In his second edition of the *Majlis* published together with the translation of the *Milal*, Jalālī Nā᾽īnī omitted all his previous insertions and published the text as one single long paragraph. Jalālī Nā᾽īnī's first two printed editions (the 1956 and 1964 editions) were based on a single manuscript (no. 593 dated 1060/1650) which he had found in the library of the Majlis (the Iranian National Consultative Assembly). It should be said that in his third edition, published in a volume entitled *Du maktūb* (1990), which was the one used by Steigerwald, many earlier errors were rectified, although some remained.

A major difficulty in preparing the edition published here was that it was necessary to read the sentences many times even after completing the collation of the manuscripts in order to establish the correct punctuation. Translating the text into English was not merely a challenge; it was also the key to finding the right punctuation and correct reading of the Persian text. While translating the text I realized that punctuation marks were sometimes in the wrong place in Jalālī Nā᾽īnī's editions. So, I have added punctuation to both the Persian text and the English translation, deciding on the correct placement of verbs and the inclusion and placement of colons and semi-colons to reflect a correct reading of the sentences. As a result, I have kept the punctuation in the Persian text to a minimum to make it easier on the eye of the modern reader.

Further to the manuscripts examined by Jalālī Nāʾīnī, in the current edition I have been fortunate to be able to refer to two other manuscripts. The first of these, which is the basis of the current edition, is from the Marʿashī library in Qumm, Iran. It is manuscript no. 12868 which was published in facsimile form in 2013 as part of a compendium of works entitled *Majmūʿa-yi Quṭb al-Dīn Shīrāzī*.[189] This manuscript is dated 685/1286 and so is the oldest one available.[190] I have referred to this manuscript as Q (ق) in the footnotes to the Persian text. The second is part of the undated manuscript no. 10117 held by the Majlis library in Tehran. I have referred to this manuscript as manuscript M (م) in the footnotes to the Persian text. In general, I have followed Jalālī Nāʾīnī's last edition of the *Majlis* but have relied mainly on manuscript Q for most of the variations comparing them also with manuscript M. However, these two manuscripts lack the first three paragraphs and part of the fourth paragraph given in the present edition. These paragraphs are the result of a collation of Jalālī Nāʾīnī's text with yet another undated manuscript from the University of Tehran Library, manuscript no. 643/24, which consists of only two folios. I have referred to this manuscript as manuscript T (ت). Manuscripts M and T are both in *nastʿalīq* script written in a very clear and legible hand. The Q manuscript is in *shikasta nastaʿlīq* and is not easily legible, but sentences or phrases have been divided by inserting a triangle of three dots at the end of each one. Since it is the

[189] Sabine Schmidtke and Reza Pourjavady, intro., *The Quṭb al-Dīn al-Shīrāzī Codex*, facsimile edition of the Marʿashī codex 12868 (Qumm, 1391 Sh./2013).

[190] Quṭb al-Dīn al-Shīrāzi was al-Ṭūsī's disciple in Marāgha. It is of considerable interest that a work by al-Shahrastānī, indicating his Ismaili connections was copied in Marāgha which happened to be the scientific centre created by al-Ṭūsī in the aftermath of Mongol invasion. Al-Ṭūsī seems to have been instrumental, quietly and shrewdly, in saving and preserving Ismaili works.

oldest manuscript and probably a close copy of al-Shahrastānī's original copy, it helps in achieving a better reading of the text. Manuscript M seems to be copied from manuscript Q which is the oldest manuscript available.

In manuscript Q, on which the current edition is based, it states that the text was copied from a manuscript copied by al-Shīrāzī in his own handwriting tracing three other manuscripts between it and the text written by al-Shahrastānī himself. Based on the latest edition of Jalālī Nāʾīnī in *Du maktūb*, I have indicated variations compared to it marking them as manuscript J (ج).

In the current edition, I have reorganized the paragraphs and numbered them accordingly, and the English translation corresponds to the Persian paragraph numbers to make it easier for the reader to follow the translation. I have broken the text down into more coherent paragraphs by adding punctuation, commas, full stops, semicolons, hyphens, etc., adding annotations from various Nizārī texts and also from al-Shahrastānī's *Mafātīḥ* to allow for a clearer reading of the text. I have also closely followed the original orthography of the text as it appears in the oldest manuscript (Q). The numbering of paragraphs is entirely mine and does not correspond to either Jalālī Nāʾīnī's editions or any of the manuscripts; it has been added so that the reader can better compare the Persian with the English and also in order to break down long sentences into shorter ones again for ease of reading. Quotation marks and brackets have been dropped with the exception of a few which I have retained from Jalālī Nāʾīnī's text. I have indicated which ones are his. All Qurʾanic verses have their references in front of them in the form of *sūra* and *āya* numbers. All traditions and *ḥadīth*s are presented in quotation marks with their references in footnotes. Also, in the second half of the book, in the Persian edition, I have highlighted in bold when either Mūsā or Khiḍr speak, in order to present the paragraphs as dialogue between the two figures. For translations of Qurʾanic verses, I have mostly used Arberry's *The*

Koran Interpreted. However, in some instances I have chosen Yusuf Ali's translation depending on the context. I have provided an index of Qur'anic citations for both the Persian and the English translation with the reference being the relevant paragraph/s. Al-Shahrastānī has a habit of providing his own Persian translation of some verses in order to articulate his point further. It is often not easy to follow a single English translation in these cases. Therefore, depending on the case, translations of verses have varied in order to remain as faithful as possible to the original text of the *Majlis*. It goes without saying that all translations are interpretations and I have endeavoured to remain as close as I can to the context of al-Shahrastānī's treatise.

All the Nizārī Ismaili texts which are referenced in the footnotes of the Persian text are Badakhchani's editions for which I have not only given page numbers but also the paragraph numbers. This makes it easier to trace the passages in question in both the Persian and English. The page numbers for the Persian edition of the *Rawḍa* are based on the version published by Mirāth-i Maktūb in Iran but the paragraph numbering is the same in all English and Persian editions. In the English, all references to published edited works are to their English texts.

Tāj al-Dīn Muḥammad b. ʿAbd al-Karīm al-Shahrastānī

Majlis-i maktūb-i munʿaqid dar Khwārazm

The Transcribed Sermon in Khwārazm

English Translation

The Transcribed Sermon in Khwārazm

In the name of God, the Merciful, the Compassionate

Here is the sermon delivered by the Imam Tāj al-Dīn Muḥammad b. ʿAbd al-Karīm al-Shahrastānī, may God have mercy upon him

[1] To God the Exalted belongs the creation and the command: 'Verily, His are the creation and the command' (7:54). To Him belongs creation, His terrestrial sovereignty and the command, His spiritual sovereignty. His command is the source of His creation; His creation is the manifestation of His command. His creation did not exist; it came into being through His command. His command did not exist; it became manifest through His creation. The existence of all creatures is through His command: 'His command, when He desires a thing, is to say to it "Be," and it is' (36:82). The manifestation of His command is through His creation: so that God might manifest His command.

[2] If you wish to make a correspondence between pre-eternity (*qidam*) and temporality (*ḥudūth*) and creation and command, then pre-eternity falls to command which carries within it the eternal and the perennial; and temporality falls to creation since creation has a beginning and an end.

[3] And when you want to attribute unity and plurality to creation and command, then unity will fall to command because it is all encompassing while plurality will be attributed to creation since creation has the properties of measure (*miqdār*) and quantity (*kammiyyat*): 'Surely We have created everything in measure. Our commandment is but one word, as the twinkling of an eye' (54:49–50).

[4] The divine command is the epithet of one of the infinite complete words [of the Lord] (*kalimāt-i tāmmāt-i bī nihāyat*): 'And the sea – seven seas after it to replenish it, yet would the Words of God not be spent' (31:27); neither is His command limited by time; nor are His words restricted by space. Neither will the passage of time bring motion to His command nor will the tranquillity of space bring rest to His words. Time and space were but two modest servants standing by the door of His creation working under the aegis of His command: And eternity is the entirety of all time; and the throne is the entirety of all space. Time has a beginning and an end; space has an outward and an inward [aspect]: 'He is the First and the Last' (57:3) so you would know that His existence is not bound by time – 'the Outward and the Inward' (57:3) so you would know that His existence is not bound by space either.

[5] You have a body and a soul. Your body is spatial (*makānī*). Your soul temporal (*zamānī*). Your body belongs to the realm of creation and your soul belongs to the realm of command: 'Say: The Spirit is of the command of my Lord' (17:85).[1] Your body is terrestrial, and your soul is spiritual: 'the spirits are His sovereignty and the bodies are His territory; He brought His sovereignty into His territory. He set conditions for the two of them and promised the two of them something. If the two[2] meet the conditions set by Him, He will also meet His pledge and promise to them'.[3] What is the condition? 'And

[1] I have used Arberry's translation here but amended it slightly. He uses 'bidding' for 'command'. There are also minor amendments to the translation of verses found later in the text.

[2] In the Persian text, al-Shahrastānī immediately translates the Arabic text but instead of using a plural subject, he translates it as 'once you meet the conditions . . .' The English translation has been revised as per the Arabic text here.

[3] According to al-Shahrastānī himself, this is a *ḥadīth* attributed to Jaʿfar al-Ṣādiq. See the *Mafātīḥ*, p. 97; English tr., T. Mayer, *Keys to the Arcana*, p. 168. In *Keys to the Arcana* the translation of the passage is slightly different: 'The spirits are His possession (*milk*) and the bodies are His dominion (*mulk*). So He causes His possession to occupy His dominion, and He has stipulations for them while they have a promise on His part. Thus if they fulfil His stipulations, He fulfils His promise to them.'

whosoever follows My guidance' (2:38); what is the promise? 'No fear shall be on them, neither shall they sorrow' (2:38).

[6] In one instance you have command and creation; in another, you have creation and guidance (*hidāyat*). Ibrāhīm, the friend of God – may the blessings of God be upon him – said: 'Who created me, and Himself guides me' (26:78). Mūsā, who spoke with the Lord – peace be upon him – said: 'He who gave everything its creation, then guided it' (20:50). Muhammad, the Chosen – may the blessings of God be upon him and his progeny – said: 'Who created and shaped, who determined and guided' (87:2–3).[4]

[7] Ibrāhīm spoke of the specific (*khāṣṣ*); Mūsā spoke about the general (*ʿāmm*); Muhammad spoke about the absolute (*muṭlaq*) – which is both specific and general. What Ibrāhīm spoke about was the origin and beginning (*mabdaʾ*); what Mūsā spoke about was the middle (*wasaṭ*); and what Muhammad spoke about was the perfection (*kamāl*). 'He who gave everything its creation, then guided it' (20:50), is more perfect than 'who created me, and Himself guides me' (26:78). And 'who created and shaped, who determined and guided' (82:7), is more perfect than 'He who gave everything its creation, then guided it'. There were two stages there: one was creation and the other was guidance. Here, there are four stages: first, creation; then, apportioning (*taswiyat*); third, determining (*taqdīr*); and fourth, guidance.

[8] In corporeal creation, the apportioning of the elements of water, earth, air and fire was required to bring about moderation: 'Who created thee and shaped thee and wrought thee in symmetry' (82:7). In spiritual determination, divine guidance is required to achieve perfection: 'Who determined and guided' (87:3). Creation and proportioning applies to the creation of the human person; determination and guidance applies to the determination of the

[4] Compare with a similar passage in the *Mafātīḥ*, tr. in *Keys to the Arcana*, p. 146.

spiritual soul. In all previous scriptures, there is an account of creation and command given by all these three eminent prophets so that by the end of *Sūra Sabbiḥ* (Sūra 87) it is said: 'Surely this is in the ancient scrolls, the scrolls of Abraham and Moses' (87:18–19).[5]

[9] He is the creator – glorified be His majesty – and He has no partner in creation: is there any creator but God? He is the guide (*hādī*) – sanctified be His names – and He has no partner in guidance: 'Had God not guided us, we had surely never been guided' (7:43). He has no partners in creation and yet He made secondary causes[6] (*asbāb*) for the affairs of creation (*khalqiyyāt*) and called them angels. He has no partners in guidance; yet He made secondary causes for the affairs of the command (*amriyyāt*) and called them prophets.

[10] The secondary causes of creation are the intermediaries in creation: the angel of life, the angel of death, the angel of wombs (*arḥām*), the angel of sustenance (*arzāq*) and the angel of terms (*ājāl*)[7] – peace be upon them. The causes of command are the intermediaries of guidance: Adam, Noah, Abraham, Moses, Jesus and Muhammad – peace be upon them.

[11] But your faith will not be right unless you subscribe to and have faith in the intermediaries of creation and the intermediaries of guidance: 'Each believes in God, His angels, His Books, and His messengers' (2:285). He put noble words on the tongues of angels and sent lofty books expressed through the tongues of the prophets; accompanying each being there is an angel and along with each angel there is an activating word.

[5] For a detailed discussion of the term 'scrolls', see P. L. Heck, 'Scrolls', *Encyclopaedia of the Qur'ān* (Leiden, 2006), vol. 4, pp. 561–579.

[6] The term *asbāb* is translated as 'secondary causes' but in some cases in the context it is translated as cause conveying the same meaning.

[7] For life, death, birth, sustenance and the duration or terms of events, there is an angel and these angels address the affairs of *this* world and thus they deal with the *khalqiyyāt*.

[12] The angel carries the burden of the word and the word activates the angel. The origin of the word '*kalima*': kāf-lām-mīm; and the origin of angel '*malak*': mīm-lām-kāf. They are mirror images of one another: in every incident, there is a decree of Almighty God and for each decree (*ḥukm*), there is a ruler (*ḥākim*) that rules by the command of God. The ruler is the perfection of the command; the command is the activator of the ruler.

[13] 'Those in authority' are 'the words of God'. The 'angels of God' are in the other world; and 'the books of God' and 'the messengers of God' are in this world. The prophets hear the words of God. The angels see the words of God. The faithful hear the book of God; and see the Messenger of God. The faith of the prophets [is described as]: 'Who believes in God and His Words' (7:158); the faith of believers [is described as]: 'Lord, we believe in what Thou hast sent down, and we follow the Messenger' (3:53). Let this ear and eye that we have see this and hear this. Or else, let them not see or hear at all:

> If I do not hear a promise from you or never catch a glimpse of you,
> then what is the benefit of my ear and eye.[8]

[14] To come back to the point: He made the natures of creatures the disciples of angels. Natural motions (*ḥarakāt-i ṭabīʿī*) are where the angels operate. Voluntary motions (*ḥarakāt-i ikhtīyārī*) are where the prophets operate.

[15] Natural motions are of three types: a motion around the centre, a centrifugal motion and a centripetal motion. Motion around the centre is circular. Centrifugal motion is upwards. Centripetal motion is downwards.

[16] Voluntary motions are also of three types: mental motion (*ḥarakat-i fikriyya*), verbal motion (*ḥarakat-i qawliyya*) and active

[8] A verse by ʿAlī b. Ḥasan al-Ṣurradurr (d. 465/1072). See his *Dīwān* (Cairo, 1995), p. 84.

motion (*ḥarakat-i fiʿliyya*). Mental motion is more akin to circular motion since thinking circles round the world: 'And reflect upon the creation of the heavens and the earth' (3:191). Verbal motion is more akin to motion upwards: 'To Him good words go up' (35:10). Actual motion is more akin to motion downwards: 'And what profits men abides in the earth' (13:17).

[17] In that realm, circular and straight motions are ordained by the command of the angels, peace be upon them. In this realm, circular and straight motions are ordained by the command of the prophets – peace be upon them. In mental motions, there is truth (*ḥaqq*) and falsehood (*bāṭil*). In verbal motions: true (*rāst*) and untrue (*durūghī*); in active motions: good (*khayr*) and evil (*sharr*). The obligation of the law (*taklīf-i sharīʿat*) says: choose the truth and forsake the falsehood; choose the true and forsake the untrue; choose the good and forsake the evil.

[18] If natural motions followed the command of the angels, then the corporeal form would be upright in this world. If voluntary motions followed the commands of the prophets, then the spiritual form in the other world would be upright. If in the realm of wombs (*ʿālam-i arḥām*) an illness or substance dominates [the sperm] – such that health moves away from moderate parameters – then the corporeal image (*ṣūrat-i jismānī*) in this world becomes defective. In the realm of decrees (*ʿālam-i aḥkām*), were whims or wishes dominant – such that the soul moved away from the moderate parameters – then the spiritual image (*ṣūrat-i rūḥānī*) in the other world would become defective.

[19] All the glorification (*tasbīḥāt*) and praising (*taḥmīdāt*) of the angels is for the rectification (*taqwīm*) of natural motions so that physical image in this world will be upright and healthy.

[20] All the worship (*ʿibādāt*) and transactions (*muʿāmalāt*) of the prophets is for the rectification of the voluntary motions so that

the spiritual image in the other world will become upright and healthy.

[21] Strange! Spiritual angels are the intermediaries of the corporeal person; and the physical prophets are the intermediaries of the spiritual soul. Angels manipulate the person to make them able to live in this world – and this life is ephemeral. The prophets manipulate the soul to make it able to live in the other world – and that life is eternal.

[22] The angels carry [people] from the origin of innate predisposition (*fiṭrat*) to the perfection of creation (*khilqat*); the prophets carry [people] from the origin of the laws of the *sharīʿat* to the perfection of the *qiyāmat* (resurrection). Mixed fluids in nature are entrusted to the discretion (*takhyīr*) of the angels; the laws of religion are entrusted to the governance (*tadbīr*) of the prophets. Say so: The natural temperament is the workshop of the angels: 'Mixed fluids that we may test him' (76:2). The result of their work is: 'And We made him hearing, seeing' (76:2). The path of the *sharīʿat* is the workshop of the prophets: 'A law and a way' (5:48). The effect of their work is: 'Surely We guided him upon the way whether he be thankful or unthankful' (76:3). They are the operators and the task is assigned to Us; as He said, 'We created' and 'We guided'. Elsewhere, We are the operators and the work is assigned to them: 'And when Thou createst out of clay ... as the likeness of a bird' (5:110) and 'And Thou, surely Thou shalt guide unto a straight path' (42:52).

[23] In the workshop of nature, all operators are compelled to perform their task; in the workshop of the *sharīʿat*, all operators have a choice and freedom. In the other workshop, there is bliss (*saʿādat*) and wretchedness (*shaqāwat*). In this workshop too there is bliss and wretchedness. The bliss and wretchedness of the other realm are concealed in the outward knowledge (*ʿilm-i ẓāhir*) but revealed in the hidden temperament (*mazāj-i makhfiyy*): 'The blessed are blessed in their mother's womb and the wretched are wretched in their mother's

womb.'[9] The bliss and wretchedness of this realm are concealed in the command but revealed in action: 'Some of them shall be wretched and some happy' (11:105).

[24] In the workshop of the other realm, the senior angels are the mentors and the junior angels are obedient disciples. In the workshop of this realm, great prophets are legislators of the laws of the *sharīʿat* and the scholars of the community (*ʿulamāʾ-i ummat*) are the exponents of the words of prophecy: 'Thou art only a warner, and a guide to every people' (13:7).

[25] At the beginning of the cycle of the sperm, there is an angel; at the beginning of the cycle of the clot [of blood], a greater angel; at the beginning of the cycle of the lump of flesh a yet greater angel and so forth till it reaches 'another creature' (23:14). The greater the task, the greater the angel.

[26] At the beginning of the cycle of names (*asāmī*), there is a prophet like Adam. At the beginning of the cycle of the meanings (*maʿānī*) of those names there is a prophet, like Noah.[10] At the beginning of the cycle of combining those names with meanings there is a prophet, like Abraham. At the beginning of the cycle of revelation (*tanzīl*), there is Moses. At the beginning of the cycle of its esoteric exegesis (*taʾwīl*), there is Jesus. At the beginning of the cycle combining revelation and its esoteric exegesis, there is Muhammad the Chosen [who says]: 'In your religion, being the creed of your father Abraham' (22:78).

[27] The angels begin with the extract (*sulāla*) and gradually take it from one stage to another until it becomes 'another creature'. The prophets begin with names and respectively carry them from one cycle to another cycle until they achieve their meanings: 'And make

[9] This is a *ḥadīth*, see note 27 in the Persian text for reference details.

[10] When al-Shahrastānī says 'like Noah', it suggests that at the beginning of each cycle there is a Prophet and he gives their names. The word 'like' (*chun*) is a figure of speech used frequently in the text.

you to grow again in a fashion you know not. You have known the first growth; so why will you not remember?' (56:61). The angels are charged with the primary formation (*nash'at ūlā*) and the prophets are charged with the secondary formation (*nash'at ukhrā*).

[28] In nature there is transformation from one stage to another and from one temperament to another and at each transformation there is a perfection. In the *sharī'at*, there is abrogation (*naskh*) in the progress from one cycle to another and from one decree to another; and at each abrogation there is a perfection.

[29] Beware! You must not consider the abrogation (*naskh*) of the ritual laws their nullification (*ibṭāl*); it is a perfection. If the sperm were to be destroyed, where would the clotted blood rest? If letters were to be destroyed, where would meanings reside? All religious laws have an origin and a perfection; the lord (*ṣāḥib*) of the origin is different from the lord of the perfection.[11]

[30] In each *sharī'at*, the origin and the perfection are different – and in this *sharī'at*, the *lā ilāha illā Allāh* is the extract (*sulāla*) of faith; acts of devotion (*'ibādāt*) and human intercourse (*mu'āmalāt*)[12] are the body of faith; knowledge (*'ulūm*) and truths (*ḥaqā'iq*) constitute the soul of faith. And in the same manner that all parts and members of a corporeal person exist in the progeny of the person as potentials capable of coming into actuality, all the laws of the *sharī'at* exist in *lā ilāha illā Allāh* potentially capable of coming into actuality. Therefore, the phrase *lā ilāha illā Allāh* is in a sense the universal of faith, in the same manner that the progeny is in a sense the universal of the person.

[11] This is a common Ismaili esoteric theme. The lord of the origin (*ṣāḥib-i sharī'at*) has a function which is different from that of the lord of perfection. The law is seen as just the beginning, like a foetus which reaches perfection when the moment of resurrection arrives. And it is the *qā'im* who is in charge of the functions of resurrection. For more details see, al-Ṭūsī, *Rawḍā*, pp. 138–139.

[12] I have followed Ismail K. Poonawala's translations of these terms in *The Pillars of Islam* (New Dehli, 2002–2004).

Hence, once you utter the *kalima*, you will have uttered the universal [concept of] religion. Thus, today [in this world], it shall bring you protection of life and property: 'When they utter *lā ilāha illā Allāh*, their property and life will be protected by me'. And tomorrow [in the hereafter], it will bring them to the realm of Paradise: 'Whoever utters the *lā ilāha illā Allāh*, will enter Paradise'. Otherwise, why should you enjoy the same status as all the believers in the universe, including the knowledgeable (*ʿālim*) and the practising (*ʿāmil*), by simply uttering these words?[13] Take heed of this point! In the same manner that the extract (*sulāla*)[14] progressed to become a complete body and the body progresses to become complete soul, the *lā ilāha illā Allāh* progresses to become a complete action (*muʿāmalat*) and action progresses to turn into complete faith (*īmān*): 'Knowledge calls upon action. If action responds to the call of knowledge, it shall stay there otherwise knowledge will turn away and leave'.[15]

[31] When the essence reaches the sperm and rests in the womb, the augmentative soul (*nafs-i nāmiyya*) will take charge of its governance. And the augmentative soul will be subject to the angel. That angel is accompanied by an activating word (*kalima-yi faʿʿāla*) so that through that word the augmentation of the augmentative soul will increase.

[32] And so, when the *kalima* of *lā ilāha illā Allāh* rests in the heart of the monotheist (*muwaḥḥid*), faith will begin to grow since faith can increase and diminish. He will be subject to the education (*taʾdīb*) of the educator (*muʾaddib*). The word of education will become his activating word so that the word augments the faith. And when the

[13] Al-Shahrastānī is defying the literal reading of it here and as earlier suggested, he is saying that one would only go to Paradise if the reality of the meaning of the *kalima* had been fulfilled within one's soul. It is only in this world where it brings protection of life and property.

[14] Different translators of the Qurʾan have given various translations from: extraction to product and quintessence. I have used 'extract' here.

[15] This is a quotation from the *Nahj al-balāgha*. See Aphorism 366 in S. J. Shahīdī, ed., *Nahj al-balāgha* (Qumm, 1372 Sh./1993), p. 425.

sperm reaches the clotted blood, the animal soul (*nafs-i ḥaywānī*) will become its governor and the angel who is the governor of the animal soul will give life to it with another word and bring the sense of touch into it.

[33] In the same manner, when the believer reaches the degree of excellence (*iḥsān*) from the degree of faith (*īmān*), the [legal] obligation (*taklīf*) of the obligated [man] (*mukallaf*) will join him. The word of obligation will become his governor so that he will progress to the senses and motions of obligation. And when clotted blood progresses to the lump of flesh, the imaginative soul (*nafs-i khayālī*) will become its governor and the angel becomes the governor of the imaginative soul.

[34] And so, when the [legally] obligated man begins the business of obligation (*muʿāmilat-i taklīfī*), the identification (*taʿrīf*) of the identifier (*muʿarrif*) joins him so that his imaginative faculty begins to work. Once these three cycles[16] are completed for the sperm, the rational soul (*nafs-i nāṭiqa*) joins him. The rational soul becomes subject to the angel and the angel becomes subject to the *kalima* so that through the *kalima* [a man's] soul achieves the perfection of the rational capacity.

[35] Similarly, when a believer progresses from submission (*islām*) to faith (*imān*) and then from faith to excellence (*iḥsān*), from there, once he reaches the degree of excellence and moves ahead, it is said that 'the ultimate stage of the steps taken is action'. Therefore, it follows from this point that in the *sharīʿat*, when one says, 'When is the resurrection?' (*matā al-sāʿa*), they say, 'The one who is asked is not more knowledgeable than the one who asks'.[17] Here is the final stage of

[16] These three cycles or stages apparently refer to *taʾdīb*, *taklīf* and *taʿrīf*.

[17] Prophetic *ḥadīth*. See Khalīl Maʾmūn Shayḥā, *Mawsūʿat al-Muʿjam* (Beirut, 2013), vol. 11, p. 289.

the *sharīʿat* and the stage above it is the stage of intellect (*ʿaql*) and the stage above intellect is the command (*amr*) and speaking of that knowledge and seeking the causes of things would be the task of the Master of the Resurrection.[18]

[36] The soul has four stages: the augmentative soul, the animal soul, the imaginative soul and the human soul. Accompanying each soul is an angel: 'over every soul there is a guardian' (86:4); and each angel is accompanied by a word.

[37] The intellects have four stages too and with each intellect there is a command. Along with each command, there is a word (*kalima*). There is a potential intellect (*ʿaql-i istiʿdādī*) that a child has. There is an obliging intellect (*ʿaql-i taklīfī*) whose function is to activate (*bi fiʿl ārad*); there is *intellectus adeptus* (*ʿaql-i mustafād*) which receives benefit; and there is *intellectus in habitu* (*ʿaql bi'l-malaka*) which gives benefit. Once the soul is complete, it will emulate human beings. Once the intellect is complete, it will emulate the angels.

[38] Any soul not nurtured by the angels is Satanic (*shayṭānī*). Any intellect not nurtured by the prophets is demonic (*ṭāghūtī*). Wherever there is rectitude either in the soul or in the intellect, there is an angel sitting beside it: 'Those who have said, "Our Lord is God" then have gone straight, upon them the angels descend' (41:30). Wherever there is discord either in the soul or the intellect, there is a demon sitting beside it: 'Shall I inform you, (O people!), on whom it is that the evil ones descend? They descend on every lying, wicked person' (26:221–222). They are lying in speech and wicked in deed.

[39] The abode of the angels is rectitude (*rāstī*) and the abode of the prophets is purity (*ṭahārat*). And the foundation of the creed of truth

[18] This paragraph bears a striking resemblence to the opening chapter of the *Milal* on Muslims, see, Shahrastānī, *al-Milal*, ed. Muhannā and Fāʿur, p. 53.

(*dīn-i ḥaqq*) is rectitude and cleanliness, *shahādat* and *ṭahārat*.[19] Sometimes rectitude comes first and cleanliness comes next. And sometimes cleanliness comes first and rectitude comes next. For a man to deserve salvation in the hereafter rectitude in form must be joined by rectitude in meaning. And when a man finds rectitude in form through the angels and does not find rectitude in meaning through the nurturing of the prophets, he will be resurrected with his head bent low in the other world: 'The guilty ones will bend low their heads before their Lord' (32:12).

[40] Since man lifted his head through innate predisposition (*fiṭrat*) in order not to resemble the reptiles, he also lifted his hands in order not to resemble cattle. He was told: You gained rectitude by the decree of innate predisposition 'in the best of moulds' (95:4), now by the decree of the *sharīʿat* find rectitude in meaning: 'Your creation was made beautiful; now make your manners beautiful.' That one I created by compulsion (*iḍṭirār*). This one, you can change by choice (*ikhtīyār*).[20] Otherwise, you will be resurrected hanging down and humiliated. 'Then do We abase him (to be) the lowest of the low, except such as believe and do righteous deeds' (95:5–6).

[41] We lifted your head from the earth by compulsion. You lower your head by choice: 'Bow down in adoration, and bring thyself the closer (to God)' (96:19). Raise your head in supplication and along with your head raise your hand. In worship, place your head on the earth. And along with your head, place your hand on the earth too. If you seek a direction (*qibla*)[21] for supplication, it is above. If you seek a

[19] The author uses these terms once again to make a distinction between the literal and exoteric aspects of faith and their esoteric meanings. The utterance of the *kalima* is the exoteric aspect of it; to acknowledge the truth of it as ablution refers to the exoteric cleanliness but all require an inner reality too.

[20] Here, 'that one' is a reference is to the physical and outward creation and 'this one' (which is a matter of choice), is a reference is to the refinement of one's character.

[21] Here the term *qibla* is not translated as the specific noun referring to the common direction of prayer towards Mecca; it is the generic meaning of the word from its Arabic root, to turn one's face towards something or someone.

direction for prostration, it is below. There is a limit for above and there is a limit for below. The limit of the above is the throne (ʿ*arsh*), not the Lord of the throne. The limit of below is the earth (*farsh*) not the Lord of the earth.

[42] O Angels! For a long time, your direction (*qibla*) was either the throne or the earth, either above or below! Now, it is time for you to turn your face towards a person (*shakhṣ*) for whom time and space are but mere modest servants at his door: 'Bow down to Adam' (2:34).[22] The throne is the universal [concept] for space; the aeon (*dahr*) is the universal for time; and Adam is the universal for mankind.

[43] The throne is the reference for governance (*tadbīr*) 'firmly established on the throne (of authority), regulating and governing all things' (10:3). The aeon (*dahr*) is the reference for determination (*taqdīr*): 'And do not curse the aeon because the aeon is God'.[23] Adam is the reference for making an image (*taṣwīr*): 'He created Adam in the image of the Merciful'.[24] And the glory of the Almighty is free from time, space and image.

[44] The direction (*qibla*) for the hand is the throne. The direction for the face is the Kaʿba. The direction for the eye, is the place of

[22] Al-Shahrastānī's narrative of this prostration is closely related to what is found in later Nizārī literature. See, for example, Ḥasan-i Maḥmūd-i Kātib, *Haft bāb*, ed. and tr. Badakhchani, pp. 52, 78–79. See also the criticism that al-Shahrastānī directs at the Ithnāʿasharīs in the *Mafātīḥ*, ed. M. A. Ādharshab, p. 280, and also referred to in the introduction in the present edition. For al-Shahrastānī, Adam is a true vicegerent of God and a symbol of the *qāʾim* and submitting to the authority of the present Imam is equivalent to the prostration of the angels before Adam. This was one of the main themes of the doctrine of *qiyāmat* during the time of Ḥasan II: turning from the ʿ*arsh* or *farsh* to the Lord of both (who is the Imam-*qāʾim*). Al-Shahrastānī's reference to 'prostration' as submission to the authority of the present living Imam is the important point here. Compare this with the paragraphs in al-Ṭūsī's *Rawḍa*, English tr., pp. 65–71.

[23] See Shayḥā, *Mawsūʿat al-Muʿjam*, vol. 11, p. 289. vol. 9, p. 784. See also, *Mafātīḥ*, p. 858. Al-Ṭūsī also quoted something similar in the *Akhlāq-i Muḥtashamī*, p. 19. From al-Shahrastānī's text to that of al-Ṭūsī,we see a shift, or a use of exegesis: the aeon and the aeon of all aeons is the Imam of the Time or the Household of the Prophet.

[24] See Shayḥā, *Mawsūʿat al-Muʿjam*, vol. 9, p. 346, with a slightly different wording. See also *Haft bāb*, paragraph 8.

prostration. The direction for the ear is the recitation of the imam. The direction for the head is Adam. The direction for the soul is the aeon (*dahr*): 'Surely in the days of your aeon (*dahr*), there are breezes'.[25]

[45] Each is engaged with a direction so that for the heart it is said: the heart of the faithful rests between two of the fingers of the All-Merciful (*raḥmān*), between two phrases (*kalima*) from the words of the All-Merciful. One phrase is *lā ilāha illā Allāh*. And one is *Muḥammad rasūl Allāh*. O Hand! You come forth empty so that you might return full. O Head! You came forth filled so that you might return empty.

[46] In the hand, there is naught but air: I have nothing and I know nothing. The head carries naught but air: I have all and I know all. Whoever says, 'I have nothing and I know nothing', will be told, 'You know all and you have all.' 'Say: I have no power over any good or harm to myself except as God willeth' (7:188), means I have nothing. And 'If I had knowledge of the unseen' (7:188) means I know nothing. O Muhammad! You have all! 'I created all things for your sake!'[26] O Muhammad! You know all, 'and He taught thee what thou Knewest not (before)' (4:113).

[47] When the Prophet raised his hand, 'he raised it such that the white area under his hand could be seen'. Holding the hand before the face in worship is tradition. Holding the hand beside the ear in the *takbīr* of worship is tradition. The hand is the means of will and power.

25 See the earlier note. This kind of reference to aeon and the Imam or the *Qā'im* is fully in line with Nizārī narratives of resurrection. The Imam's breath is like the breath of Jesus who gives life to those who are lying dead in the graves of their body and it is the life of knowledge which brings them back to life even though they are not physically dead. Regarding the *ḥadīth* itself, that which is found in most sources has the word '*li rabbikum*' instead of '*lakum*'. See for example, al-Ghazālī, *Iḥyā' 'ulūm al-Dīn*, ed. 'Abd al-Raḥīm b. Ḥusayn al-'Irāqī (Cairo, [1967–68?]), vol. 2, p. 134.

26 See Muḥammad b. Ḥasan Ḥurr al-'Āmilī, *al-Jawāhir al-saniyya fi'l-aḥādith al-qudsiyya* (Beirut, 1982), p. 284. The reference here in most works of *ḥadīth* is to Man in general but al-Shahrastānī takes this as addressing the Prophet.

Distance yourself from your own will and power: *lā ḥawla wa lā quwwat illā bi'llāh* [there is no will and no power save in God].[27]

[48] The ear is the location of hearing and obedience. Keep them both next to each other in the *takbīr* or prayer so that you acknowledge both the accomplished (*mafrūgh*) and the inchoative (*musta'naf*). You will turn away from free will (*qadar*) by saying *lā ḥawla wa lā quwwata illā bi'llāh* and you will also turn away from predestination (*jabr*) by saying, 'We hear and we obey' (5:7). And you shall not enter the sanctuary of worship if you do not keep these two decrees side by side.

[49] Yet again, the face turns to what is opposite (*muqābala*). The face (*wajh*), direction (*jihat*) and confrontation (*muwājaha*) are all from the same root. And direction seeks a finitude and the finitude seeks a limit and the limit seeks a man standing opposite (*muqābala*). And the hand, too, seeks a direction but upwards: 'And towards you I raised my hands'. Keep your hands in front of the face in supplication so that each one becomes the limit of the other and each becomes the direction (*qibla*) of the other.

[50] The hand says: I am on the same level with the face in seeking and I relinquished the upward direction. The face says: I am on the same level with the hand in seeking and I relinquished opposition. The hand is then told: 'I am indeed close (to them): I listen to the prayer of every suppliant when he calleth on Me' (2:186). And tomorrow [in the hereafter] the face is told: 'Some faces, that Day, will beam (in brightness and beauty); Looking towards their Lord' (75:22–23).

[51] What an astonishing business! If you speak of direction in knowledge (*ma'rifat*), then the knowledge will no longer be knowledge. And in worship (*ṭā'at*),[28] if you pay no heed to direction,

[27] See Muḥammad b. Aḥmad al-Dhahabī, *Siyar a'lām al-nubalā'*, ed. S. Arna'ūṭ (Beirut, 1994), vol. 6, p. 261.

[28] Literally, the word '*ṭā'at*' means obedience but in this case, since it refers to ritual worship, I have chosen the latter translation given the context here.

then your worship will not be deemed worship. Knowledge has to do with the spirit and the spirit does not have directions nor does it seek directions. Worship (and its rituals) have to do with the body and the body dwells in [a place with] directions and it seeks directions. The body is corporeal. It seeks a direction and a specific direction so that worship will be deemed correct otherwise you will not be among the people of the *qibla* (*ahl-i qibla*). The spirit is incorporeal. Knowledge does not depend on direction to be true, were it not the case you would not be deemed to be among the people of unity (*ahl-i tawḥīd*).[29] How can I understand these two contradictory rules? How do I order these contradictory rules? How do I reconcile 'Whithersoever you turn, there is the Face of God' (2:115) with 'And wherever you are, turn your faces towards it' (2:144)? If you do not speak of 'all places' it is wrong. If you speak of 'in all places', wrong again. If you speak of a specific place, you are wrong. If you do not turn your face to a specific place, you will be wrong again. You should not cover your hands while praying. You should not bare your hands and feet in prostration. You should not cover your head and feet in the sanctuary of the Kaʿba. You should not bare your head and feet in the toilet. You do not know what wisdom lies underneath each decree! You do not know what truth each face[30] carries![31]

[52] Tell the cause-seeking intellect that if it wishes to become an angel, it must say: 'We know not save what Thou hast taught us' (2:32) and tell the direction-seeking sense that if it wishes to acquire a

[29] It is important to note the esotericism of al-Shahrastānī here. For him physical acts of worship are bound by time and space and therefore they require a direction but knowledge and the esoteric meaning of worship is above and beyond time and space and requires turning one's entire existence to face towards to the one and only true Lord. So, we have *sharīʿat* vs. *qiyāmat* as we have *ṭāʿat* vs. *maʿrifat* (or the exoteric vs. the esoteric). See also, al-Ṭūsī, *Rawḍa,* p. 110.

[30] The original term is *ṣūrat* here but in light of the earlier verse quoted, I have used 'face' here instead of 'image'.

[31] Compare this paragraph with a similar description – there are even some sentences reproduced verbatim – in the *Mafātīḥ:* see, ed. M. A. Ādharshab, p. 646.

spiritual quality, it must say: 'We hear, and obey' (2:258). Build a scale with the intellect by which to measure the spirit:

> He is the one who measures the intellect and the soul; how would he be captured by profound reflection?![32]

'God the Almighty created His religion on the basis of His creation so that by its allegory people can seek signs from His creation to reach His religion and from His religion to reach His unicity.'[33]

The reciter recited, 'In the name of God, the beneficent, the merciful.'

> O comrades! The soil lying on the bed of the valley and the palm in it smell like camphor and the trunk of the tree smells like sandalwood.
>
> Because Umayma, in the company of friends, was passing through the valley gently like a breeze.[34]
>
> The scent of the Mūlīyān river is breathing in; it is the scent of the graceful beloved that breathes in.[35]

[53] It is the scent of prophecy that emanates from these words said by the descendant[36] of the Prophet: 'God created His religion on the

[32] This is one of the opening verses of the *Shāhnāma* of Firdawsī.

[33] In *Jāmiʿ al-ḥikmatayn* Nāṣir-i Khusraw attributed this tradition to the Prophet; see, *Nasir-e Khosraw Kitâb-e Jâmiʿal-Hikmatain: Le livre réunissant les deux sagesses*, ed. Henry Corbin and M. Moʿin (Tehran, 1953), p. 154. The Nizārīs used this phrase later but given the context here, it appears that al-Shahrastānī explicitly traces it back to Jaʿfar al-Ṣādiq (and he talks about the descendant of the Prophet); see *Mafātīḥ*, p. 97, T. Mayer, tr., *Keys*, p. 168). Eric Ormsby has translated it as follows: 'God the Exalted established his religion on the analogy with His creation so that one might be guided from His creation to His religion and from there be led to His oneness', in Ormsby, tr., *Between Reason and Revelation: Twin Wisdoms Reconciled.* An annotated English translation of Nāṣir-i Khusraw's *Kitāb-i Jāmiʿ al-ḥikmatayn* (London, 2012), p. 145. See also al-Ṭusī, *Rawḍa*, p. 138 and al-Muʾayyad fi'l-Dīn al-Shīrāzī, *al-Majālis al-Muʾayyadiyya* (Mumbai, 1422/2002), p. 108. But all known Ismaili sources attribute this to the Prophet.

[34] These two verses are from an Arabic poem by Kuthayyir ʿAzza (d. 105/723), and are also quoted, with slight variation, in al-Zamakhsharī's *Rabīʿ al-abrār wa nuṣūṣ al-akhbār* (Beirut, 1412/1992), vol. 1, pp. 285–286. On the biography of the poet, see Iḥsān ʿAbbās, 'Kuthayyir b. ʿAbd al-Raḥmān', *EI2*, Consulted online on 1 June 2020 http://dx.doi.org.iij.idm.oclc.org/10.1163/1573-3912_islam_SIM_4587.

[35] This is a verse by the Persian poet Rūdakī (d. 329/940–941).

[36] The term used by al-Shahrastānī here is '*sulālay-i nubuwwat*' which literally means 'that which is drawn from the loins of the Prophet'. See note 33 on the provenance of the *ḥadīth*.

basis of His creation' – this is the same foundation of creation and the command. The command and religion (*dīn*) belong to one category; creation and the *sharīʿat* belong to another category.[37] Angels are the intermediaries of creation. Prophets are the intermediaries of *dīn*. The command is the source (*maṣdar*) of creation. Creation is the manifestation (*maẓhar*) of the command. *Dīn* is the source of creation. Creation is the manifestation of *dīn*. Does the intellect belong to the category of creation or that of the command? You would inevitably say it belongs to creation. Therefore, the command is the source of the intellect and the intellect is the manifestation of the command. And the intellect is both created and assigned a command. 'When God created the intellect, He told him to turn his face towards Him and he did so. Then, He told him to turn his face away, and he did so'.[38] The intellect obeyed both commands. Therefore, the intellect is both created and assigned a command.

[54] The *mutakallims* had three approaches to creation and the command. The Muʿtazilīs said that creation and the command are both the same, in the sense that His creation is created and His command is also created but the command is speech and composed of letters and it subsists on a tree.[39] The Karrāmīs said that the creation

37 It is interesting that al-Shahrastānī makes a clear distinction between religion (*dīn*) and its legal prescriptions (*sharīʿat*): the first belongs to the realm of command while the second belongs to the realm of creation. The first is more 'esoteric' while the second has to do with the exoteric and bound by time and space.

38 See Muḥammad b. Yaʿqūb al-Kulaynī, *al-Uṣūl min al-kafī*, ed. ʿAlī Akbar Ghaffārī (Beirut, 1401/1980–81), vol. 1, p. 10.

39 This is a reference to 'And God spoke to Moses in plain speech' (4:164). The Muʿtazila believed that the speech of God does not rely and subsist on God himself but on something else created by God. In this case, the speech of God, subsists on a tree out of which the voice came and spoke to Moses (see also 28:30). Hence, according to the Muʿtazila, the speech of God does not subsist on God but on a tree (apparently because the only single reference to God's speech with a human being is the case of Moses as related in the Qurʾan). In the *Milal*, Shahrastānī mentions the same thing about the Muʿtazila without reference to the tree: 'And they all agreed that divine speech is a temporal one created in a location (*maḥall*)'; the location in question, then, is the tree mentioned in our text. The active agent here is the tree even though eventually the existence of the sounds goes back to God. In other cases, the agent on whom the speech subsists could be Gabriel or the Prophet. Al-Shahrastānī, *al-Milal*, ed. Fāʿur and Muhannā, p. 57.

and the command are both the same, yet His creation is not created and His command is temporal speech and letters, but is self-subsistent. The Ashʿarīs said that His creation is created and subsists not in its essence; and His command is not created but subsists in His existence.[40]

[55] None of them knew the truth of either creation or the command. They knew neither the relationship of creation, nor that of the command, to Him. And the Qurʾan says: 'To Him belongs creation and the command' (7:54). If they were both the same, why are there two different terms for them? If one of them did not derive its subsistence from Him, and one did, why would there be common references here? If 'belonging to Him' refers to sovereignty, then why do you describe attributes of the command? If 'belonging to Him' refers to attributes, then why do you not describe the attributes of creation?

[56] Nay, nay, you ought to say it the way the man of the book and the one who is the companion of the book[41] said: To Him belongs creation, His terrestrial sovereignty and the command, His spiritual sovereignty. He is the Lord of the spiritual and terrestrial realms: the spirits are His sovereignty and the bodies are His territory; He brought His sovereignty into His territory. He set a condition for the two of them and promised the two something. If the two meet the conditions set by Him, He will also meet His pledge and promise to them. What is my condition? 'Children of Adam! If there should come to you

[40] Here, al-Shahrastānī is making a clear distincion between these three theological schools and the Nizārī belief that God is beyond and above his command. The major area of difference concerns how these groups attributed creation and command to the 'essence' of God. See also, al-Ṭūsī, *Contemplation and Action*, pp. 34–38.

[41] Here, 'the man of the book' and 'the companion of the book' refer to Jaʿfar al-Ṣādiq, based on the *ḥadīth thaqalayn*. See the first instance of the citation of this *ḥadīth* in footnote 3, paragraph 5 above (and its explicit reference to Jaʿfar al-Ṣādiq in the *Mafātīḥ*). See the reference to the Shiʿi Imam as '*al-tālī li kitāb Allāh*', '*aḥād al-thaqalayn*' and '*ab al-sibṭayn*' in the *Mafātīḥ*, ed. M. A. Ādharshab, p. 277.

Messengers from among you, relating to you My signs, then whosoever is godfearing and makes amends' is the condition which is followed by the pledge that 'no fear shall be on them, neither shall they sorrow' (7:35). The territory and sovereignty are His: 'O God! Master of sovereignty' (3:26). The celestial and terrestrial sovereignty are His: 'Unto God belongs sovereignty over the heavens and the earth' (3:189). The celestial and terrestrial hosts are His: 'To God belong the hosts of the heavens and the earth' (48:4). The celestial and terrestrial keys are His: 'To Him belong the keys of the heavens and the earth' (42:12). The celestial and terrestrial treasuries are His: 'Unto God belong the treasuries of the heavens and of the earth' (63:7). To the kingdom (*mulk*), hosts. To the hosts, a treasury. To the treasury, a key. The key is in the hand of the unseen: 'To God belongs the Unseen in the heavens and the earth' (11:123).[42]

[57] The celestial sovereignty is the world of His determination; the world of the causes of creation. The terrestrial sovereignty is the realm of His obligation (*ʿālam-i taklīf*); the world of causes [used] by the command. The celestial host is the angels and the favoured ones (*muqarrabān*). The terrestrial host is the Prophets, holders of authority (*ūlu'l-amr*) and Lords of command (*khudāwandān-i farmān*).[43] In the celestial treasuries are the secrets of His determination. In the terrestrial treasuries are the secrets of the obligation[44] to Him. The key to those treasuries is *lā ilāha illā Allāh* and the key to these treasuries is *Muḥammad rasūl Allāh*. The key to Paradise is *lā ilāha illā Allāh, Muḥammad rasūl Allāh* – and indeed the key to all conquest and opening: In the same manner that in uttering the phrase *lā ilāha illa*

[42] In this paragraph, al-Shahrastānī quotes Qurʾanic verses and then immediately offers a translation/interpretation of them.

[43] The Prophets and the Shiʿi Imams are considered to be the terrestrial hosts or divine agents on earth while angels and the favoured ones operate in the celestial realm but with contrasting objectives. The terrestrial ones gesture to the celestial realm while the celestial ones are destined to serve the terrestrial (see earlier paragraphs of the *Majlis*).

[44] Here 'the obligation' and 'His obligation' refers to obligations set forth by God for man.

Allāh the lips do not touch each other, no sky will ever block another sky until the phrase reaches the foot of the Throne and seeks forgiveness for the one who has uttered it. Then it is said: You have come alone! Go back and bring your comrade with you to be received! O key of opening! Bring the keychain with you so that the speaker of it may find salvation (*rahāyish*) since the key for the opening (*gushāyish*) of the door of Paradise is *lā ilāha illā Allāh*; and the key for the locking the door of Hell is *Muḥammad rasūl Allāh.*[45] The door of Paradise shall not be opened until you have closed the door of Hell.

[58] By uttering *Muḥammad rasūl Allāh* people will be saved from Hell and by *lā ilāha illa Allāh* they will reach Paradise. By uttering these two statements with your tongue, here in this world you will have an opening and a salvation (*gushāyish wa rahāyish*); this will bring immunity to property and life. But it will only bring you salvation tomorrow if you have said it with a pure heart; therefore, a *qāʾim* is required to make the distinction between a pure believer (*muʾmin-i mukhliṣ*) and a hypocritical disbeliever (*munāfiq-i murāʾī*) and to separate the people of Paradise from those of Hell ... Today: 'We would not know the *muʾmīn* from the *munāfiq* except through love for ʿAlī or hostility towards him', says Saʿīd-i Musayyib.[46] And tomorrow: 'O ʿAlī! You are the one who consigns people to Paradise or Hell';[47] therefore, you will sit at the fork of the road and say, 'This one is mine' and you will send him to Paradise. And the fire says, 'This one is mine' and will throw him into Hell.[48] The difference between a monotheist (*muwaḥḥid*) and a polytheist (*mushrik*) is known through

[45] The terms chosen for salvation and opening by al-Shahrastānī here were also used by Nāsir-i Khusraw as the title of one of his books, *Gushāyish wa rahāyish*.

[46] See ʿAbd al-Ḥusayn Amīnī, *al-Ghadīr fi'l-kitāb wa'l-sunna wa'l-adab*, vol. 1, pp. 257 ff. Amīnī's work is a thorough collection of Shiʿi traditions on the status and position of ʿAlī b. Abī Ṭālib. Saʿīd-i Musayyib, or Saʿīd b. Musayyib (d. 93 or 94/712–13), was one of the early traditionists of the Successors and an authority on jurisprudence.

[47] Ibid., vol. 1, p. 329.

[48] These are all references to ʿAlī b. Abī Ṭālib.

the utterance of *lā ilāha illā Allāh*; the Muslim is distinguished from the infidel (*kāfir*) through the utterance of *Muḥammad rasūl Allāh*; and the difference between a *muʾmin* and a *munāfiq* is through love for or hostility towards ʿAlī which is the criterion for going to Paradise or Hell.

[59] We shall show our heavenly kingdom (*malakūt*) to our friend Ibrāhīm: 'So We were showing Abraham the kingdom of the heavens and earth, that he might be of those having sure faith' (6:75). O rotation of night and day! Draw a pitch black veil for a while over the heads of earthly creatures: 'When the night covered him over' (6:76). O bearers of spiritual ranks! Put on your faces the masks of star, moon and sun, and display yourselves each to the pure eye of our friend Ibrāhīm. Tell him in the language of lessons (*bi zabān-i iʿtibār*) that we are your instructors who seek to be viewed so that we take you from rank to rank until you say to each: 'This is my Lord' (6:76). And once each of these [heavenly bodies] sets and disappears, Ibrāhīm tells one of them: 'I love not those that set' (6:76). He then tells another: 'Unless my Lord guide me, I shall surely be among those who go astray' (6:77) and another: 'O my people! I am indeed free from your (guilt) of giving partners to God' (6:78). His head does not bow before the nurturing of the bearers of spiritual rank. You may imagine that he was referring to star, moon and sun, saying of each, 'This is my Lord' and 'This is my Lord'; each of these three is a spiritual entity (*rūḥāniyyat*) which governs him. He wished to give his hand in education to them so that he might ascend to his rank of prophethood. Neither star, moon nor the sun helped him; nor did the spirituality of their [physical] limits, souls and intellects.[49] This was because: I ascend to the height of my own voluntary rank (*marātib-i ikhtiyārī*) and they

[49] These terms, *ḥadd*, *nafs* and *ʿaql*, are found in earlier Ismaili thought of the Fatimid era. See for instance, F. Daftary, *The Ismāʿīlīs: Their History and Doctrines* (2nd ed., Cambridge, 2007), pp. 229–230.

descend to the depth of their involuntary rank (*marātib-i qasrī*). How could they help me? How do they deserve to be my tutors? If the first tutor does not help me, 'I shall surely be among those who go astray' (6:77).

[60] O Ibrāhīm! We are not your tutor and teacher; we are each a polished mirror so that you might see the celestial kingdom (*malakūt*) in us which is the world of determination. You will see the Lord of the celestial kingdom in the celestial kingdom and say, 'This is my Lord', and you will be right. He said: I would not want a mirror which declines. I would need a mirror which is constantly in ascendance and has no descent and decline: 'I have set my face' (6:79). My own face is the mirror of my face because the face of innate predisposition turns towards the Creator of the heavens and the earth. Perfection is where pristine faith (*ḥanīfiyyat*)[50] and Islam are: *ḥanīfiyyat* is observing perfection in men – and anything other than this is all polytheism and misguidedness to him. Then the final step of Ibrāhīm becomes the first step of Muhammad so that in worship, the first thing he recites is 'I have set my face' (6:79) and the end of all the steps taken by the prophets before him was just the beginning of the steps he would take and a prelude to his grace.[51]

[61] O Ibrāhīm! You have a cave. O Muhammad! You have a cave. *O Ibrāhīm! Step out of the cave, O Muhammad! Step into the cave! O Ibrāhīm! Move and open your eyes and you will see the kingdom* (malakūt) *of the heavens and the earth. O Muhammad! Lower your eyes and you will see the sovereignty* (jabarūt) *of the heavens and the earth.*[52] O Ibrāhīm! Step out of the cave! O Muhammad! Step into the cave! O Ibrāhīm! You move. O Muhammad! You rest. O Ibrāhīm! You

[50] For *ḥanīfiyyat* see the Introduction pp. 13, 51–53.
[51] This appears to be a quotation but I could not find its source.
[52] There are Arabic phrases here which appear to be quotations but I could not find any reference to these in sources of *ḥadīth*.

open your eyes! O Muhammad! You close your eyes! O Ibrāhīm! You watch the celestial kingdom (*malakūt*) to see what you see. O Muhammad! You watch the earthly sovereignty (*jabarūt*) to see what you see. O Ibrāhīm! You have three spiritual beings who come forth in three corporeal forms to nurture you. O Muhammad! You have three words which come forth as three persons to nurture you. One is the *sakīna*[53] as a friend in corporeal form. One is endorsement and assistance in the form of the spiritual hosts. The other is the superiority of the word (*ʿuluww-i kalima*) in the form of a divine *kalima*: 'Then God sent down on him His *sakīna*, and confirmed him with hosts you did not see; and He made the word of the unbelievers the lowest; and God's word is the uppermost' (9:40). First the *sakīna*, and last the *kalima*. The hosts are between the *sakīna* and the *kalima*. O Ibrāhīm! You have the star and we have the *sakīna*. You have the moon and we have the encampment. And for 'this is greater' you have the sun. We have the words of *lā ilāha illā Allāh* and *Allāhu Akbar*.

[62] Out of these three indications of Ibrāhīm, three offspring were brought forth. One was Isḥāq, one was Yaʿqūb and one was Yūsuf. And those three signs were hints (*ishāra*) for him. One was a star, one was the moon and the other was the sun. They were taken to the door of the abode of the third offspring so that all prostrated before him: 'I saw eleven stars, and the sun and the moon; I saw them bowing down before me' (12:4) so that the one prostrated to becomes the prostrator. And out of that one hint of Ibrāhīm to the sign on his chest, an offspring was brought forth called Ismāʿīl so that he would carry the *ḥanīfiyyat* from the loins of the pure (*aṣlāb-i pāk*) to the wombs of the pure (*arḥām-i pāk*) until it manifests itself in Muhammad the Chosen

[53] For a detailed discussion of this term and its equivalent, see Reuven Firestone, 'Shekhinah', *Encyclopaedia of the Qurʾān*, vol. 4, pp. 598–591. For more on the subject of this paragraph see Qur'an 11: 69 ff., Qur'an 15: 51 ff. and Genesis 18:1 ff.

One – may the blessings of God be upon him and his progeny – such that he says: '*I was sent forth by the mild and magnanimous* ḥanīfiyyat' and the *ḥanīfiyyat* is acknowledging only the deputyship (*niyābat*) of men (*rijāl*) and *ṣabwa*[54] is [acknowledging only] the deputyship of spiritual entities.[55]

[63] Two lights remained as the legacy of Ibrāhīm. One apparent (*ẓāhir*) light. One concealed (*mastūr*) light. 'O Our Lord! Truly Thou dost know what we conceal and what we reveal' (14:38). 'What we conceal' refers to the state of Ismāʿīl and 'what we reveal' refers to the state of Isḥāq.

[64] In the apparent light, a perfection for Yaʿqūb and Yūsuf. And a perfection for Mūsā and Hārūn. A perfection for Dāʾūd and Sulaymān. And a perfection for Yaḥyā and ʿĪsā. In the concealed light, one perfection was the sum of all perfections. Whatever Yaʿqūb and Yūsuf had of suffering and prosperity is with us. Whatever Mūsā and Hārūn had of the knowledge of *tanzīl* and *taʾwīl* is with us. Whatever Dāʾūd and Sulaymān had of the knowledge of the Book and wisdom is with us. Whatever Yaḥyā and ʿĪsā had of contraction (*qabḍ*) and expansion

54 The word *ṣabwa* refers to the practice of the Sabians (*al-Ṣābiʾā*) and the root of the word means to grow forth and to rise out of. Al-Shahrastānī devoted a significant section of his *al-Milal* to a debate between the Ṣābiʾa and the Ḥunafāʾ. It is interesting that one of the meanings of *Ṣābiʾ* is 'the one who departs from his religion to another religion' and the term was applied to any individual of 'a certain sect of the unbelievers, [the Sabians,] said to worship the stars secretly and openly to profess themselves to belong to the Christians' (see Lane, *An Arabic-English Lexicon*, p. 1640). In this context, the stars are the equivalents of spiritual entities as discussed here by al-Shahrastānī. Basically, for al-Shahrastānī, submitting to the authority of a present living Imam who appears in physical form is an integral part of having a pristine faith and he equates it with prostration before Adam, using the story of creation as an allegory to refer to surrendering to the authority of a personified Imam not an abstract ideal. Therefore the idea of '*shakhṣ*' and '*tashakhkhuṣ*' is critical in his narrative, just as it is in the doctrine of *qiyāmat* expounded by Ḥasan II.

55 This is the distinction that al-Shahrastānī makes between *ḥanīfiyyat* and the faith of the Sabians (*Ṣabwa*). He discusses this extensively in the *Mafātīḥ*. See ed. M. A. Ādharshab, pp. 633–635. The *ḥunafāʾ* prefer men over spiritual beings as opposed to the Sabians. The term he uses for men is *rijāl* and *ashkhāṣ*. This idea of *shakhṣ* and personification is critical to the doctrine of *qiyāmat* later developed by Ḥasan II.

(*basṭ*) is with us.[56] But whatever we have of the arcana (*asrār*) and of the signs (*āyāt*) is with no other person.[57]

[65] He is the compendium of all words (*jawāmiʿ al-kalim*). If you interpret the compendium of all words as the Qurʾan, that is right because all the arcana and the signs are in it. If you interpret the compendium of all words as the phrase of *lā ilāha illā Allāh* that is right again. Whatever is in the Qurʾan entire is in this phrase of the *kalima* also.

[66] And the reciter recited: 'The All-merciful has taught the Qurʾan' (55:1–2)

[67] We have a workshop and We have a court. The world is Our workshop and Adam is Our court. You came to Our workshop. Now it is time you entered Our court or We shall expel you from the workshop. O Angels! You have come through Our gates. Now it is time you came to Our court: 'Prostrate before Adam' (2:34). Whosoever obeys is an angel and whosever does not is Satan!

[68] In other words, 'Our workshop' is the world of creation and the affairs of creation. 'Our court' is the world of the command and the affairs of the command. 'Our court' is: 'And he taught the Qurʾan' (55:2) and 'Our workshop' is 'He created the human being' (55:3).

[69] No one can ever challenge Him as the creator: 'And if you asked them who has created them, they would say God' (43:87). If they lay

56 This refers to the conversation between Īsā and Yaḥyāʾ. As recounted in al-Zamakhsharī, Jesus met John and smiled at him. John said to him, 'Why do I find you smiling? It is as if you think you are immune [to divine testing].' And Jesus responded by saying, 'Why do I not find you smiling? It is as if you are despondent about divine mercy and benevolence.' Jesus is reported to be in a state of *basṭ* while John is in a state of *qabḍ*. See, Maḥmūd b. ʿUmar al-Zamakhsharī, *Rabīʿ al-abrār wa nuṣūṣ al-akhbār*, ed. ʿAbd al-Amīr Muhannā (Beirut, 1412/1992), vol. 5, p. 113. See also, Ibn ʿAsākir, *Taʾrīkh madīnat Dimashq*, ed. ʿUmar al-ʿAmrawī (Beirut, 1417/1997), vol. 47, p. 467.

57 Al-Shahrastānī's reference to *asrār* and *ayāt* concerns how he employs *taʾwīl*. The former has to do with esoteric exegesis while the latter refers to the *tafsīr* of the verses, thus his *taʾwīl* is a combination of the *ẓāhir* and the *bāṭin*.

claim to anything, it will be only to the command and the commandments: 'I do not know any deity for you but Myself' (28:38). The Creator is none other than Me, the commander is other than Me. Iblīs did not rebel against Him as the Creator at all: 'You created me from fire and create him from clay' (7:12). His dispute was in regard to the command and he disagreed with the intermediary of the command so that it was said: 'What prevented you from prostrating once I commanded you to do so?' (7:12). If you present a thousand arguments (*ḥujjat*), none of them shall be a response to 'once I commanded you' (7:12). If this is imitation (*taqlīd*), then what is insight? What I am saying here is insight.[58]

[70] There are established premises and the conclusion follows of necessity. It is established that He has created me of fire. It is established that He has created Adam of clay. It is established that fire is nobler than clay. Why then must I prostrate before him? Why then is he superior to me? When You say, 'Go forth from it! Surely thou art outcast' (15:34), it is utterly unfair. Yet again, when You say: 'And surely upon thee is the curse until the Day of Judgment' (15:35), it is absolute injustice.

[71] O Cursed One! Do you give Me a premise (*muqaddima*) and conclusion (*natīja*)? Have you become a logician? Do you consider fire nobler than clay? Have you become a natural philosopher? Do you consider that the simple (*basīṭ*) comes before the compound (*murakkab*) and have you become a metaphysician? Do you give Me the creed of the philosophers? Once you established that I am the ruler and the decree belongs to Me, why then do you set decrees for Me? If I am the commander, then the decree is Mine. Why do you command Me? 'Once I commanded you' (7:12) is a response to

[58] Here, al-Shahrastānī argues that this act of submission and surrender is not blind imitation but the very gist of insight and submission out of knowledge. It is the opposite of arrogance using the pretext of knowledge and reason. Here is a subtle response to the critics of the Nizārīs who submit to the instruction of an Imam and their detractors call this 'imitation'.

all misgivings (*shubahāt*). 'He said, "Because Thou hast caused me to err, I shall surely lie in wait for them on Thy straight path"' (7:16). I will approach them from the fore and the back, the right and the left to lead them astray.

[72] O Cursed One! You formulate a contradiction. If you attribute misleading to Me, why then would you lie in wait? If you lie in wait to mislead them, why then do you attribute misleading to Me?

[73] You speak of both predestination and free will. The creed of the believers in predestination arises from the word of 'Thou hast caused me to err'. The creed of the believers in free will arises from the word of 'I shall lie in wait' (7:16). Both groups shall be entangled within the traps of Iblīs and will be thrown into the fire of Hell.

[74] Approaching from the fore is teaching: 'teaching the people sorcery' (2:102). Approaching from behind is being a disciple: 'From them they learned how they might divide a man and his wife' (2:102). Approaching from the right is to proclaim asceticism (*zāhidī*) and divine law (*nāmūs*): 'Not remembering God save a little' (4:142). Approaching from the left is to proclaim ungodliness (*fāsiqī*) and antinomianism (*ibāḥat*): 'Thou wilt not find most of them thankful' (7:17).

[75] Wherever there is misgiving (*shubhat*), it is a temptation of the devil. Wherever there is temptation, it arises from the misgiving of that Cursed One. His misgiving is either anthropomorphism (*tashbīh*) or negation (*ta ʿṭīl*). It is either predestination or free will. It is either reason (*ʿaql*) or aural instruction (*samʿ*).

[76] The Anthropomorphists (*mushabbiha*) held there was an essence and a face for God; and their proof was [the tradition] which says: And He created Adam in the image of God.[59] The Karrāmīs maintained

[59] See Shayḥā, *Mawsūʿat*, vol. 9, p. 346.

there is a physical locus and a direction for God or [considered Him] subsisting in an essence or primordial attribute (*jismī ou jihatī*). Their proof was: 'He is Omnipotent over His servants' (6:18). The Ashʿarīs, an essence and eight pre-eternal attributes. Their proof: 'Nor shall they compass aught of His knowledge except as He willeth' (2:255). The Muʿtazilīs, an essence [for God] and attributional characteristics (*aḥkām-i ṣifātī*). Their proof: 'The Living, the Self-subsisting' (2:255). The philosophers, an essence and negative and relative attributes. Their proof: intellect.[60] And at the root of each denomination an anthropomorphism is implied and a negation is necessitated.

[77] Then again on the issue of creation and the command, the Muʿtazilīs said: The command and creation are both the same and are both created temporally. The Karrāmīs said: Creation and the command are both the same and temporal in the essence of the Almighty. The Ashʿarīs did not consider them one and the same. They called the creation temporally created and the command not created but pre-eternal and yet in the essence of the Almighty.

[78] And all of this is neither found in the Qurʾan, nor in the scripture and the tradition (*kitāb wa sunnat*). We are the people of 'thus said God and thus said the Messenger of God.'[61] It is said in the Book of Command and Creation:[62] 'To Him belongs creation', i.e. His terrestrial dominion 'and the command' (7:54), i.e. His spiritual sovereignty. Bodies are terrestrial creation: 'We created man' (23:12). The spirits belong to His command: 'Say: "The Spirit (cometh) by command of my Lord"' (17:85).[63]

[60] This is found also in al-Ṭūsī's *Sayr wa sulūk*. See *Contemplation and Action*, pp. 34–44.

[61] This is one of the key themes in the teachings of Ḥasan-i Ṣabbāḥ, viz., that he would not go beyond what God and his Prophet said. See al-Shahrastānī's *al-Milal*, ed. Muhannā and Fāʿur, p. 234.

[62] Here, al-Shahrastānī is apparently referring to a specific book titled '*Khalq wa amr*', but it is not clear who the author is. Judging by the context and the wording, this should contain the sayings of a Shiʿi Imam.

[63] Yusuf Ali's translation is used here.

[79] Whatever is of creation dwells in space, time and matter. 'It is an extraction of clay', refers to matter. 'Then We set him, a drop' (23:13) refers to time. And 'in a receptacle secure' (23:13) refers to space. In the genesis of spirits, there is neither time, nor space nor matter: 'And our command is naught but an instant' (54:50) in which it is said, '"Be" and then it is' (2:117).

[80] Bodies are nurtured by a physical meal: food and drink. Spirits are nurtured by a spiritual meal: the *tanzīl* and the *taʾwīl*. Bodies are made of earth and water and their meal is also made of these. Spirits are made of the command and the word (*kalima*) and hence is their meal made of the word.

[81] If you eat ten portions (*man*) of food, you will not become a scholar. If you learn ten pieces of knowledge, you will not become fat. Hunger is useful for prophets and having a bellyful is harmful to them. '*One day I will be hungry and one day full*.'[64] This is because they nurture the spirit not the body. Those who possess the world benefit from having a full belly and suffer from hunger. They 'eat as cattle eat' (47:12) because they nurture the body not the spirit. When death arrives, your body will rest in the grave; what is the use of being fat? The spirit will go to the spiritual world; what damage does thinness cause it? In that world, being thin is no fault for a scholar.

[82] Moses – peace be upon him – could find a royal meal as long as he was by the side of Pharaoh and he would have become fat. He was told: if you seek [to learn from] the knowledge of Shuʿayb, set yourself on the road. Sit underneath a tree in hunger and weariness and say: 'O my Lord, surely I have need of whatever good Thou shalt have sent down upon me' (28:24). You will serve for ten years to learn ten points of knowledge [from him]. If you seek the knowledge of

[64] A Prophetic *ḥadīth*. See Shayḥā, *Mawsūʿat*, vol. 1, p. 641.

Khiḍr[65] – peace be upon him – you have to undertake a quest around the world for a year: 'Bring us our breakfast; indeed, we have encountered weariness from this our journey' (18:62). He said: We had nothing but the fish and we forgot about it. The fish slipped through my hands and went into the sea. And as it went the sea closed over it. He said: Now we have found the sign of the knowledgeable man. Rise and let us go to his abode. He did not find the spiritual meal until the physical meal slipped through his hands into the sea: 'Then they found one of Our servants' (18:65). They found a servant of Ours on whom We had bestowed Our special grace and taught him special knowledge. What was that grace? Being patient about what he did not know until such time that he was taught about it and then he would know it. This was the quality given to him but not to Moses.

[83] Moses says: 'Shall I follow thee so that thou teachest me, of what thou hast been taught, right judgment.' (18:66). Here, there are six submissions of respect in humility, following and discipleship. First of all, 'shall I' speaks of enquiry not of certainty. Then 'I follow' refers to following as opposed to companionship. 'So that thou teachest me' refers to 'thou' being a teacher and a master and 'me' being a disciple and a novice. And 'of what' refers to part of the knowledge not its entirety. And 'what thou hast been taught' refers to what has been taught to you not what you have come to know. And 'right judgment' refers to the measure of my degree of merit not to the measure of your ability and power.

[84] He made these six humble submissions and yet the response to him was harsh: 'Assuredly thou wilt not be able to bear with me patiently' (18:67), and 'How shouldst thou bear patiently what thou hast never encompassed in thy knowledge?' (18:68).

[65] On the figure of Khiḍr see J. Renard, 'Khaḍir/Khiḍr', *Encyclopaedia of the Qur'ān*, vol. 3, pp. 81–84.

[85] Yet, again Moses submitted in humility: 'Yet thou shalt find me, if God wills, patient; and I shall not rebel against thee in anything' (18:69). O harshness of Moses! What happened to you?! Yes, when I had to speak to Aaron, I was the teacher and he the disciple: 'And laid hold of his brother's head, dragging him to him' (7:150). I showed that harshness and he showed patience. Here, I am the disciple and Khiḍr is the teacher. It is befitting of him to be harsh and befitting of me to be patient: 'Yet thou shalt find me, if God wills, patient', so that I will not disobey you in any command. He said: Since you will follow, then do not ask me any questions of anything that I do until such time when I tell you the secret and the story of it.

[86] On three occasions, he did three things: one was to wreck a boat belonging to poor people for no reason. The other was murdering a child, not full grown, innocent of any crime. The third was repairing an old wall and receiving no reward from anyone.

[87] Moses says: Wrecking the boat with no reason is tampering with someone else's property without having the right to and this is not allowed in the law of the *sharīʿat*. Killing a child, not full grown, innocent of any crime, is shedding someone's blood with no reasonable cause (*bī qiṣāsī*) and this is not allowed in the law of the *sharīʿat* either. Repairing a neglected wall for no wages is putting your own self in hardship for no reason and this is not allowed in the law of the *sharīʿat* either.

[88] Khiḍr says: Since a usurper was on his way to confiscate the boat, I damaged the boat so that the usurper would not take it. And in your law, it is allowed to keep the whole even though a part may be corrupt – just as in leprosy, you cut off the hand to keep the whole body from corruption. This is the response for wrecking the boat. About the other event: once the child had become full grown he would have become an unbeliever and his unbelief (*kufr*) would lead

to harming his believing parents. Killing the child is allowed here so that by sacrificing the branch you keep the root – just like cutting off a dead branch from a tree to allow a new branch to grow – and this is allowed both by reason and in religious law. Regarding the third event: choosing the interest and benefit of the other over one's own interest is a virtuous characteristic. That wall was a marker for a hidden treasure for a pair of orphans. If the sign had collapsed, the treasure would have stayed unused and the two orphans would have been deprived of it. And their father was a decent man.

[89] Moses says: First of all, you tamper with someone's property without seeking their permission at that time because a usurper is to appear at some time later. In that moment, it is you who is the usurper, no less a tyrant. That usurper may or may not come. In the second instance, you are violating someone's life who at this moment is not a criminal because he is to become an infidel in the future. At that moment, you are a murderer and a tyrant. That unbelief might or might not come about. And in the third instance, you are putting yourself through hardship while you are hungry and weary, doing something for nothing. That wall might or might not collapse. And had you sought some recompense for doing it, it would have been better.

[90] Khiḍr says: 'Might be' and 'might not be' belongs to you, Moses, since you dwell in the realm of 'might be' and 'unless' in the world of doubt and misgiving. I am in the world of certainty: 'That is the Book, wherein is no doubt' (2:2) – whatever is doubtful for you is certain for me. Whatever is contingent for you is necessary for me. You say: May be the usurper will not come and even if he comes he might not seize the boat; this child may mature and not become an infidel and even if he does, he might not harm his parents; that wall might not collapse and even if it does, someone may rebuild it. I know for certain that the tyrant will come and the child will become an infidel and the wall will collapse. My decree is based on certainty and yours is based on doubt.

You need to wait until your doubt turns into certainty. I do not have to wait.

[91] Moses says: These decrees you make are decrees of the future. What I decree is the decree of this moment. For the incident of today, you need a decree of today and for that of tomorrow, you need a decree for tomorrow. The usurper has not come yet; how can you make a decree?! The child has not matured yet and nor has he become an infidel; how do you decide he has become an infidel?! The wall has not collapsed yet; how do you take it for a collapsed wall?!

[92] Khiḍr says: Yesterday, today and tomorrow are temporal. You are a man of time – you must rule according to time. I am not a man of time. For me, yesterday, today and tomorrow are all the same. Whatever is to happen in the future, has already happened for me. The usurper who is yet to come has already come in my world. The unbelief of the child which is yet to come has already happened for me. I do not pass a verdict based on time; my verdict is beyond and above time because my rule transcends time. You need to be in quest for a year to find me. I can find you in an instant. I can reach the west from the east in an instant. Time and space are beneath me. I am above time and above space. Any verdict I pass is not time-bound.

[93] Moses says: That is true, but in order to pass a verdict based on causes, those causes should exist in the first place. When the cause of an event has not yet come into existence; how do you pass a verdict? There is no unbelief yet; how do you call it unbelief?! The wall has not collapsed yet; how do you assume it has collapsed?! No one has ever seen the passing of verdicts [on an affair] before it actually happens through its cause.

[94] Khiḍr says: In the world of causes, causes precede verdicts. In the world of no causes, the verdict is passed without a cause. There the verdict takes place by decree. The verdict is passed by knowledge, by

Providence (*mashiyyat*): They will all follow Your providence without You ever uttering a word and they will stop what they are doing by Your desire without You ever preventing them from it.[66] Thus, what is known has a verdict for it. What is desired will inevitably happen.

[95] Moses says: Then why is any legal obligation required? What is the need for sending prophets? What is the point of commandments and prohibitions? How do I then make laws and issue verdicts? Where is justice and where is the *sharīʿat* here?! You destroy the property of the destitute with no reasonable cause! You shed blood unlawfully, with no cause! You work for people without asking for a wage! And you say that you act based on knowledge and you pass a verdict based on desire and providence: 'And I desired to damage it' (17:89); 'We desired that their Lord should give to them in exchange one better than him in purity, and nearer in tenderness' (18:81); 'And thy Lord desired that they should come of age' (18:82). What happens to my obligation here? What happens to the verdict of the *sharīʿat* here? How can we ever speak of 'do' and 'don't' here?

[96] Khiḍr says: Moses! Your error is that you only know of one decree! Almighty God has two decrees for verdicts as they happen. One is the accomplished (*mafrūgh*) and the other is the inchoative (*mustaʾnaf*).[67] One is already processed and other is being processed. One is the determination (*taqdīr*) and the other is the obligation (*taklīf*).[68] One is: 'Perfect are the words of thy Lord in truthfulness and justice; no man can change His words' (6:115). The other is: 'And He made the word of

[66] This is a phrase from a *duʿā* by ʿAlī b. al-Ḥusayn in the *Ṣaḥifa al-Sajjādiyya* (Duʿā no. 7). Editor's translation.

[67] These two terms are part of the system of dyads constantly used by al-Shahrastānī. The term *mafrūgh* refers to affairs in the realm of *qiyāmat* or the world of command, while *mustaʾnaf* refers to affairs or rules in the realm of the *sharīʿat* where these are time-bound and depend on causes in the world of creation. See also T. Mayer, tr., *Keys*, pp. 113–118, where al-Shahrastānī devotes an entire chapter to the explanation of these terms.

[68] In *Keys to the Arcana* these two terms are translated as 'decree' and 'ordinance'. For instance, see pp. 63–64.

the unbelievers the lowest; and God's word is the uppermost' (9:40). One is: 'The Word is not changed with Me' (50:29). The other is: 'And when We exchange a verse in the place of another verse' (16:101). Just as there are two verdicts, there are also two judges. One judge acts based on his own verdict. The other judge requires two men to be witnesses and he needs to take an oath from them for him to work. One is the judge of the *sharī'at* and the other is the judge of the resurrection (*qiyāmat*). The justice of the *sharī'at* relies on witnesses and oath. The justice of the resurrection depends on knowledge (*'ilm*) and providence (*mashiyyat*). You are the judge of the *sharī'at*; do not pass a verdict unless you have seen or heard something. I am the deputy of the judge of the resurrection; I will pass a verdict once I know it. I acted as I wished. For you, what applies is work and you will be rewarded. You will not be given a wage until you work. You will not work unless you are paid a wage. I work without a wage; I receive a wage without working: *everyone is prepared for what he is created for*.[69]

[97] Moses says: In this case, what is the point of legal obligation? If all acts are already accomplished (*pardākhtah*), what is the point in engaging in accomplishing (*pardākhtan*) things? If someone is already a Muslim, what is the point of telling them: 'Become a Muslim!'? If they are already infidels, what is the point of telling them, 'Do not become an infidel!'? If it is true that 'alike it is to them whether thou hast warned them or thou hast not warned them, they do not believe', then what is the point of 'arise, and warn!' (74:2)? If the word has already been uttered and it cannot be revoked, what is the point of this other verdict then? If this verdict does not nullify the other one, then requiring obligation would be necessarily unjust.

[98] And Khiḍr says: Obligation (*taklīf*) is the manifestation of determination (*taqdīr*). And determination is the source of obligation.

[69] A Prophetic *ḥadīth*. See Shayḥā, *Mawsū'at*, vol. 18, p. 150.

What is hidden in determination will not be revealed except through obligation. What is embedded in obligation will not come into existence except through determination.[70] This is the point of all this. The accomplished will be revealed in the inchoative and the inchoative will emerge from the accomplished. So, the accomplished and the inchoative together are both accomplished and yet, the accomplished is the accomplished and the inchoative is the inchoative. I am the ruler of the accomplished and you are the ruler of the inchoative. I am the man of the esoteric (*taʾwīl*) and you are the man of the exoteric (*tanzīl*). I pass verdicts based on the inward (*bāṭin*) and you pass verdicts based on the outward (*ẓāhir*). My verdict nullifies not yours; nor does your verdict nullify mine. And both verdicts are right: And every jurisprudent is right (*kull mujtahid muṣayyib*). My verdict does not necessitate powerlessness (*ʿajz*); nor does yours necessitate injustice. 'The Word is not changed with Me' (50:29), so that you know there is no incapacity. 'I wrong not My servants' (50:29), so that you know that there is no injustice. Since in this world there is good and there is evil in the absolute and real sense (*muṭlaq*) and there is good and evil in the relative sense (*bi iḍāfat*), what is absolute good is an essence which will not change and what is absolute evil is also an essence which will not change. And whatever is relative good and evil will change and transform. Therefore, and as a result, whatever is good and does not change is the accomplished and whatever changes is the inchoative.[71]

[70] This appears to be a revised theory which lies between the Ashʿarī version of the theory of acquisition which says while God creates every act of man, he makes him responsible for its consequences. On the other hand, the Muʿtazila would say that a man chooses how to act and then God 'creates' the act for him. But here, God is not involved in 'creation'; all creation goes back to the Command.

[71] Here the argument presented through this narrative about Khiḍr is that there are two realms which should not be mixed together. Both can be true at the same time; they run parallel to one another. The entire encounter, as we have seen earlier in the text, is an exercise in teaching Moses something new: that there is a realm beyond what he knows and that is the realm of the *mafrūgh* or *qiyāmat*. But Moses is not authorized, as a prophet, to act based on this knowledge because it is the *qāʾim,* who has the knowledge of the Command and the *qiyāmat,* who can act according to his knowledge without necessarily obviating the role of the prophet.

[99] The two orphans who had a treasure were in the category of absolute good. Therefore, two prominent people were required to work for them despite any weariness and hunger so that the marker to their treasure would remain hidden [until the time comes for it to be revealed]. And that immature child was in the category of absolute evil: 'The young child killed by Khiḍr was predisposed in his nature to unbelief.' Therefore, he was beheaded in his childhood. Now, look at the sign written all over him: predisposed to unbelief (*kāfir-i maṭbūʿ*). And the boat of the poor people at sea which was desired by the usurper was only a contingent and it fell to the realm of relative good and relative evil: 'This is the interpretation of that thou couldst not bear patiently' (18:82).

[100] Moses says: These two decrees and the two realms you speak about are now established for me. Now, there is only one more question left. Which decree is the original and which is the secondary? Which word precedes and which one succeeds? Which decree takes precedence over the other? Which decree circumscribes and which one is the circumscribed? Which one is the universal and which one is the particular? Or are both decrees equal in weight?

[101] Khiḍr says: Questions will continue to come until one is told to cease and desist. If you have surrendered to me and accepted me as a teacher and acknowledged that you are the disciple, then at all times you must submit, because I know something that you do not. And do something that you would find unpleasant. If you object, you will have violated your submission. And if you remain silent, you will be deprived of the knowledge of that message. 'Being patient about what you do not know until you are taught is hard.' It is the undertaking of exceptional men. Here, when you called yourself a disciple and called me the teacher, you acknowledged the accomplished and the inchoative, because the accomplished is the perfection and the inchoative is the incomplete moving towards perfection. The

accomplished is the [adult] man in perfect creation and the inchoative is the sperm moving towards perfection. The accomplished is the scholar and the inchoative is the disciple. The accomplished is the prophet and the inchoative is the community (*ummat*). The scholar is the circumscriber and the disciple is the circumscribed. The prophet is the whole and the community is the part. The whole precedes the part and the part comes after the whole.

[102] The *tanzīl* and the *ta'wīl*, the beginning and the end, the outward and the inward are also similarly arranged. And recognize the hierarchy (*tarattub*) between the two so that you have no doubts at any time on any issue, because anyone who does not recognize these two decrees and two realms will always remain in the darkness of misgiving. Sometimes anthropomorphism pulls him towards the realm of similitude (*mushābahat*). Sometimes negation pulls him towards the realm of distinction (*mubāyanat*). Sometimes predestination takes him to the realm of the accomplished and he will inevitably need free will. Sometimes free will pulls him towards the realm of the inchoative and he will inevitably need predestination. Sometimes aural instruction (*sam'*) pulls him towards the deputyship of aural instruction; sometimes reason (*'aql*) pulls him towards the deputyship of reason.[72]

[103] And the misgivings of the people of the world are confined to these three issues: either anthropomorphism or negation [i.e. negative theology]; either predestination or free will; either aural instruction or reason. All misgivings arise from these three issues. All knowledge is made clear. And anyone who passes only one verdict, is blind in one eye: '[Everything then depends] on the eye chosen for viewing'.

[72] Al-Shahrastānī is suggesting a realm beyond both aural instruction and rationality (i.e. the theories of the Ash'arīs and the Mu'tazilīs). By deputyship, he means submitting to the higher authority. He has explained this in paragraph 62 where he makes a distinction between *ṣabwa* and *ḥanīfiyyat*. What matters to him is the deputyship of *rijāl* and these are persons, individuals with divine authority (he refers to the Shi'i Imams here), who are present, living and accessible.

[104] When this debate between Moses and Khiḍr had concluded and they were about to part, a gazelle appeared from the desert and stood between the two of them. One side of the gazelle was cooked and one side was raw. The cooked side was facing Khiḍr and the raw side was facing Moses.

[105] Khiḍr said: O Moses! If you wish to eat its meat, rise and light a fire and cook the raw meat so that you can eat it. And Khiḍr himself stretched out his hand and started eating the cooked side.

[106] I used to read in the commentaries about this in my youth. I wondered what this allegory meant until I heard the story about predestination and free will which took place between Abū Bakr and ʿUmar when the Prophet – may the blessing of God be upon him and his progeny – disagreed with them and said: *Is this what you were commanded to speak about? An Angel God created which is made half of fire and half of snow. The fire does not melt the snow and the snow does not extinguish the fire. The glorification of the angel is: glorified is the one who brought together fire and snow*. The angel who is half fire and half snow is the same gazelle which is half cooked and half raw.

[107] O Moses! Since you are in the world of secondary causes, you have the deputyship of rawness and the deputyship of the inchoative. Rise and bring fire, cook the meat and eat it! Since I am in the world of no causes, I am the deputy of maturity, the deputy of the accomplished. Hence, I can eat the cooked meat. In my world, everything is mature and done. All trees have borne fruit and all fruits are ripe. All that is ever to be, has come into existence. All intellects are perfect (*kāmil*). All spirits are complete (*tamām*). All natures are in balance. If I damage a boat, I damage a fine one. If I kill a child, I kill one with no crime. If I restore a wall, I restore a treasure. You are Moses and you have seen all these three stages in yourself. The boat was your body. The logs of the boat were parts of your body. The poor people were [symbols for] the meanings in your body. The usurper

was Pharaoh. Khiḍr was Gabriel. When he took your hand to put the fire in your mouth, your tongue burnt. And your tongue was one of the logs of the boat of your body. The usurper released you. And the boat was left for the poor. The other event was the murder of the young child. It was like killing the Egyptian man (*qibṭī*) whom you killed with a punch for no crime. You had to flee and you reached the rank of prophecy then. The other event was the case of the wall: you had travelled a long way. You were tired and hungry. You reached a well where shepherds were watering their sheep. Despite your weariness and hunger, you helped the two daughters of Shuʿayb to water their sheep. And yet you did not ask for any wage. Why was that? 'And our father is passing old' (28:23). It is as I said: *and their father was a decent man*. When all of these had already happened to yourself, why did you object to what I was doing? And all of these three conditions happen to everyone. The heart of a believer is best when broken: 'And I am near the ones with a broken heart'.[73]

[108] [One will go through] some stages with the devil but the heart eventually remains with those who dwell in the heart. The tempting soul (*nafs-i hawā*) of the believer has to be killed lest it gain power. If it gains power, it will mislead the parents, who are the intellect and speculation (*naẓar*), and will draw them towards its temptation. Then, instead of that tempting soul, we give him the soul at peace (*nafs-i muṭmaʾinna*). Yet again, the wall of his will and power has to be destroyed and renovated because underneath the wall there is a treasure: 'There is no will and power except through God; and this [phrase] is a treasure from the treasures of Paradise'.[74] And that treasure is made of two phrases and both of them are orphans from the other world. One is the phrase of *tawḥīd* and the other is the phrase of *nubuwwat*. One is the *lā ilāha illā Allāh* and the other is *Muḥammad*

73 A *ḥadīth qudsī*, see al-Ghazālī, *Iḥyāʾ ʿulūm al-Dīn* (Cairo, 1950), vol. 6, p. 1014.
74 See para 46, note 26 above.

rasūl Allāh. And their father is the First Command.[75] And if you speak of father and mother, then they are the Pen and the Tablet[76] where one of them is a man and the other is a receiver. One of them is the active subject and the other is the passive receiver. Yet again, the treasure filled with gems is the Qurʾan. The wall which is the sign of the treasure is man. 'The All-Merciful has taught the Qurʾan. He created man' (55:1–3). Whenever the wall is about to collapse, two prominent people (*du shakhṣ-i buzurgawār*) will restore it. Sometimes man is the sign of the Qurʾan and the Qurʾan is the treasure. Sometimes the Qurʾan is the sign of man and man is the treasure. *Amīr al-muʾminīn* ʿAlī – peace be upon him – collected the Qurʾan underneath which there was a treasure for two orphans. That is, for Ḥasan and Ḥusayn – peace be upon them. 'And their father was a decent man – and their father was better than them.' One treasure was the exoteric (*tanzīl*) and the other treasure was the esoteric (*taʾwīl*).[77] One of them was the stationary treasure and the other was the moving treasure. 'They are both Imams whether they rise or they sit.'[78] And may the blessings of God be upon Muhammad and his pure progeny.

***

This was cited from a manuscript in the handwriting of the Imām Tāj al-Dīn Muḥammad b. ʿAbd al-Karīm al-Shahrastānī. And yet, this manuscript was incomplete and I rectified whatever was possible while copying it.

75 He is referring to ʿAlī as the First Command. The early Ismailis would have used the term *asās*.

76 For more on the Tablet and the Pen see D. A. Madigan, 'Preserved Tablet', *Encyclopaedia of the Qurʾān*, consulted online on 16 July 2020 http://dx.doi.org.iij.idm.oclc.org/10.1163/1875-3922_q3_EQSIM_00339.

77 I have used *exoteric* and *esoteric* to refer to the literal and allegorical exegesis of the Qurʾan in Shiʿi and Sufi traditions.

78 See al-Ṭūsī, *Talkhīṣ al-muḥaṣṣal*, ed. ʿAbd Allāh Nūrānī (Tehran, 1359 Sh./1980), p. 461.

Appendix

Dyads

khalq	*amr*
ḥudūth	*qidam*
kathrat	*waḥdat*
mushābahat	*mubāyanat*
maẓhar	*maṣdar*
milk	*mulk*
jasad	*rūḥ*
tan	*jān*
ʿālam-i asbāb	*ʿālam-i bī sababī*
ẓāhir	*bāṭin*
farīshtigān	*payāmbarān*
mustaʾnaf	*mafrūgh*
taklīf	*taqdīr*
sharīʿat	*qiyāmat*
ism	*maʿnā*
tanzīl	*taʾwīl*
ṭāʿat	*maʿrifat*
ahl-i qibla	*ahl-i tawḥīd*
ṣabwa	*ḥanīfiyya*

Triads

taḍādd	*tarattub*	*waḥdat/tawḥīd*
ʿāmm	*khāṣṣ*	*muṭlaq*
khalq	*dīn*	*waḥdāniyya*
madbaʾ	*wasaṭ*	*kamāl*
Mūsā	*Ibrāhīm*	*Muḥammad*
mulk	*malakūt*	*jabarūt*
islām	*imān*	*iḥsān*
nafs-i ḥaywānī	*nafs-i khayālī*	*nafs-i nuṭqī*

ʿarsh	*dahr*	*Ādam*
tadbīr	*taqdīr*	*taswīr*
makān	*zamān*	*insān*

Tetrads

khalq	*taswiyat*	*taqdīr*	*hidāyat*
nafs-i nāmiyya	*nafs-i ḥaywānī*	*nafs-i khayālī*	*nafs-i insānī*
ʿaql-i istiʿdādī	*ʿaql-i taklīfī*	*ʿaql-i mustafādd*	*ʿaql-i biʾl-malaka*
mulk	*lashkar*	*kalīd*	*khazīna*

Ibrāhīm	*Isḥāq=nūr-i ẓāhir*	*Yaʿqūb=miḥnat* *Yūsuf=niʿmat*
		Dāʾūd=kitāb *Sulaymān=ḥikmat*
		Yaḥyā=qabḍ *ʿĪsā=basṭ*
		Mūsā=tanzīl *Hārūn=taʾwīl*
	Ismāʿīl=nūr-i mastūr	*Muḥammad=asrār & āyāt*

shubahāt	*tashbīh vs. taʿṭīl* *jabr vs. qadar* *samʿ vs. ʿaql*

Bibliography

Encyclopaedia of Islam, 2nd edn, ed. P. Bearman, Th. Bianquis, C. E. Bosworth, E. van Donzel, W. P. Heinrichs (online edition, Brill).

Encyclopaedia of the Qur'ān, ed. Jane Dammen McAuliffe. Leiden, 2006.

Abū Isḥāq Quhistānī. *Haft bāb*, ed. and tr. W. Ivanow. Bombay, 1959.

Adhkāʾī, Parvīz. 'Nukātī chand az tafsīr-i Shahrastānī', *Maʿārif*, 15 (1982), pp. 117–126.

Alí-de-Unzaga, Omar, ed. *Fortresses of the Intellect: Ismaili and other Islamic Studies in Honour of Farhad Daftary*. London, 2011.

Amīnī, ʿAbd al-Ḥusayn. *al-Ghadīr fi'l-kitāb wa'l-sunna wa'l-adab*. Qumm, 1416/1995.

Amir-Moezzi, Mohammad Ali, ed. *Islam: Identité et Alterété: Hommage à Guy Monnot*. Turnhout, 2013.

Badakhchani, S. J. 'Shahrastānī's Account of Ḥasan-i Ṣabbāḥ's Doctrine of Taʿlīm', in Mohammad Ali Amir-Moezzi, ed., *Islam: Identité et Alterété: Hommage à Guy Monnot*. Turnhout, 2013, pp. 27–55.

Badakhchani, S. J. 'The Paradise of Submission: A Critical Edition and Study of *Rawzeh-i Taslim* commonly known as *Tasawwurat* by Khwajeh Nasir al-Din-i Tusi 1201–1275', PhD, University of Oxford, 1989.

Bahrāmī, Muḥammad. 'Girāyish-i madhhabī-yi Shahrastānī, ṣāḥib-i tafsīr-i Mafātīḥ al-asrār', *ʿUlūm-i Qurʾān wa Ḥadīth: Pazhūhishhāy-i Qurʾānī*, 21–22 (2000), pp. 354–383.

Daftary, Farhad. *The Ismāʿīlīs: Their History and Doctrines*. 2nd edn, Cambridge, 2007.

Farmānīyān, Mahdī. 'Shahrastānī: sunnī-yi Ashʿarī yā Shiʿi-yi bāṭinī', *Haft-āsimān*, 7 (2000), pp. 135–182.

al-Ghazālī, Muḥammad. *al-Munqidh min al-ḍalāl*, ed. Jamīl Ṣalībā and Kāmil ʿAyyād. Beirut, 1967.

Ḥasan-i Maḥmūd-i Kātib. *Dīwān-i qāʾimiyyāt*, ed. S. J. Badakhchani. Tehran, 2011.

—— *Haft bāb*, ed. and tr. by S. J. Badakhchani as *Spiritual Resurrection in Shiʿi Islam: An Early Ismaili Treatise on the Doctrine of Qiyāmat*. London, 2017.

Hourani, George. *Reason and Tradition in Islamic Ethics*. Cambridge, 1985.

al-Ḥurr al-ʿĀmilī, Muḥammad b. Ḥasan. *al-Jawāhir al-saniyya fi'l-aḥādith al-qudsiyya*, Beirut, 1982.

Ibn al-Jawzī, Abu'l-Faraj ʿAbd al-Raḥmān b. ʿAlī al-Ḥanbalī. *al-Mudhish*, ed. ʿAbd al-Karīm Muḥammad Munīr Tattān and Khaldūn ʿAbd al-ʿAzīz Makhlūṭa. Damascus, 1435/2014.

Jalālī Nāʾīnī, Muḥammad Riḍā. *Du maktūb az Muḥammad b. ʿAbd al-Karīm Shahrastānī*. Tehran, 1369 Sh./1990.

—— *Sharḥ-i ḥāl wa āthār-i ḥujjat al-ḥaqq Muḥammad b. ʿAbd al-Karīm b. Aḥmad Shahrastānī*. Tehran, 1343 Sh./1964.

al-Kirmānī, Ḥamīd al-Dīn Aḥmad b. ʿAbd Allāh. *Rāḥat al-ʿaql*, ed. M. K. Ḥusayn and M. M. Ḥilmī. Cairo, 1953.

Lane, Edward William. *An Arabic-English Lexicon*. London, 1863.

Lewisohn, Leonard. 'From the "Moses of Reason" to the "Khiḍr of the Resurrection": The Oxymoronic Transcendant in Shahrastānī's *Majlis-i maktūb . . . dar Khwārazm*', in Omar Alí-de-Unzaga, ed., *Fortresses of the Intellect: Ismaili and Other Islamic Studies in Honour of Farhad Daftary*. London, 2011, pp. 403–429.

Mir-Kasimov, Orkhan, ed. *Intellectual Interactions in the Islamic World: The Ismaili Thread*. London, 2020.

Mitha, Farouk. *al-Ghazālī and the Ismailis: A Debate on Reason and Authority in Medieval Islam*. London, 2001.

Mohammad Poor, Daryoush. 'Extra-Ismaili Sources and a Shift of Paradigm in Nizārī Ismailism', in Orkhan Mir-Kasimov, ed. *Intellectual Interactions in the Islamic World: The Ismaili Thread*. London, 2020, pp. 219–245.

—— *Authority without Territory*. New York, 2014.

Monnot, Guy. 'Al-Shahrastānī', *EI2*, vol. 9, pp. 214–216.

al-Muʾayyad fi'l-Dīn al-Shīrāzī, Abū Naṣr Hibat Allāh b. Abī ʿImrān Mūsā. *al-Majālis al-Muʾayyadiyya*, ed. Ḥātim Ḥamīd al-Dīn. Mumbai, 1422/2002.

Nāṣir-i Khusraw. *Kitāb-i Jāmiʿ al-ḥikmatayn*, tr. Eric Ormsby as *Between Reason and Revelation: Twin Wisdoms Reconciled*. London, 2012.

Öztürk, Mustafa. 'The different stances of al-Shahrastānī: a study of the sectarian identity of Abū l-Fatḥ al-Shahrastānī in relation to his Qurʾānic commentary, Mafātīh al-asrār', *Ilahiyat Studies*, 1/2 (2010), pp. 195–239.

Pourjavady, Reza, and Sabine Schmidtke, intro. *The Quṭb al-Dīn al-Shīrāzī Codex, facsimile edition of the Marʿashī codex 12868*. Qumm, 1391 Sh./2013.

Sanāʾī Ghaznawī, Majdūd b. Ādam. *Dīwān-i Sanāʾī Ghaznawī*, ed. M. T. Mudarris Raḍawī. Tehran, 1362 Sh./1983.

al-Shahrastānī, Muḥammad b. ʿAbd al-Karīm. *al-Milal wa'l-niḥal*, ed. Amīr ʿAlī Muhannā and ʿAlī Ḥasan Fāʿūr. Beirut, 1414/1993; Persian translation as *Tarjuma-yi kitāb al-milal wa'l-niḥal*, facsimile edition, intro. Muḥammad ʿImādī Ḥāʾirī. Tehran, 1395 Sh./2016.

—— *Mafātīḥ al-asrār wa maṣābīḥ al-abrār*, ed. M. A. Ādharshab. Tehran, 1386 Sh./2008; tr. by Toby Mayer as *Keys to the Arcana: Shahrastānī's esoteric commentary on the Qur'an; A translation of the commentary on* Sūrat al-Fātiḥa *from Muḥammad b. ʿAbd al-Karīm al-Shahrastānī's* Mafātīḥ al-asrār wa maṣābīḥ al-abrār. Oxford, 2009.

—— *Muṣāraʿat al-falāsifa*, ed. and tr. by Wilferd Madelung and Toby Mayer as *Struggling with the Philosopher: A Refutation of Avicenna's Metaphysics*. London, 2001.

—— *Nihāyat al-aqdām fī ʿilm al-kalām*, facsimile edition, intro. Muḥammad ʿImādī Ḥāʾirī. Tehran, 1391 Sh./2012.

—— *Nihāyat al-aqdām fī ʿilm al-kalām*, ed. and tr. by Alfred Guillaume as *The Summa Philosophiae of al-Shahrastānī*. London, 1934.

Shayḥā, Khalīl Maʾmūn. *Mawsūʿat al-Muʿjam al-mufahras li-alfāẓ al-ḥadīth al-nabawī al-sharīf li'l-kutub al-sitta: Ṣaḥīḥayy al-Bukhārī wa-Muslim wa'l-Sunan li-Abī Dāwūd wa'l-Tirmidhī wa'l-Nasāʾī wa-Ibn Mājah. Wa-maʿahu sharḥ Gharīb al-ḥadīth li-Ibn al-Athīr*. Beirut, 2013.

Steigerwald, Diane. 'Al-Shahrastānī's Contribution to Medieval Islamic Thought', in Todd Lawson, ed., *Reason and Inspiration in Islam: Theology, Philosophy and Mysticism in Muslim Thought: Essays in Honour of Hermann Landolt*. London, 2005.

—— *Majlis: Discours sur l'Ordre et la création*. Saint-Nicolas, Québec, 1998.

al-Suḥaybānī, Muḥammad b. Nāṣir b. Ṣāliḥ. *Manhaj al-Shahrastānī fī kitābih al-Milal wa'l-niḥal*. Riyadh, 1997.

al-Ṭūsī, Khwāja Naṣīr al-Dīn Muḥammad b. Muḥammad. *Sayr wa sulūk*, ed. and tr. by S. J. Badakhchani as *Contemplation and Action: The Spiritual Autobiography of a Muslim Scholar*. London, 1998.

—— *Rawḍa-yi taslīm*, ed. and tr. by W. Ivanow. Leiden, 1950; ed. and tr. by S. J. Badakhchani as *Paradise of Submission: A Medieval Treatise on Ismaili Thought*. London, 2005.

—— *Talkhīṣ al-muḥaṣṣal*, ed. ʿAbd Allāh Nūrānī. Tehran, 1359 Sh./1980.

—— *Tawallā wa tabarrā, Maṭlūb al-muʾminīn and Āghāz wa anjām*, ed. and tr. by S. J. Badakhchani as *Shiʿi Interpretations of Islam: Three Treatises on Theology and Eschatology*. London, 2010.

—— *Akhlāq-i Muḥtashamī*, ed. M. T. Dānishpazhūh. Tehran, 1982.

Wensinck, Arent J. *Concordance et indices de la tradition musulmane*. Leiden, 1936–1971.

al-Zamakhsharī, Abu'l-Qāsim Maḥmūd b. ʿUmar. *Rabīʿ al-abrār wa nuṣūs al-akhbār*, ed. ʿAbd al-Amīr Muhannā. Beirut, 1412/1992.

Zarrīnkūb, ʿAbd al-Ḥusayn. 'Shahrastānī wa hamnashīn-i Farsī-yi ū', *Nāmah-yi furūgh-i ʿilm*, 2 (1950), pp. 35–42.

Index

Abraham (Ibrāhīm, prophet), 75, 80, 95–8
abrogation (*naskh*), 81
absolute (*muṭlaq*), 75
Active intellect (*ʿaql-i faʿʿāl*), 48–51
Active motion, 77–8
Adam, 32, 80, 86, 99, 100, 101–2
Ādharshab, Muḥammad ʿAlī, 8, 28, 31, 32, 66
Adhkāʾī, Parvīz, 14–15, 19
aeon (*dahr*), 86
Āghāz wa anjām (al-Tusi), 36, 56
Akhbārī (Shiʿi traditionist), 30
ʿAlī b. al-Ḥusayn (Zayn al-ʿĀbidīn), early Shiʿi Imam, 63–4
Alamūt (seat of the Nizārī Ismaili state and fortress in northern Persia), 65
Amīnī, ʿAbd al-Ḥusayn, 37
angels, 76–7, 78, 79, 80–1, 93
abode of, 84
  becoming, 89–90
  direction, 86
  intermediaries of creation, 91
Anṣārī, Abu'l-Qāsim, 2, 19
anthropomorphism, 101–2, 112
Anthropomorphists (*mushabbiha*), 101–2
Antinomianism (*ibāḥa*), 27
arḥām, 76
arzāq, 76
Asʿad Mīhanī, 4
asās al-taʾwīl, 56, 58
Ashāʿira (theological movement), 55–66
Ashʿarīs (proponents of Ashāʿrism), 9–10, 92, 102
aural instruction (*samʿ*), 101, 112
autonomy, 61
ʿAyn al-Quḍāt Ḥamadānī (Sufi shaykh and author), 17–18, 23

Badakhchani, Jalal, 23
Baghdad, 4, 4–5
Bahrāmī, Muḥammad, 33, 36
Bayhaqī, Ẓahīr al-Dīn, 1
bliss (*saʿādat*), 79–80
bodies, 103
body, 74–5
Buzurg-Umīd, Kiyā (Nizārī Ismaili lord of Alamūt), 6, 8, 18, 26, 55

causes
  secondary, 76, 113
  and verdicts, 107–8
celestial sovereignty, 93–4
centrifugal motion, 77
centripetal motion, 77
commandments, 108
compendium of all words, the, 99
compound (*murakkab*), 100
compulsion, 85–6
contraction (*qabḍ*), 98
contrariety (*taḍādd*), 8–9, 22
cosmology, 13
creation (*khalq*), 9, 12, 13, 24–5, 73, 99–100, 102
  apportioning of the elements, 75–6
  and command, 91–2
  Imam at centre of, 25
  perfection of, 79
  primary cause, 48–9

Daftary, F., 20
dāʿī (summoner), 10, 18, 25, 28, 34, 35–6, 48, 54
dāʿī al-duʿāt (chief *dāʿī*), 20–1, 23, 30, 36, 46, 48

Dā'ūd (prophet), 98
da'wa (mission), 35, 38, 46, 48, 51, 55
al-da'wa al-jadida, 9
death of ignorance (*mawt al-jahl*), 40
deputyship of men (*niyābat al-rijāl*), 51
determination, 109–10
direction, 86–9
discretion (*takhyīr*), 79
Divine command (*amr*), 9, 12, 25, 48–51, 73, 74, 84, 91–2, 102

earthly sovereignty, 97
education, 82–3
elements, the, 75–6
eternal people (*unās sarmadiyyūn*), 51, 52
ethical voluntarism, 58–9, 59–66
ethics, 59–66
evil, 56, 61, 110
excellence, 83–4
expansion (*basṭ*), 98

faith, 25, 45–6, 76, 77, 81–3, 96
falsehood, 78
faqīh, 33
Farmāniyān, Mahdī, 30, 31, 34–6
Fatimid precedents, 54–5
first effect, 25, 48
free will, 101, 112, 113
Fuṣūl-i mubārak (Epistles of the Nizārī Ismaili Imam, Ḥasan II), 22, 51–2

Gabriel, 114
al-Ghazālī, Muḥammad (Sunni theologian and author), 4
Ghaznawī, Sanā'ī, 17, 21, 23
Gimaret, Daniel, 41
God, 76
  celestial sovereignty, 93–4
  as Creator, 99–100
  engagement with the concept of, 9
  face of, 101–2
  knowing, 12, 24–5
  knowledge of, 33, 62
  omnipotence, 101–2
  prostration before, 32
  purity in the worship of, 32
  spiritual sovereignty, 102
  terrestrial sovereignty, 73, 92–3
good and evil, 56, 61, 110
governance, 32
gradual hierarchy (*tarattub*), 8
guidance, intermediaries of, 76

Haft bāb (title of two Nizārī Ismaili works of the Alamūt period), 39, 45, 53
hajj, the, 4
Ḥamawī, Yāqūt (medieval Muslim traveller and author), 1
ḥanīfiyyat (pristine faith), 13, 45–6, 51, 53
Hārūn (Aaron), 98
Ḥasan II, *'alā dhikrihi al-salām* (4th lord of Alamūt and Nizārī Ismaili Imam), 8, 8–9, 16–17, 21–2, 23, 24, 26, 26–7, 39, 45, 55
Ḥasan-i Ṣabbāḥ (1st lord of Alamūt and founder of the Nizārī state), 7, 10, 12, 18, 19, 24, 25–6, 35, 38–9, 44, 47–8, 65
heart, the, 114
Hell, 94–5
heretics, 27
hierarchy (*tarattub*), 22, 25, 26, 27, 30, 35, 54, 112
Hourani, George, 59, 60–1, 62, 64
ḥudūth (temporality), 73
human reason, 24, 61–2
ḥunafā', 53

Ibn al-Sam'ānī (Muslim scholar and biographer), 1, 2, 4
Ibn Khallikān (Muslim scholar and biographer), 1–2
Ibn Sīnā (Avicenna), 7, 9

Ibn Taymiyya (Sunni author), 29
imamate, the, 8, 13, 39, 45, 58
 and creation, 25, 50–1
 deputyship of, 51
 doctrine of, 53
 Ismaili, 57
 knowledge of, 25–6
 the living, 47–8
 relationship to, 22
 role of, 12
 status, 64–5
 temporary absence of, 48
Imāmiyya, 30, 31, 37, 51
independence, 61
innate predisposition (*fiṭrat*), 79, 85, 96
intellect, 84, 89–90, 91
Intellectus adeptus, 84
inter-textuality, 37–54
involuntary rank, 96

ʿĪsā (Jesus), 80
al-Iṣfahānī, Afḍal al-Dīn Ṣadr Turka (medieval Persian translator of al-Shahrastānī's *al-Milal*), 14
Isḥāq (Isaac), 97
Ismāʿīl (6th Ismaili Imam; also name of the son of Ibrāhīm in Islamic tradition), 97–8
Ismailism, 56–8, 62
Ithnā ʿasharīs (also called Twelvers), 27, 42–4
Ivanow, Wladimir, 16, 22–3, 45

Jalālī Nāʾīnī, Muḥammad Riḍā, 14–16, 37, 67, 68, 69
justice, 108–9

Kaʿba, 86, 89
al-Kahf, Surat, 12
kalam, 7
Kalima (Divine word), 9, 77, 82–4, 87, 97
kammiyyat (quantity), 73
Karrāmīs (theological movement), 9–10, 91–2, 101–2
Khiḍr (prophet), 12, 54, 58, 60, 69, 103–14
Khurāsān, 5
Khwāfī, Abu'l-Muẓaffar Aḥmad, 2
Khwārazm, 4
al-Khwārazmī, Ibn Arsalān (medieval Persian historian), 2, 3, 3–4
al-Kirmānī, Ḥamīd al-Dīn (Ismaili *dāʿī* and author), 35, 61
Kitāb al-iṣlāḥ (by Abū Ḥātim al-Rāzī), 54
knowledge (*maʿrifat*), 81–2, 88–9, 103–14
al-Kulaynī (early Imāmī *muḥaddith*), 53

lā ilāha illā Allāh, 81–3, 93–4, 114–5
Landolt, Hermann, 38, 41–2

Madāʾinī, Abu'l-Ḥasan, 2–3
Madelung, Wilferd, 20, 42, 46–7, 48
Mafātīḥ al-asrār wa maṣābīḥ al-abrār (by al-Shahrastānī), 7–9, 12–15, 21, 23, 26, 30–4, 36–40, 41, 42–4, 47–9, 51, 53, 56, 65–6, 69
Mafrūgh, 11, 22, 38, 54, 60, 88, 108
Mahdi, the, 31–2
Majlis-i Khwārazm/maktūb, 73–115
 completed, 7
 content, 11–16
 edition, 66–70
 encounter between Mūsā and Khiḍr, 54–5, 58, 60, 69
 footnotes, 69
 genre, 11
 manuscript, 14
 manuscripts, 68–9
 narrative, 27
 paragraph numbers, 69
 Qurʾanic verse references, 69
 reading, 12
 significance, 9–10

terminology, 21–2, 23, 26–7, 30
text, 1942, 14–15
theme, 9
translation, 66, 67–8
makānī (spatial), 74
manifestation (*maẓhar*), 91
Marw, in Khurāsān, 4
al-Marwazī, Naṣīr al-Dīn Maḥmūd (Saljūq vizier), 5
Marw-i Shāh-i Jahān, 5
matter, 103
Mayer, Toby, 66
mental motion, 77–8
messiah, 38, 39
al-Milal wa'l-niḥal (heresiographical work by al-Shahrastānī), 1, 5–7, 9, 12, 14, 19–20, 23, 34, 36, 41, 43-4, 47-8, 51, 53, 67
miqdār (measure), 73
misgiving (*shubhat*), 101

misguidedness, 4
Monnot, Guy, 20–1, 43
Muhammad, the Prophet, 44–5, 75, 80, 87–8, 97–8, 115
Muḥammad III, ʿAlāʾ al-Dīn (Nizārī Ismaili Imam), 44
Muḥammad b. Buzurg-Umīd (3rd Lord of Alamūt), 8, 55
mulk (sovereignty) , 73, 92–4, 97, 102
Mūsā (Moses), 12, 54, 58, 60, 69, 75, 80, 103–14
al-Mūsawī, Majd al-Dīn ʿAlī (*naqīb* of the ʿAlids of Tirmidh), 5, 7
Mushabbiha, criticism of, 10
mustaʾnaf, 11, 22, 38, 54, 60, 88, 108
Mustanṣir bi'llāh (Ismaili Imam-caliph), 4, 18
Mutakallim, 10, 12
Muʿtazila (Sunni theological movement), 9–10, 55–6, 61, 91
Muʿtazilī (proponent of Muʿtazilism), 102

natural motions, 77, 78
negation (*taʿṭīl*), 112
negative theology, 112
Nihāya, 29–30
Nihāyat al-aqdām (by Shahrastānī), 5, 58
Niʿmatullāhī Order (Sufi *ṭarīqa*), 57–8
Nīshābūr, in Khurāsān, 2–3, 4
Niẓām al-Mulk (Saljūq vizier), 3
Niẓāmiyya madrasa/s, 2–3
Nizārī doctrine, 13
influence on, 16–23
Nizārī/s, Nizārī Ismailis, 6
Noah, 80
nullification (*ibṭāl*), 81
al-Nuʿmān, al-Qāḍī Abū Ḥanīfa (Ismaili *dāʿī* and foremost Fatimid jurist), 54

obedience, 88
obligation (*taklīf*), 83, 93, 108–10
obliging intellect, 84
Öztürk, Mustafa, 30–1, 37

Paradise, 81–2, 94–5
pardākhtah (accomplished, *mafrūgh*), 109
perfection, 96, 98–9
Persia, 18
personification (*tashakhkhuṣ*), 45
philosophy, seven issues in, 7
plurality, 73
potential intellect, 84
predestination, 101, 112, 113
pre-eternity (*qidam*), 73
premise (*muqaddima*), 100
primary cause, 48–9
prohibitions, 108
property, 105, 106
Prophet, the, 39
role of, 12
prophets, the, 77–8, 78–9, 80, 84, 91, 93

prostration, 85–6, 89
providence, 108

qā'im (lit., riser), 30, 54, 60, 88, 108
qidam (pre-eternity), 73
qiyāmat (resurrection) , 8–9, 13, 21, 22, 23
 declaration of, 17, 24, 26, 39, 55
 doctrine of, 24–7, 41, 45
 perfection of, 79
Qur'anic approach, 13
Qur'anic verses, 11–12
Qushayrī, Abū Naṣr (Sunni scholar), 2

Rawḍa-yi taslīm (by Naṣīr al-Dīn al-Ṭūsī), 8, 16, 33, 38, 40–1, 49–50, 51, 53, 63, 65–6, 70
al-Rāzī, Abū Ḥātim (Ismaili *dā'ī* and author), 54
realm of distinction (*kawn-i mubāyanat*), 112
realm of similitude (*kawn-i mushābahat*), 112
reason (*'aql*), 112
rectification (*taqwīm*), 78
rectitude (*rasti*), 84–5
relative (*bi iḍāfat*), 110
resurrection, 8–9, 40–1
 day of, 16–17
 justice of, 108–9
Resurrection, Sermon of, 26
Risāla dar ḥaqīqat-i dīn (post Alamūt Nizārī work), 57
Rūdakī (Persian poet), 90
Rūmī (Sufi master and Persian poet), 11

Sa'dī (Persian poet), 11
Sa'īd-i Musayyib (early traditionist), 94
Saljūqs (Turkish dynasty), 3, 7
salvation, 94
Sanā'ī Ghaznawī (Sufi and Persian poet), 17, 21, 23
Sanjar (Saljūq sulṭān), 5–7
ṣabwa, 13
Sayr wa sulūk (spiritual biography of Naṣīr al-Dīn al-Ṭūsī), 8, 10, 12–13, 16, 20, 30, 32–3, 46, 48, 50
secondary causes (*asbāb*), 76, 113
al-Shāfi'ī (Sunni theologian and eponymous founder of the Shāfi'ī school of jurisprudence), 59
al-Shahrastānī, Muḥammad b. 'Abd al-Karīm 18–19
 al-Milal wa'l-niḥal, 19–20
 Ash'arī tendencies, 58–9
 biographies and source material, 1–2
 birth, 1, 1–2
 critique of Ḥasan-i Ṣabbāḥ, 47–8
 critique of the philosophers, 49–50
 death, 8
 early life, 2–3
 education, 2–3
 faith, 28–37, 56
 fall from grace at court, 6
 family, 2
 Fatimid precedents, 54–5
 honorifics, 1
 influence, 16–23
 Ismaili adherence, 20–1
 Ismaili affiliations, 29, 31, 34–6, 42–3, 47–8, 53–4, 56–8
 Ismaili connections, 13–16
 most important works, 5, 7
 performs the *hajj*, 4
 popularity, 19–20
 posthumous connections with Nizari Ismailis, 8–9
 scholarly activity, 3–7
 terminology, 21–2, 23, 26–7, 30–1, 34–6, 37–9, 54
 title, 46
 tomb, 8
 writings, 1

Shahristāna, 7
sharī'at (sacred law of Islam), 27, 62, 79, 81, 83–4, 91, 105, 108, 108–9
Shihāb al-Dīn Shāh, 57
simple (*basīṭ*), 100
al-Shīrāzī, al-Mu'ayyad fi'l-Dīn (Ismaili chief *dā'ī* and author), 11, 62
al-Sijistānī, Abū Ya'qūb (Ismaili *dā'ī* and author), 10, 24–5
sorcery, 101
soul, 74–5
  perfection of, 82–3
  Satanic, 84
  stages, 84
space, 74, 103
spirit, 89
spiritual sovereignty, 102
Steigerwald, Diane, 42–3, 54–5
al-Subkī (Sunni biographer and author), 2
Sufi (a Muslim mystic), 11–16, 17
Sufism (*tasawwuf*), 57–8
Sulaymān (prophet), 98

taḍādd (contrariety), 8, 22, 25, 34, 60
ta'līm (teaching, especially the Ismaili Nizārī teaching of the Alamūt and post-Alamūt era), 12–13, 24–6, 50, 64
tanzīl (revelation), 80, 98, 103, 110, 112, 115
taqdīr (determining), 11, 60, 75, 86, 108, 109
taqiyya (precautionary dissimulation of belief), 7
tarattub (hierarchy), 22, 25, 26, 27, 30, 35, 54, 112
taswiyat (apportioning), 75
tawḥid (unicity of God), 25, 44–5, 62
ta'wīl (esoteric interpretation), 33, 56, 98, 112, 115
temptation, 101, 114
terrestrial sovereignty, 73, 92–3
theistic subjectivism, 62–6
throne, the, 86
time, 74, 103, 107
Tirmidh, 5, 7, 29, 36, 43
transformation, 81
truth, 78, 108
al-Ṭūsī, Naṣīr al-Dīn (Ismaili author and polymath), 8, 10, 12, 16, 20, 23, 27, 30, 32, 38–9, 40–1, 46, 48–3, 63, 64

unas sarmadiyyun, 51–4
unity, 8–9, 22, 73

values, 62
verbal motion, 77–8
verdicts, and causes, 107–8
Virani, Mumtaz, 66
voluntary motions, 77, 77–8, 78–9
voluntary rank, 95–6

waḥdat, 45
walayat al-faqih, 32
Word of God, the, 9
worship (*tā'at*), 85–9
wretchedness (*shaqāwat*), 79–80

Ya'qūb (descendent of the prophet Ibrāhīm), 97, 98
Yāqūt al-Hamawī (medieval Islamic geographer), 4
Yūsuf (prophet), 97, 98

zamānī (temporal), 74
Zarrīnkūb, 'Abd al-Ḥusayn, 15

Index of Qur'anic citations

Text	Sura	Verse	Paragraph
And whosoever follows My guidance.	2	38	5
No fear shall be on them, neither shall they sorrow.	2	38	5
Each believes in God, His angels, His Books, and His messengers.	2	285	11
Bow down to Adam.	2	34	42
I am indeed close (to them): I listen to the prayer of every suppliant when he calleth on Me.	2	186	50
Whithersoever you turn, there is the Face of God.	2	115	51
And wherever you are, turn your faces towards it.	2	144	51
We know not save what Thou hast taught us.	2	32	52
We hear, and obey.	2	258	52
Prostrate before Adam.	2	34	67
Teaching the people sorcery.	2	102	74
From them they learned how they might divide a man and his wife.	2	102	74
Nor shall they compass aught of His knowledge except as He willeth.	2	255	76
The Living, the Self-subsisting.	2	255	76
'Be' and then it is.	2	117	79
That is the Book, wherein is no doubt.	2	2	90
Lord, we believe in what Thou hast sent down, and we follow the Messenger.	3	53	13
And reflect upon the creation of the heavens and the earth.	3	191	16
O God! Master of sovereignty.	3	26	56

Text	Sura	Verse	Paragraph
Unto God belongs sovereignty over the heavens and the earth.	3	189	56
And He taught thee what thou Knewest not (before).	4	113	46
Not remembering God save a little.	4	142	74
A law and a way.	5	48	22
And when Thou createst out of clay . . . as the likeness of a bird.	5	110	22
We hear and we obey.	5	7	48
So We were showing Abraham the kingdom of the heavens and earth, that he might be of those having sure faith.	6	75	59
When the night covered him over.	6	76	59
This is my Lord.	6	76	59
I love not those that set.	6	76	59
Unless my Lord guide me, I shall surely be among those who go astray.	6	77	59
O my people! I am indeed free from your (guilt) of giving partners to God.	6	78	59
I shall surely be among those who go astray.	6	77	59
I have set my face.	6	79	60
He is Omnipotent over His servants.	6	18	76
Perfect are the words of thy Lord in truthfulness and justice; no man can change His words	6	115	96
Verily, His are the creation and the command.	7	54	1, 78
Had God not guided us, we had surely never been guided.	7	43	9
Who believes in God and His Words.	7	158	13
Say: I have no power over any good or harm to myself except as God willeth.	7	188	46
If I had knowledge of the unseen.	7	188	46

To Him belongs creation and the command.	7	54	55
Children of Adam! If there should come to you Messengers from among you, relating to you My signs, then whosoever is godfearing and makes amends, no fear shall be on them, neither shall they sorrow.	7	35	56
You created me from fire and create him from clay.	7	12	69
What prevented you from prostrating once I commanded you to do so?	7	12	69
once I commanded you.	7	12	69, 71
He said, 'Because Thou hast caused me to err, I shall surely lie in wait for them on Thy straight path'.	7	16	71
Thou wilt not find most of them thankful.	7	17	74
And laid hold of his brother's head, dragging him to him.	7	150	85
Then God sent down on him His Shekhina, and confirmed him with hosts you did not see; and He made the word of the unbelievers the lowest; and God's word is the uppermost.	9	40	61
And He made the word of the unbelievers the lowest; and God's word is the uppermost.	9	40	96
Firmly established on the throne (of authority), regulating and governing all things.	10	3	43
Some of them shall be wretched and some happy.	11	105	23
To God belongs the Unseen in the heavens and the earth.	11	123	56
I saw eleven stars, and the sun and the moon; I saw them bowing down before me.	12	4	62

Text	Sura	Verse	Paragraph
And what profits men abides in the earth.	13	17	16
Thou art only a warner, and a guide to every people.	13	7	24
O Our Lord! Truly Thou dost know what we conceal and what we reveal.	14	38	63
Go forth from it! Surely thou art outcast.	15	34	70
And surely upon thee is the curse until the Day of Judgment.	15	35	70
And when We exchange a verse in the place of another verse.	16	101	96
Say: The Spirit is of the command of my Lord.	17	85	5
Say: 'The Spirit (cometh) by command of my Lord'.	17	85	78
And I desired to damage it.	17	89	95
Bring us our breakfast; indeed, we have encountered weariness from this our journey.	18	62	82
Then they found one of Our servants.	18	65	82
Shall I follow thee so that thou teachest me, of what thou hast been taught, right judgment.	18	66	83
Assuredly thou wilt not be able to bear with me patiently.	18	67	84
How shouldst thou bear patiently what thou hast never encompassed in thy knowledge?	18	68	84
Yet thou shalt find me, if God wills, patient; and I shall not rebel against thee in anything.	18	69	85
We desired that their Lord should give to them in exchange one better than him in purity, and nearer in tenderness.	18	81	95
And thy Lord desired that they should come of age.	18	82	95

This is the interpretation of that thou couldst not bear patiently.	18	82	99
He who gave everything its creation, then guided it.	20	50	6, 7
In your religion, being the creed of your father Abraham.	22	78	26
Another creature.	23	14	25
We created man.	23	12	78
Then We set him, a drop.	23	13	79
In a receptacle secure.	23	13	79
Who created me, and Himself guides me.	26	78	6, 7
Shall I inform you, (O people!), on whom it is that the evil ones descend? They descend on every lying, wicked person.	26	221–222	38
I do not know any deity for you but Myself.	28	38	69
O my Lord, surely I have need of whatever good Thou shalt have sent down upon me.	28	24	82
And our father is passing old.	28	23	107
And the sea – seven seas after it to replenish it, yet would the Words of God not be spent.	31	27	4
The guilty ones will bend low their heads before their Lord.	32	12	39
To Him good words go up	35	10	16
His command, when He desires a thing, is to say to it 'Be', and it is.	36	82	1
Alike it is to them whether thou hast warned them or thou hast not warned them, they do not believe. (?)	36	10	97
Those who have said, 'Our Lord is God' then have gone straight, upon them the angels descend.	41	30	38

Text	Sura	Verse	Paragraph
And Thou, surely Thou shalt guide unto a straight path.	42	52	22
To Him belong the keys of the heavens and the earth.	42	12	56
And if you asked them who has created them, they would say God.	43	87	69
Eat as cattle eat.	47	12	81
To God belong the hosts of the heavens and the earth.	48	4	56
And our command is not but an instant.	50	54	79
The Word is not changed with Me.	50	29	96
The Word is not changed with Me.	50	29	98
I wrong not My servants.	50	29	98
Surely We have created everything in measure. Our commandment is but one word, as the twinkling of an eye.	54	49–50	3
The All-merciful has taught the Qur'an.	55	1–2	66
And he taught the Qur'an.	55	2	68
He created the human being.	55	3	68
The All-Merciful has taught the Qur'an. He created man.	55	1–3	108
And make you to grow again in a fashion you know not. You have known the first growth; so why will you not remember?	56	61	27
He is the First and the Last.	57	3	4
The Outward and the Inward.	57	3	4
Unto God belong the treasuries of the heavens and of the earth.	63	7	56
Arise, and warn!	74	2	97
Some faces, that Day, will beam (in brightness and beauty); Looking towards their Lord.	75	22–23	50
Mixed fluids that we may test him.	76	2	22

And We made him hearing, seeing.	76	2	22
Surely We guided him upon the way whether he be thankful or unthankful.	76	3	22
Who created thee and shaped thee and wrought thee in symmetry.	82	7	8
Over every soul there is a guardian.	86	4	36
Who created and shaped, who determined and guided.	87	2–3	6, 7
Who determined and guided.	87	3	8
Surely this is in the ancient scrolls, the scrolls of Abraham and Moses.	87	18–19	8
In the best of moulds.	95	4	40
Then do We abase him (to be) the lowest of the low, except such as believe and do righteous deeds.	95	5–6	40
Bow down in adoration, and bring thyself the closer (to God).	96	19	41

www.ingramcontent.com/pod-product-compliance
Lightning Source LLC
Chambersburg PA
CBHW051809230426
43672CB00012B/2670
* 9 7 8 0 7 5 5 6 0 2 9 7 1 *

مجلس مکتوب منعقد در خوارزم

تاج الدین محمّد بن عبدالکریم شهرستانی
(م. ۱۱۵۳/۵۴۸)

به کوشش:
داریوش محمّدپور

بسم اللّه الرّحمن الرّحیم

هذا مجلس عقده الإمام تاج الدّین محمّد بن عبدالکریم الشهرستانی تغمّده اللّه بغفرانه

[۱] ایزد را - تعالی - خلق است و امر: أَلَا لَهُ الْخَلْقُ وَالْأَمْرُ (۵۴:۷). آفرینش و فرمان او راست: له الخلق مِلکاً و الامر مُلکاً. امر او مصدر خلق اوست؛ خلق او مظهرِ امرِ او. خلق او نبود، بامر او در وجود آمد. امر او بود[۱]، بخلق او در ظهور آمد.[۲] وجود خلایق بامر اوست: إِنَّمَا أَمْرُهُ إِذَا أَرَادَ شَيْئًا أَن يَقُولَ لَهُ كُن فَيَكُونُ (۸۲:۳۶). ظهور امر او، بخلق اوست: حَتَّىٰ أظهر اللّه أمره.[۳]

[۱] ج: نبود؛ ت: بود. از مضمون بند بعدی (هم‌عنان دانستن امر با قدم) و هم‌چنین اشاره به ظهور، کلمه باید «بود» باشد.
[۲] این نکته مهم‌ترین وجه شباهت آراء شهرستانی و نفوذ آن بر تفکر بعدی نزاریان در زمینه‌ی خلق و امر است. بنگرید به *سیر و سلوک* طوسی (صص. ۱۱-۸) و *مفاتیح* شهرستانی (صص. ۲۷۷-۲۷۶) در نقد موضع فلاسفه.
[۳] ج: حتی ظهر أمر اللّه.

[۲] اگر قِدَم و حدوث را قسمت کنی بر خلق و امر، قدم نصیب امر آید که ابدیّت و سرمدیّت او راست؛ حدوث نصیب خلق آید که بدایت، و نهایت او راست.

[۳] و چون وحدت و کثرت را قسمت کنی بر خلق و امر، وحدت نصیب امر آید که احاطت او راست، و کثرت نصیب خلق که مقدار و کمیّت او راست: انَّا كُلَّ شَيْءٍ خَلَقْنَاهُ بِقَدَرٍ وَمَا أَمْرُنَا إِلَّا وَاحِدَةٌ كَلَمْحٍ بِالْبَصَرِ (۵۰: ۴۹-۵۴).

[۴] امر قدسی، صفتِ یکی کلماتِ تامّاتِ بی‌نهایت: وَالْبَحْرُ يَمُدُّهُ مِن بَعْدِهِ سَبْعَةُ أَبْحُرٍ مَّا نَفِدَتْ كَلِمَاتُ اللَّهِ (۳۱:۲۷). نه امر او بزمان محدود[۴] گشت، نه کلمات او بمکان محصور. نه گردش زمان امر او را در گردش آورد؛ نه آرامش مکان کلمات او را در آرامش آورد. زمان و مکان دو غلامک بودند بر در سرای صنع او، در تحت[۵] فرمان امر او: والدّهر کلّ الزّمان، والعرش کلّ المکان. زمان را اولی و آخری؛ مکان را

---

[۴] ج و ت: معدود؛ به قرینهٔ کلمهٔ محصور، این کلمه باید محدود باشد.

[۵] صفحه‌بندی نسخهٔ م از این‌جا آغاز می‌شود. جملات و عبارات قبل از این در نسخهٔ م موجود نیست.

ظاهری و باطنی. هُوَ الْأَوَّلُ وَالآخِرُ (۳:۵۷)، تا بدانی که وجودش زمانی نیست. وَالظَّاهِرُ وَالْبَاطِنُ (۳:۵۷)، تا بدانی که وجودش مکانی نیست.

[۵] تو را تنی و جانی: تن تو، مکانی؛ جان تو، زمانی. تن تو، خلقی؛ جان تو، امری: قُلِ الرُّوحُ مِنْ أَمْرِ رَبِّي (۸۵:۱۷). تن تو مِلکی، جان تو مُلکی: الأرواح مُلکُه، والاجساد مِلکُه وأحلّ مُلکُه في مِلکه؛ وله علیهما شرطٌ، ولهما عنده[۶] وعدٌ؛ فإن وفوا بشرطه، وفي لهم بوعده[۷]. جان‌ها مُلک اوست، تن‌ها مِلک اوست. او مُلک خود را در مِلک خود کشید. او را بر ایشان شرطی؛ ایشان[۸] را با او وعدی. چون بشرط[۹] او وفا کنی، او بوعدهٔ خود وفا کند. شرط چیست؟ فَمَن تَبِعَ هُدَايَ (۳۸:۲). وعده چیست؟ فَلَا خَوْفٌ عَلَيْهِمْ وَلَا هُمْ يَحْزَنُونَ (۳۸:۲).

---

[۶] در همهٔ نسخه‌ها، «قبله» آمده است. در بندهای بعدی «عنده» است که به همین شکل تصحیح شده است. در متن *مفاتیح* اما به شکل «قبله» آمده است. بنگرید به *مفاتیح*، ص. ۹۷.

[۷] شهرستانی این عبارات را حدیثی از امام جعفر صادق می‌داند. بنگرید به *مفاتیح، ص. ۹۷*.

[۸] ج: و ایشان.

[۹] ج: تو بشرط

[۶] این‌جا که خلق و امر آمده است، جایی دیگر خلق و هدایت آید. ابراهیم خلیل – صلوات الله علیه – گفت: الَّذِي خَلَقَنِي فَهُوَ يَهْدِينِ (۷۸:۲۶). موسی کلیم – علیه السّلام[۱۰] – گفت: الَّذِي أَعْطَىٰ كُلَّ شَيْءٍ خَلْقَهُ ثُمَّ هَدَىٰ (۵۰:۲۰). محمّد مصطفی – صلوات الله علیه و علی آله[۱۱] – گفت: الَّذِي خَلَقَ فَسَوَّىٰ وَالَّذِي قَدَّرَ فَهَدَىٰ (۸۷: ۲-۳).

[۷] ابراهیم خاص گفت؛ موسی عام. محمّد مطلق، هم خاص و هم عام. آن‌چه ابراهیم گفت، مبدأ بود. و آن‌چه موسی گفت، وسط. و آن‌چه محمّد گفت، کمال.[۱۲] الَّذِي أَعْطَىٰ كُلَّ شَيْءٍ خَلْقَهُ ثُمَّ هَدَىٰ [۱۳]کامل‌تر از آن که الَّذِي خَلَقَنِي فَهُوَ يَهْدِينِ.

---

[۱۰] کذا در ت. ج: صلوات اللّه علیه.

[۱۱] ت: صلی اللّه علیه و سلم.

[۱۲] طوسی در *آغاز و انجام* تعبیری بر همین سیاق دارد. در *آغاز و انجام* موسی مرد مبدأ است و صاحب تنزیل و صاحب غرب. عیسی مرد معاد است و صاحب تأویل و صاحب شرق. محمد، جامع هر دو است. طوسی در این بندها سخنی از ابراهیم به میان نمی‌آورد. عین عبارات در صص. ۴۲-۴۳، بند ۱۱ روایت مبسوط‌تر طوسی را دارد.

[۱۳] نسخهٔ ت از ابتدای متن تا این‌جا را دارد و سپس ناگهان عباراتی نامربوط در نسخه در ادامه ظاهر می‌شود که ربطی به متن *مجلس* ندارند (برگ ۱۳۴). بخش‌هایی از ادامهٔ متن در حاشیهٔ برگ بعدی آمده است و

الَّذِي خَلَقَ فَسَوَّىٰ وَالَّذِي قَدَّرَ فَهَدَىٰ کامل‌تر از الَّذِي أَعْطَىٰ كُلَّ شَيْءٍ خَلْقَهُ ثُمَّ هَدَىٰ. آن‌جا دو مرتبه بود: یکی خلق؛ یکی هدایت. این‌جا چهار مرتبه[۱۴]: یکی، خلق. دیگر، تسویت. سیوم، تقدیر. چهارم، هدایت.

[۸] در خلق جسمانی، تسویهٔ اجزاء آب و خاک و هوا و آتش ببایست تا اعتدال حاصل آید: الَّذِي خَلَقَكَ فَسَوَّاكَ فَعَدَلَكَ (۸۲:۷). در تقدیر روحانی، هدایت ربانی ببایست تا کمال حاصل آید: وَالَّذِي قَدَّرَ فَهَدَىٰ.[۱۵] خلق و تسویه در خلق شخص انسانی. تقدیر و هدایت در تقدیر نفس روحانی. در همهٔ کتاب‌های گذشته، تقریر خلق و امر آمده و این سه پیامبر بزرگوار بیرون داده تا در آخر سورت سبّح این آمد که :إِنَّ هَٰذَا لَفِي الصُّحُفِ الْأُولَىٰ صُحُفِ إِبْرَاهِيمَ وَمُوسَىٰ (۸۷: ۱۸-۱۹).

تکرار ابتدای بند ۷ است و به جای «کامل‌تر» در نسخه «گاه» ضبط شده است و متن ادامه پیدا می‌کند.

[۱۴] ج: مرتبه است.

[۱۵] نسخهٔ ق تا این‌جا را ندارد. ابتدای نسخه (ص ۳۳ نسخهٔ چاپی عکسی) از این‌جا به بعد آغاز می‌شود.

[۹] خالق اوست – جل جلاله – و او را در خلق شریک نه، هل من خالق غیر اللّٰه؟ هادی اوست، تقدّسَت أسمائه، و او را در هدایت شریک نه: وَمَا كُنَّا لِنَهْتَدِيَ لَوْلَا أَنْ هَدَانَا اللَّهُ (۴۳:۷). بی آن که او را شریک گویی در خلق، اسباب ساخت در خلقیّات و ایشان را فریشتگان نام نهاد. با آن که او را شریک نیست در هدایت، اسباب ساخت در امریّات و ایشان را پیامبران نام نهاد.

[۱۰] اسباب خلقی متوسطان در خلق: مَلَک الحیات، مَلَک الموت، مَلَک الارحام، مَلَک الارزاق، مَلَک الآجال – علیهم السّلام. اسباب امری، متوسطان در هدایت: آدم، نوح، ابراهیم، موسی، عیسی، محمّد – علیهم السّلام.

[۱۱] و تو را ایمان درست نیاید تا بمتوسطان خلق، و متوسطان هدایت نگروی و ایمان نیاوری: الْمُؤْمِنُونَ كُلٌّ آمَنَ بِاللَّهِ وَمَلَائِكَتِهِ وَكُتُبِهِ وَرُسُلِهِ (۲:۲۸۵). کلماتی شریف در زبان فریشتگان نهاد، کتاب‌های عزیز بر زبان پیامبران فرستاد: مع کُلّ موجودٍ مَلَکٌ ومع کُلّ مَلَکٍ کلمة فعّالة – با هر موجودی مَلَکی، با هر مَلَکی کلمه‌ای.

[۱۲] مَلَک، حمّالِ[۱۶] کلمه. کلمه، فعّالِ مَلَک. فریشته بار کلمه می‌کشد. کلمه کار فریشته می‌کند. اصلِ کلمه، کاف، لام، میم. و اصلِ ملک، میم، لام، کاف؛ هر دو مقلوب یکدیگر: في كلّ حادثةٍ للّه تعالى حكم، وعلىٰ كلّ حكمٍ حاكمٌ يحكُمُ بأمره. حاکم، کمالِ امر؛ امر، فعّالِ حاکم.

[۱۳] اولو الأمر: کلمات الله. ملائکة الله در آن عالم؛ کتب الله، رسل الله[۱۷]، در این عالم. پیامبران کلمات الله می‌شنوند، ملائکة الله می‌بینند. مؤمنان کتاب الله می‌شنوند، رسول الله می‌بینند. ایمان پیامبران: الَّذِي يُؤْمِنُ بِاللَّـهِ وَكَلِمَاتِهِ (۷:۱۵۸)؛ ایمان مؤمنان: رَبَّنَا آمَنَّا بِمَا أَنزَلْتَ وَاتَّبَعْنَا الرَّسُولَ (۳:۵۳). این سمع و بصر که ما داریم، این بیند، و این شنود. و اگر نه مبیناد و مشنواد:

إذا لم أَفُزْ منكمْ بوعْدٍ ونَظْرَةٍ | إليكم فما نَفْعي بسمعي وناظري[۱۸]

---

[۱۶] نسخه‌ها: کمال. ما ضبط مرجح ج را اختیار کردیم به قرینهٔ جملهٔ بعدی.

[۱۷] نسخهٔ ت در این جا تمام می‌شود.

[۱۸] بنگرید به: دیوان صرَّ دُرّ، (قاهره ۱۹۹۵)، ص. ۸۴. معنای بیت به فارسی چنین است: «مرا چه حاجت به گوش و دیدگانم اگر از شما عهدی

[۱۴] با سر سخن آی! طبایعِ موجودات را بشاگردی فریشتگان فرستاد و عقولِ[۱۹] مکلَّفان را بشاگردی پیامبران فرستاد. حرکاتِ طبیعی، کارگاه فریشتگان آمد، حرکاتِ اختیاری کارگاه پیامبران آمد.

[۱۵] حرکات طبیعی سه نوع[۲۰]: حركة علي المركز، حركة من المركز، حركة الي المركز. حرکت بر مرکز، حرکت دوری؛

نگیرم و یا نظری بر جمال روی شما نیفکنم؟». از محمد تقی کرمی بابت تصحیح و ویرایش ترجمهٔ این بیت به فارسی سپاسگزارم. همچنین بنگرید به: ابن فضل اللّه العمری، شهاب الدین احمد بن یحیی، *مسالک الأبصار فی ممالک الأمصار*، ج. ۱۳، ص. ۳۲۱ (بیروت ۱۹۷۱). نویسنده این بیت منسوب به علی ابن حسن الصردر (م. ۱۰۷۲/۴۶۵) را از ابن الجوزي (م. ۵۹۷ ق.)، به شکلی که در نسخ خطی ما آمده نقل کرده است. ابن الجوزی نیز در *المدهش* این بیت را با اندک تفاوتی به همراه این مصرع آورده است:

متى غنّت الورقاء كانت مدامتي

دموعي وزفَرَاتي حَنينَ مَزاهري

(بنگرید به: *المدهش*، ص. ۶۲۷ تصحیح عبدالکریم محمد منیر تتان و خلدون عبدالعزیز مخلوطة، دمشق ۲۰۱۴/۱۴۳۵).

[۱۹] ج: عقل مكلفانرا.

[۲۰] ج: نوع [است].

حرکت از مرکز، حرکت [به] بالا؛ حرکت بمرکز، حرکت [به] زیر.[۲۱]

[۱۶] حرکت اختیاری نیز سه آمد: حرکت فکریّة، حرکت قولیّة، حرکت فعلیّة. حرکت فکری بحرکت دوری مانندهتر که فکرت گرد عالم می‌گردد: وَيَتَفَكَّرُونَ فِي خَلْقِ السَّمَاوَاتِ وَالْأَرْضِ (۳:۱۹۱). حرکت قولی بحرکت [به] بالا مانندهتر: إِلَيْهِ يَصْعَدُ الْكَلِمُ الطَّيِّبُ (۳۵:۱۰). حرکت فعلی بحرکت [به] زیر مانندهتر: أَمَّا مَا يَنفَعُ النَّاسَ فَيَمْكُثُ فِي الْأَرْضِ (۱۳:۱۷).

[۱۷] آن‌جا حرکات دایر و مستقیم مقدّر بر فرمان فریشتگان علیهم السّلام؛ این‌جا حرکات دایر و مستقیم مقدّر بر فرمان پیغامبران – علیهم السّلام. در حرکات فکری، حقی و باطلی. در حرکات قولی، راستی و دروغی. در حرکات فعلی، خیری و شرّی. و تکلیف شریعت می‌گوید: حق گزین، باطل بگذار؛ راست گزین، دروغ بگذار؛ خیر گزین، شرّ بگذار.

---

[۲۱] عبارات داخل قلاب تصحیح قیاسی جلالی نائینی است و در نسخه‌ها موجود نیست. بر اساس ج افزوده شد.

[۱۸] اگر حرکات طبیعی بر وفق فرمان فریشتگان آمد، صورت جسمانی در این عالم راست. و اگر حرکات اختیاری بر وفق فرمان پیغامبران آمد، صورت روحانی در آن عالم راست. اگر در عالم اَرْحام علّتی یا مادّتی مستولی گشت - چنان‌که مزاج از حد اعتدال برفت - صورت جسمانی در این عالم ناقص آمد. اگر در عالم احکام هویٰ یا امل مستولی گشت - چنان‌که نفس از حد اعتدال برفت - صورت روحانی در آن عالم ناقص گشت.

[۱۹] همهٔ تسبیحات و تحمیدات فریشتگان - علیهم السّلام - از جهت تقویمِ حرکاتِ طبیعی،[۲۲] تا صورت جسمانی در این عالم راست و درست آید.

[۲۰] همهٔ عبادات و معاملات پیغامبران - علیهم السّلام - از جهت تقویم حرکات اختیاری،[۲۳] تا صورت روحانی در آن عالم راست و درست خیزد.

---

[۲۲] ج: طبیعی [است].
[۲۳] ج: اختیاری [است].

[۲۱] عجبا! فریشتگانِ روحانی، متوسطِ شخصِ جسمانی؛ پیغامبران جسمانی، متوسطِ نفسِ روحانی. فریشتگان در شخص متصرّف تا در این عالم زندگانی تواند کرد - و این زندگی[۲۴] فانی. پیامبران در نفس متصرّف تا در آن عالم زندگانی تواند کرد[۲۵] - و آن زندگی باقی.

[۲۲] فریشتگان از مبدأ فطرت، بکمال خلقت می‌رسانند؛ پیغامبران از مبدأ شریعت، بکمال قیامت می‌رسانند. امشاج طبیعت، در تخییر فریشتگان - علیهم السّلام؛ احکام شریعت، در تدبیر پیغامبران - علیهم السّلام. چنین گوی: کارگاه فریشتگان، مزاج طبیعت: أَمْشَاجٍ نَّبْتَلِيهِ (۲:۷۶)؛ اثر کار ایشان: فَجَعَلْنَاهُ سَمِيعًا بَصِيرًا (۲:۷۶). کارگاه پیغامبران، منهاج شریعت: شِرْعَةً وَمِنْهَاجًا (۴۸:۵). اثر کار ایشان: إِنَّا هَدَيْنَاهُ السَّبِيلَ إِمَّا شَاكِرًا وَإِمَّا كَفُورًا (۳:۷۶). کارکنانْ ایشان، کار با ما حواله که إنّا خلقنا، إنّا هَدَیْنا. جایی دیگر کارکنانْ

[۲۴] ج: زندگانی.
[۲۵] ج: کرد(ن)

مایم و کار با ایشان حواله: وَإِذْ تَخْلُقُ مِنَ الطِّينِ كَهَيْئَةِ الطَّيْرِ (۱۱۰:۵) وَإِنَّكَ لَتَهْدِي (۵۲:۴۲).

[۲۳] در کارگاه طبیعت، کارکنان همه مجبور؛ در کارگاه شریعت، کارکنان همه مختار. در آن کارگاه، سعادتی و شقاوتی. در این کارگاه سعادتی و شقاوتی. آن سعادت و شقاوت در علم ظاهر مخفی، در مزاج مخفی ظاهر : السعید من سعد في بطن أمّه والشقي من شقي في بطنِ أمّه.[۲۶] این سعادت و شقاوت در امر مخفی، در عمل ظاهر: فَمِنْهُمْ شَقِيٌّ وَسَعِيدٌ (۱۰۵:۱۱).

[۲۴] در آن کارگاه، فریشتگانِ بزرگ استادِ کارفرمای؛ فریشتگانِ خُرد شاگرد فرمان‌بردار. در این کارگاه، پیغامبرانِ

[۲۶] حدیث نبوی است. بنگرید به ونسنک (۱۹۳۶)، *المعجم المفهرس لألفاظ الأحادیث النبوي*، ج ۳، ص. ۱۶۴. و هم‌چنین در صحیح مسلم (قدر، ۳). شهرستانی در *مفاتیح* نیز این روایت را آورده است. بنگرید به *مفاتیح* (تحقیق آذرشب)، صص. ۵۵ و ۶۰۴.

بزرگ، شارعِ احکام شریعت؛ علماء امت، شارحِ کلام نبوت: إِنَّمَا أَنتَ مُنذِرٌ وَلِكُلِّ قَوْمٍ هَادٍ (۷:۱۳)[۲۷].

[۲۵] بر سر دور نطفه، فریشته‌ای؛ بر سر دور علقه، فریشته‌ای بزرگ‌تر؛ بر سر دور مضغه، [فریشته‌ای][۲۸] بزرگ‌تر. و همچنین تا به خَلْقًا آخَرَ (۱۴:۲۳)، هر چند کار بزرگ‌تر، فریشته شریف‌تر.

[۲۶] بر سرِ دورِ اسامی، پیغامبری چون آدم؛ بر سرِ دورِ معانیِ آن اسامی، پیامبری چون نوح؛ بر سر دورِ جمعِ آن اسامی و

---

[۲۷] در متون اسماعیلی بعدی، منذر اشاره به پیامبر دارد و هادی اشاره به امام. یعنی در رتبهٔ اول در کارگاه این‌جهانی پیامبران شارع‌اند و صاحبان تنزیل ولی امامان – علماء – شارح‌اند و صاحبان تأویل. حاجتی به گفتن نیست که چنان‌که از خلال همین متن شهرستانی و تفسیر او بر می‌آید مراد او از علما نه فقهاست و نه مفسران. اشارت او ناگزیر به امامان شیعی است. مقایسه کنید با *آغاز و انجام* طوسی. طوسی در این‌جا منذر را هم‌عنان با قائم آورده است. عین عبارت بدین قرار است: «سرّ قیامت سرّی بزرگ است، انبیاء را به کشف آن اجازه ندادند. چون انبیاء اصحاب شریعت‌اند، اصحاب قیامت دیگرند: إِنَّمَا أَنتَ مُنذِرٌ وَلِكُلِّ قَوْمٍ هَادٍ (۱۳:۷). محمّد علیه السلام به قرب قیامت مخصوص است: أنا والساعةً کهاتین. حالش با قیامت آن است که يَسْأَلُونَكَ عَنِ السَّاعَةِ أَيَّانَ مُرْسَاهَا فِيمَ أَنتَ مِن ذِكْرَاهَا...إِنَّمَا أَنتَ مُنذِرُ مَن يَخْشَاهَا (۷۹، آیات ۴۲، ۴۳ و ۴۵)» (ص. ۴۵، بند ۱۴).

[۲۸] ج: مضغه (فرشته‌ای). مانند ج، کلمه را در کروشه افزوده‌ایم.

معانی، پیغامبری چون ابراهیم. بر سر دور تنزیل، موسی. بر سر دور تأویل، عیسی. بر سرِ دورِ جمعِ تنزیل و تأویل، محمّد مصطفیٰ - صلوات الله علیهم اجمعین - علیٰ مِّلَّةَ أَبِيكُمْ إِبْرَاهِيمَ (۲۲:۷۸).

[۲۷] فریشتگان از سلاله درگرفته و بتدریج طوراً بعد طور بخلقاً آخر می‌رسانند. پیغامبران از[۲۹] اسامی درگرفته و بترتیب دوراً بعد دور بمعانی می‌رسانند: وَنُنشِئَكُمْ فِي مَا لَا تَعْلَمُونَ وَلَقَدْ عَلِمْتُمُ النَّشْأَةَ الْأُولَىٰ فَلَوْلَا تَذَكَّرُونَ (۵۶: ۶۱-۶۲) - فریشتگان[۳۰]، بر نشأة اولیٰ؛ پیغامبران، بر نشأة اُخریٰ.

[۲۸] در طبیعت، استحالتِ طوری بطوری؛ و حالی بحالی و در هر استحالتی[۳۱] کمالی. در شریعت، نسخِ دوری بدوری؛ و حکمی بحکمی و در هر نسخی کمالی.

---

[۲۹] م: ندارد.

[۳۰] در این بند، در نسخهٔ م ضبط «فریشتگان» به صورت «فرشتگان» آمده است. در نسخهٔ مزبور هم فرشتگان آمده و هم فریشتگان. در متن حاضر همه جا از ضبط «فریشتگان» پیروی کرده‌ایم.

[۳۱] ج این کلمه را به شکل «استحالت» ضبط کرده است.

[۲۹] زنهار! تا نسخ احکام را ابطال ندانی، اکمال دانی. اگر نطفه باطل گشتی، علقه بر کجا نشستی؟ اگر اسامی باطل گشتی، معانی بر کجا نشستی؟[۳۲] جملهٔ شرایع را مبدایی و کمالی؛ صاحب مبدأ جدا و صاحب کمال جدا.

[۳۰] و در هر شریعتی جداگانه مبدأیی و کمالی. و در این شریعت، لا إله إلّا اللّه، سلالهٔ دیانت. عبادات و معاملات، تن دیانت. علوم و حقایق، جان دیانت. چنان‌که جملهٔ اجزاء و

[۳۲] همین مضمون با عباراتی کمابیش مشابه در *روضهٔ تسلیم* (از این پس در متن فقط با عنوان *روضه* از آن یاد می‌شود) آمده است: «و حکم هر پیمبری که به سر احکام پیمبر پیشین درآمده است غرض آن اِکمال بوده است نه ابطالش، اما آن اکمال از راه ظاهر و شکل به ابطال مانسته است نه به اکمال. زیرا تا چیزی را از حالی به حالی نگردانند، صورت که غایت کمال آن چیز باشد در او نتوان پوشید. مثلاً تا نطفه به استحالت حوالی و تغیرات از حالی به حالی نگردد، آن صورت که بر آن ایستاده باشد باز نگذارد و به مراتب علقه و مضغه و لحم و عظام – که به هر مقام از این که رسید به جان نزدیک‌تر شد – برنگذرد و هرگز به تمام صورت انسانی نتواند رسید. حال اکمال و ابطال شرایع هم‌چنین تصور باید کرد که اگر حکم پیمبر اول بر حال خود بماند و حکم پیمبر دیگر پس از آن نیاید و در نهایت قائم قیامت تصرف نکند، محکومان آن حکم هرگز از راه به مقصد و از اسم به معنی و از مشابهت به مباینت و از اضافه به حقیقت و از شریعت به قیامت نتوانند رسید» (صص.۱۲۰-۱۱۹، بندهای ۴۱۸-۴۱۷).

اعضاء شخص در سلاله موجود است، وجودی باستعداد قوت، همچنین جملهٔ احکام شریعت در کلمهٔ لا إله إلّا اللّه موجود است، وجودی باستعداد قوت. پس کلمهٔ لا إله إلّا اللّه بوجهی کلیِ دیانت آمد، چنان‌که سلاله بوجهی کلیِ[۳۳] شخص آمد. تا چون کلمه بگویی، کلی دیانت بگفته باشی و در حریم عصمت نفس و مال آمده امروز: فاذا قالوها عصموا منی دمائهم وأموالهم. و در حریم بهشت رفته فردا: من قال لا إله إلّا اللّه دخل الجنة. و الا چرا بایستی که بدین کلمه که بگویی با همهٔ مؤمنان عالَم، عالِم و عامِل، برابر گردی؟ نکته بشناس! چنان‌که سلاله می‌رود تا تنِ تمام شود، و تن می‌رود تا جانِ تمام شود، همچنین کلمه می‌رود تا معاملتِ تمام شود و عمل می‌رود تا

---

[۳۳] در م «دیانت آمد... به وجهی کلی» مفقود است. ق و ج به همین شکل ضبط شده‌اند.

ایمانِ[۳۴] تمام شود: يَهْتِفُ العلمُ بالعمل فإن أجابَهُ والّا إرتحَلَ عنهُ.[۳۵]

[۳۱] چون سلاله بنطفه رسید و در رحم قرار گرفت، نفس نامیه مدبّر او گشت و فریشته، مدبّر نفس نامیه و با آن فریشته، کلمهٔ فعّاله تا بآن کلمه، نفس نامیه را در زیادت نمو می‌آرد.

[۳۲] و همچنین چون کلمهٔ لا إله إلّا اللّه در دل مُوحِّد قرار گرفت، ایمان در زیادتی آمد که الایمانُ یزید و ینقُص. تأدیب

---

[۳۴] ج: (ایمان) جان؛ ق: جان؛ م: ایمان. ولی گویا باید اصل کلمه «علم» باشد با توجه به روایتی که از *نهج البلاغة* نقل شده است. در متن همان ضبط نسخهٔ م را حفظ کرده‌ایم ولی در ترجمهٔ انگلیسی کلمه‌ای را که صحیح‌تر به نظر می‌رسد آورده‌ایم.

[۳۵] از *نهج البلاغة*، کلمات قصار، شمارهٔ ۳۶۶. در نهج البلاغهٔ چاپ و ترجمهٔ سید جعفر شهیدی، این سخن به این صورت ضبط شده است: العِلْمُ مَقرونٌ بالعملِ فمَن عَلِمَ عَمِلَ. والعِلْمُ يَهْتِفُ بالعملِ فإن أجابَهُ وإلّا ارتحَلَ عنهُ، یعنی: علم را با عمل همراه باید ساخت، و آن که آموخت به کار بایدش پرداخت، و علم عمل را خوانَد اگر پاسخ داد، و گرنه روی از او بگرداند (*نهج البلاغة*، ترجمهٔ سید جعفر شهیدی، تهران ۱۳۷۲، ص. ۴۲۵). شهرستانی این سخن امام علی را در *مفاتیح* نیز آورده است: «وقيل: أثبت العلم للأحبار، ونفاه عن العوام أو أثبته للشياطين ونفاه عن اليهود؛ وقيل: معناه لم يعملوا بما علموا فصاروا كمن لا يعلم، كما ورد في الخبر: «يهتف العلم بالعمل؛ فإن أجاب وإلّا ارتحل عنه»...» (*مفاتیح*، ص. ۴۸۹).

مؤدِّب، مدبّر او گشت و کلمهٔ تأدیب، کلمهٔ فعالهٔ او آمد تا بدان کلمه ایمان را زیادتی گرداند[۳۶] و چون نطفه بعلقه رسید، نفس حیوانی مُدبّر او گشت و فریشته، مُدبّر نفس حیوانی، با کلمهٔ دیگر او را حیات می‌دهد و حسّ لمس در او می‌آرد.

[۳۳] همچنین، چون[۳۷] مرد مؤمن از درجهٔ ایمان بدرجهٔ احسان رسید، تکلیفِ مُکَلِّف بدو پیوست و کلمهٔ تکلیف مدبّر او گشت تا در حس و حرکت تکلیفی آمد و چون علقه بمضغه رسید، نفس خیالی مدبّر او گشت و فریشته، مدبّر نفس خیالی.

[۳۴] همچنین چون مرد مکلَّف در معاملت تکلیفی آمد، تعریف مُعرِّف بدو پیوست تا در تخیّل و توهّم آمد و چون سه دور تمام گشت بر نطفه، نفس ناطقه بدو پیوست[۳۸] و فریشته مدبّر نفس ناطقه و کلمه مدبّر فریشته تا بدان کلمه او را کمال نفس نطقی می‌دهد.

---

[۳۶] ج: زیادت می گرداند.

[۳۷] م: ندارد.

[۳۸] عبارت «تا در تخیل و توهم آمد... بدو پیوست» در ج موجود نیست ولی در نسخه‌های م و ق موجود است.

[۳۵] همچنین مرد مؤمن چون از مرتبهٔ اسلام بایمان آمد، و از ایمان باحسان رسید، دیگرباره خواهد که از درجهٔ احسان قدم فرا[۳۹] نهد. گویند: نهایةُ الأقدام أعمالٌ. از حکم شریعت، این جاست. تا گوید: «متی الساعة»، گویند: «ما المسؤولُ عنه بأعلم من السائل».[۴۰] اینجاست نهایتِ شریعت. و از اینجا برتر، عقل است و از عقل برتر، امر است و آن علوم گفتن و عللِ اشیاء جستن، کارِ حاکمِ قیامت.[۴۱]

[۳۶] مراتب نفس چهار بود: نفس نامیه، نفس حیوانی، نفس خیالی، نفس انسانی. و با هر نفسی، فریشته. إِن كُلُّ نَفْسٍ لَّمَّا عَلَيْهَا حَافِظٌ (۴:۸۶)؛ و با هر فریشته، کلمه.

---

[۳۹] ج: فرا(تر).

[۴۰] حدیث نبوی. بنگرید به: خلیل مأمون شیحا (بیروت: ۲۰۱۳)، *موسوعة المعجم المفهرس لألفاظ النبوي الشريف لمكتب الستة*، ج. ۱۱، ص. ۲۸۹. بخش پاسخ سؤال به این شکل روایت شده است: ما المسؤولُ عنها بأعلمَ من السائل.

[۴۱] بنگرید به یادداشت ذیل بند ۲۵ در بالا و نقل قول از *آغاز و انجام* طوسی. هم‌چنین مقایسه کنید با بند دیگری از *آغاز و انجام*: ص. ۴۵ بند ۱۵.

[۳۷] مراتب عقول هم چهار آمد، و با هر عقلی، امری؛ و [با] هر امری، کلمه. عقل استعدادی که طفل دارد. عقل تکلیفی که بفعل آرد. عقل مستفاد که فایده می گیرد. عقل بالملکة که فایده می‌دهد.[۴۲] چون نفس[۴۳] تمام شود،[۴۴] با آدمیان همسری کند. چون عقل تمام شود با فریشتگان هم‌بری کند.

---

[۴۲] در *روضه* نیز تعابیری مشابه آمده است: عقل هیولانی، عقل ملکی، عقل به فعل و عقل مستفاد. عین عبارات *روضه* به شرح زیر است: «عقل هیولانی قوّتی است که قبول صورت ها می کند مجرّد از مواد، اما هنوز قبول آن صورت‌ها نکرده باشد ولیکن شایستگی آن [را] دارد که قبول کند. مثلاً چون کودک طفل که دبیری نتواند، اما استعداد و امکان دارد که دبیر شود. عقل مَلَکی قوّتی است که چون قابل این صورت‌های مجرّد شود که به اول گفته آمد، آن صورت‌ها در او قرار گیرد و از ضروریّات به نظریّات و از نظریّات به ضروریّات تواند آمد به آسانی. و عقل به فعل قوّتی است که قبول صورت مجرّده و شدن از ضروریّات به نظریّات و از نظریّات به ضروریّات او را به فعل حاصل آید، نه به انفعال. و هر وقت که خواهد مطالعه آن کند. و عقل مستفاد قوّتی است که چون همهٔ این کمالات که گفته شد او را حاصل آمده باشد، میان او و آن عقل که او را از قوّت به فعل می‌آورد مناسبتی پدیدار آید چنان که هر صورت معقول که در او باشد در این یک بر مثال آینه زدوده که در برابر شخصی بدارند بی زیادت و نقصان پدیدار آید» (ص. ۲۷، بندهای ۷۴-۷۱).

[۴۳] نسخهٔ م و ق، این کلمه را به شکل «نفوس» ضبط کرده‌اند. ما از ضبط نسخهٔ ج یعنی «نفس» پیروی کرده‌ایم.

[۴۴] در نسخه‌ها، «شد» آمده است که به قرینهٔ جملهٔ بعدی، «شود» ضبط کردیم.

[۳۸] هر نفس که نه پروردهٔ فریشتگان آمد، شیطانی. هر عقل که نه پروردهٔ پیغامبران آمد، طاغوتی[٤٥]. هر جا که استقامتی است در نفس یا در عقل، فریشته بر او نشسته: إِنَّ الَّذِينَ قَالُوا رَبُّنَا اللَّـهُ ثُمَّ اسْتَقَامُوا تَتَنَزَّلُ عَلَيْهِمُ الْمَلَائِكَةُ (۳۰:۴۱). هر جا که دوری است در نفس یا در عقل، شیطانی برو نشسته: هَلْ أُنَبِّئُكُمْ عَلَىٰ مَن تَنَزَّلُ الشَّيَاطِينُ تَنَزَّلُ عَلَىٰ كُلِّ أَفَّاكٍ أَثِيمٍ (۲۶: ۲۲۱-۲۲۲). افاک فی القول اثیم فی الفعل.

[۳۹] فریشتگان را منزل‌گاه راستی، پیغمبران را منزل‌گاه پاکی. و دین حق بنا بر راستی و پاکی، شهادت و طهارت. گاهی راستی در پیش[٤٦]، [و] پاکی باز پس. و گاهی پاکی در پیش و راستی باز پس. راستی در صورت با راستی در معنی جمع باید تا مرد شایستهٔ سعادت آخرت گردد. و چون راستی در صورت یافت بتوسط فریشتگان و راستی در معنی نیافت از تربیت

[٤٥] ضبط ج. در نسخه‌های م و ق کلمه شباهت به «هوی» یا «غوی» دارد.
[٤٦] ج: پیش (و).

پیامبران علیهم السّلام[۴۷]، در آن عالم منکوس خیزد: نَاكِسُوا رُؤُسِهِمْ عِندَ رَبِّهِمْ (۱۲:۳۲).

[۴۰] چون آدمی از حکم فطرت سر از زمین برداشت تا مار صفت نباشد، هر دو دست هم برداشت تا چهارپاصفت نباشد. گفتند: از حکم فطرت، راست‌قامت آمدی: فِي أَحْسَنِ تَقْوِيمٍ (۴:۹۵). از حکم شریعت، راست‌معنی شو: حَسُنَت خَلقَک فحَسِّن خُلقَک. آن یکی من آفریدم باضطرار. آن دگر تو کن باختیار و الا نگونسار خیزی و خاکسار. ثُمَّ رَدَدْنَاهُ أَسْفَلَ سَافِلِينَ إِلَّا الَّذِينَ آمَنُوا وَعَمِلُوا الصَّالِحَاتِ (۹۵: ۵-۶).

[۴۱] سرت را از زمین برداشتم[۴۸] باضطرار. تو سر با زمین آر باختیار: وَاسْجُدْ وَاقْتَرِب (۱۹:۹۶). در دعا سر بردار، با سر دست بردار. در نماز سر بر زمین نه، با سر دست بر زمین نه. اگر[۴۹] در دعا قبله خواهی، فوق. اگر در سجود قبله خواهی، تحت. فوق

---

[۴۷] م: ندارد.
[۴۸] م: برداشتیم.
[۴۹] ج: و اگر.

را نهایتی، تحت را نهایتی. نهایتِ فوق، عرش، نه ذوالعرش. نهایتِ تحت، فرش نه ذوالفرش.

[۴۲] ای فریشتگان! مدتی دراز قبلهٔ شما عرش بود یا زمین یا فوق بود یا تحت! اکنون وقت آن آمد که روی بشخصی آرید

که مکان و زمان غلامکان در سرای اویند: اسْجُدُوا لِآدَمَ (۲:۳۴).[۵۰] عرش، کل مکان؛ دهر[۵۱]، کل زمان. آدم، کل انسان.[۵۲]

[۴۳] عرش حواله‌گاه تدبیر: اسْتَوَىٰ عَلَى الْعَرْشِ يُدَبِّرُ الْأَمْرَ (۱۰:۳). دهر، حواله‌گاه تقدیر: لا تَسُبُّوا الدّهرَ فإنَّ اللهَ هو

[۵۰] این بند را می‌توان مقایسه کرد با بندهای مشابهی از *هفت باب* حسن محمود و هم‌چنین *روضه* و نقل قول‌هایی از *علیٰ ذکره السلام*. هم‌چنین با متن *مفاتیح* مقایسه شود در تفسیر استکبار ابلیس. در *هفت باب*، ضمن نقل عبارتی از *علیٰ ذکره السلام* آمده است: «چون به قیامت خدای مشخص و معین باشد، پس چه بماند که نه معین و نه مشخص باشد؟» (چاپ بدخشانی، ص. ۳۳، بند ۶۶). یکی از مفاد و مضامین کلیدی دعوت قیامت *علیٰ ذکره السلام* همین تکیه بر تشخص است، یعنی روی آوردن از قبلهٔ عرشی یا زمینی به قبلهٔ شخصی که شخص در این میانه امام یا قائم است. شهرستانی در *مفاتیح* در شرح سجده در برابر آدم می‌آورد: «وكما أنّ إبليس خرج على خليفة الحقّ كذلک الخوارج في هذه الأمة خرجوا على أمام الوقت؛ وكما أنّ إبليس نازع اللّه في حكمه وقدره، كذلک القدرية خصماء اللّه في القدر؛ وكما أن إبليس لم يقل بالإمام الحاضر الحي القائم كذلک العامة والشيعة المنتظرة لم يقولوا إلّا بالإمام الغائب المنتظر» (ص. ۲۸۰). تعبیر او از سجود اقرار به امامت و ولایت امام حی و حاضر و قائم است. این تعریض تند او به امامیه، آشکارا او را به اسماعیلیان نزاری نزدیک‌تر می‌کند. در *روضه* بنگرید به صص. ۵۱-۵۶ (بندهای ۱۶۱-۱۸۱).

[۵۱] در نسخه‌ها «دور» آمده است ولی از سیاق عبارات بعد مشخص است که اصل کلمه همان «دهر» است. ج هم دهر آورده است.. در عبارات پیشین هم شهرستانی، دهر به کار برده در اشاره به کلیِّ زمان.

[۵۲] یعنی عرش، کلیِّ مکان است؛ دور، کلیِّ زمان؛ و آدم، کلیِّ انسان.

الدَّهْرُ.[٥٣] آدم حواله‌گاه تصویر: خلق آدم علی صورة الرحمن.[٥٤] و جلال احدی منزه از زمان و مکان و صورت.

---

[٥٣] بنگرید به: خلیل مأمون شیحا (بیروت: ۲۰۱۳)، *موسوعة المعجم المفهرس لألفاظ النبوي الشريف للكتب الستة*، ج. ۹. ص. ۷۸۴. شهرستانی در *مفاتیح* هم این روایت را آورده است به شرح زیر: «فقد قال – صلی اللّه علیه وآله - «لا تسبّوا الدّهر؛ فإن اللّه هو الدّهر» وقد قال رجل من أهل بيته: «أنا دهر الدّهور» وقد قال النبي – صلی اللّه علیه و آله -: «من سبّ أهل بيتي فقد سبني ومن سبني فقد سبّ اللّه» فمن سبّ الدّهر وهو رجل فقد سبّ اللّه، والدّهر رجل والشهر رجل» (ص. ۸۵۸). طوسی نیز در *اخلاق محتشمی* روایتی با همین مضمون نقل کرده است: «أنا سبت السّبوت ودهر الدّهور. نحن أناسٌ سرمديّون وشيعتنا منّا» (*اخلاق محتشمی*، ص. ۱۹). در *روضه* نیز عباراتی از *علیٰ ذکره السلام* نقل شده است که بخش دیگری از روایت مزبور را آورده است: نحن أناس سرمديّون (ص. ۱۰۴، بند ۳۵۶). در همین بند، باز هم از زبان *علیٰ ذکره السلام*، آمده است که: «و گفته‌اند آسمان و زمین از جای بشود و حکم شنبه از جای بنشود» (همان). این عبارات در بخش‌هایی از خطبهٔ قیامت *علیٰ ذکره السلام* آمده‌اند. در شرح ترتیب خطبهٔ قیامت، ابو اسحاق قهستانی نقل می‌کند که: «... بعد از آن نسخهٔ نامه‌ای که اولش این است، نحن الحاضرون الموجودون، بخواند و دیگر خطبهٔ اول بخواند و لحظه‌ای بنشست و برخاست و خطبهٔ دویم بخواند...» (*هفت باب ابو اسحاق*، صص. ۴۲-۴۱).

[٥٤] بنگرید به: خلیل مأمون شیحا (بیروت: ۲۰۱۳)، *موسوعة المعجم المفهرس لألفاظ النبوي الشريف للكتب الستة*، ج. ۹، ص۳۴۶. در موسوعه، به شکل: «خلق آدم علی صورته» آمده است. بنگرید به *هفت باب* حسن محمود، بند ۸.

[۴۴] دست را قبله، عرش. روی را قبله، کعبه. چشم را قبله، سجده‌گاه. گوش را قبله، قرائت امام. سر را قبله، آدم. نفس را قبله، دهر: إن لکم في أيام دهرکم نفحات.

[۴۵] هر یک را بقبله‌ای مشغول تا دل را گویند: قلب المؤمن بين إصبعين من أصابعِ الرّحمن، بين كلمتين من كلمات الرحمن. یک کلمه، لا إله إلّا اللّه. یک کلمه، محمّد رسول الله. ای دست! تو تهی آی تا پر باز گردی. ای سر! تو پر می‌آی تا تهی بازگردی.

[۴۶] دست را بادی بدست: هیچ چیز ندارم، هیچ چیز ندانم. سر را بادی در سر: همه چیز دارم، همه چیز دانم. هر که گوید: «هیچ[۵۵] ندارم، هیچ[۵۶] ندانم»، گویندش: «همه تو داری، همه تو دانی».[۵۷] قُل لَّا أَمْلِكُ لِنَفْسِي نَفْعًا وَلَا ضَرًّا إِلَّا مَا شَاءَ اللَّـهُ (۱۸۸:۷)، هیچ چیز ندارم است. وَلَوْ كُنتُ أَعْلَمُ الْغَيْبَ (۱۸۸:۷)، هیچ چیز ندانم است. ای محمّد! همه تو داری!

---

[۵۵] ج و م: هیچ چیز.
[۵۶] ج و م: هیچ چیز.
[۵۷] در م: داری و دانی جا به جاست.

خلقتُ الاشیاء لأجْلِک! ای محمّد! همه تو دانی! وَعَلَّمَكَ مَا لَمْ تَكُن تَعْلَمُ (۱۱۳:۴)!

[۴۷] مصطفی چون دست برداشتی، چنان برداشتی که سپیدی زیر دست او بدیدندی[۵۸]: و کان یُریٰ بَیاضُ إبْطَیه. دست با روی برابر داشتن در نماز سنت است. دست با گوش برابر داشتن در تکبیر نماز سنت است. دست، آلتِ حول و قوت است. از حول و قوّهٔ خویش بیزار شو: لا حول ولا قوة الا باللّه.

[۴۸] گوش، محل سمع و طاعت است. هر دو را با هم برابر دار در تکبیر احرام، تا هم بمفروغ گفته باشی و هم بمستأنف. هم از قَدَر بیزار شده که لا حول ولا قوة الا باللّه هم از جَبْر بیزار شده که سَمِعْنَا وَأَطَعْنَا (۷:۵). و در حریم نماز نیایی تا این دو حکم برابر نکنی.

[۴۹] دیگر باره روی طالبِ جهت است در مقابله. وجه، و جهت، و مواجهه از یک باب. و جهت نهایتی[۵۹] خواهد. و نهایت

[۵۸] ضبط ج و نسخهٔ ق این است. نسخهٔ م به شکل «بدندی» ضبط کرده است.

[۵۹] نسخهٔ م: و جهتی نهایتی خواهد.

حدی. و حدی مردی در مقابله. و دست هم طالب جهت است و لیکن بجهت فوق: و إلیک رَفَعْتُ الأیدي. دست در برابر روی آر در دعا، تا هر یکی حد دیگری بود، هر یکی قبلهٔ دیگری.

[۵۰] دست می گوید: من با روی برابرم در طلب و بترک فوق بگفتم. روی می‌گوید: من با دست برابرم در طلب و بترک مقابله بگفتم. دست را گویند: فَإِنِّي قَرِيبٌ أُجِيبُ دَعْوَةَ الدَّاعِ إِذَا دَعَانِ (۲:۱۸۶). روی را گویند فردا: وُجُوهٌ يَوْمَئِذٍ نَّاضِرَةٌ إِلَىٰ رَبِّهَا نَاظِرَةٌ (۷۵: ۲۲-۲۳).

[۵۱] عجبا کارا! اگر در معرفت جهت گویی، معرفت نه معرفت؛ و اگر در طاعت جهت نگویی، طاعت نه طاعت. معرفت راه بجان دارد و جان نه در جهت نه جهت‌جوی؛ طاعت ره[60] بتن دارد و تن هم در جهت و هم جهت‌جوی. تن جسمانی است، جهت خواهد و جهتی معین تا طاعت درست آید، و اگر نه اهل قبله‌ات نخوانند. جان روحانی است، جهت نخواهد تا

[60] ج: (و) طاعت ره.

معرفت درست آید، و اگر نه اهل توحیدت نخوانند[٦١]. این دو حکم متضاد چون دانم؟ این احکام بر تضاد چون رانم؟ فَأَيْنَمَا تُوَلُّوا فَثَمَّ وَجْهُ اللَّـهِ (۲:۱۱۵) با وَحَيْثُ مَا كُنتُمْ[٦٢] فَوَلُّوا وُجُوهَكُمْ شَطْرَهُ (۲:۱۴۴) چون جمع کنم؟[٦٣] اگر بکل مکانٍ نگویی، خطا؛ اگر في کل مکانٍ گویی خطا؛ اگر[٦٤] در مکان معین گویی،

---

[٦١] این تفاوتی که شهرستانی میان اهل توحید و اهل قبله می گذارد، موازی است با تفاوت میان اهل قیامت و اهل شریعت. اهل شریعت جهت‌جوی‌اند و مقید به زمان و مکان. اهل قیامت فارغ‌اند از جهت و تا حجاب جهت و زمان و مکان بر نخیزد، طاعت و معرفت قیامت درست نیاید. مراجعه کنید به تعبیری که طوسی از طاعت شریعت و طاعت قیامت دارد. در *روضه* آمده است: «زمان شریعت را که آن وقت طاعت به شرط تعیین اوقات فرمایند و دعوت با ظاهر اعمال جسمانی کنند و استغراق طاعات باشد در اوقات، دور ستر خوانند و به پیمبران علیهم السلام خاص باشید. و زمان قیامت را که آن وقت طاعت به رفع تعیین اوقات فرمایند و دعوت با خدا و خدای کنند و استغراق اوقات باشد در طاعات، دور کشف [خوانند] و به امام لذکره السلام خاص باشد» (ص. ۹۳، بندهای ۳۲۰ و ۳۲۱).

[٦٢] در همهٔ نسخ، به جای و حیث ما کنتم آمده است: فأینما کنتم.

[٦٣] بنگرید به مفاتیح: «أنّ الحکم المستأنف في الجهة أنّه لا تصحّ منك العبادة إلاّ إلی جهة وقبلة؛ والحکم المفروغ فیها أنّه لا تصحّ منك المعرفة إذا کانت إلی جهة وقبلة. فمن حکم المستأنف: وَحَيْثُ مَا كُنْتُمْ فَوَلُّوا وُجُوهَكُمْ شَطْرَهُ ومن حکم المفروغ: فَأَيْنَمَا تُوَلُّوا فَثَمَّ وَجْهُ اللّٰه، وحکم المستأنف یتبدّل تشریعه وشریعته، وأمّا حکم المفروغ فلا یتطرّق إلیه التبدیل» (ص. ۵۲۹)

[٦٤] ج: (و) اگر.

خطا؛ اگر روی بمکانی معین نیاری، خطا. نشاید که دست پوشیده داری در دعا. نشاید که سر و پا برهنه داری در سجود. نشاید که سر و پا پوشیده[۶۵] داری در حرم. نشاید که سر و پا برهنه داری در مبرز. تو خود چه دانی در زیر هر حکمی چه حکمت است! تو خود چه دانی که با هر صورتی چه حقیقت است!

[۵۲] عقلِ علّت‌جوی را بگوی اگر می‌خواهی که فریشته‌صفت شوی، بگوی: لَا عِلْمَ لَنَا إِلَّا مَا عَلَّمْتَنَا (۳۲:۲). و حس جهت‌جوی را بگوی اگر می‌خواهی که روحانی‌صفت شوی، بگوی: سَمِعْنَا وَأَطَعْنَا (۵۱:۲۴). از عقل ترازوی ساز تا جان را بدان بسنجی:

خرد را و جان را همی سنجد او
در اندیشهٔ سخته کی گنجد او؟![۶۶]

---

[۶۵] م: برهنه.

[۶۶] بیت از شاهنامهٔ فردوسی است.

إن اللّه تعالیٰ أسّس دینَه علیٰ مثالِ خَلْقِه لِیُسْتَدلّ بخَلقِه علیٰ دینه و بدینه علیٰ وحدانیّته.[۶۷]

قرأ القاری بسم اللّه الرحمن الرحیم:

خلیلي إنّ الجزع أضحیٰ ترابه | من الطیبِ کافوراً وعیدانه رَنْداً

---

[۶۷] ناصر خسرو در *جامع الحکمتین* می گوید: «وضع دینِ خدای بر مثال دنیاست از بهر آنک دنیا را وجود بعقل خدای است و دین را وضع بفرمان خداست، و هم آفرینش و هم فرمان مر او راست چنانک گفت: قوله الا له الخلق و الامر تبارک اللّه رب العالمین. و شناختِ مراتبِ خلقی مردم را از بهر آن باید تا بدان شناخت مر او را شناختِ مراتبِ امری به حاصل آید، و از دنیا بر دین دلیل گیرد تا تأمل و تفکرش باطل نشود. و خبر است از رسول – علیه السلام – که گفت «خدای تعالی مر دین خویش را بنیاد بر مثال آفرینش دنیا نهاد، تا از آفرینش او بر دین او دلیل گیرند، و از دین او بر یگانگی او دلیل یابند،» بدین خبر *إن اللّه أسّس دینه علی مثال خلقه لیستدل بخلقه علی دینه وبدینه علی وحدانیته*. پس هر که مرین مراتب را که موجودات خلقی راست بشناسد، باید که بر مراتب دین دلیل گیرد، و مراتب اندر عالم دین هم برین مثالست که اندر دنیاست» (*جامع الحکمتین*، ص. ۱۵۴). ابوحاتم رازی مضمون این روایت را به این شکل در *أعلام النبوة* آورده است: «وأُمرنا ان ننظرَ في خلقه، ونعتبر به، ونعرف الٰهیته وربوبیته وتوحیده بخلقه، ونستدلَّ علیه بصنعه؛ فأن في ما خلق من سماواته وأرضه وما بینهما من عجائب الصنع، ما یدل علی إنیته ووحدانیته؛ وفي ذلک عبرة للمعتبرین ودلیلٌ للمتفکرین» (*أعلام النبوة*، ص. ۳۸). همین روایت را نیز المؤید في الدین الشیرازی در *مجالس المؤیدیه* نقل کرده است و آن را منسوب به پیامبر می‌داند (*مجالس المؤیدیه*، ص. ۱۰۸). ناصر خسرو نیز گویا به اقتفای استاد خود روایت را منسوب به پیامبر نقل کرده است.

وما هي إلا أن مَشَتْ بجَنابه | أُميمةُ في سِرْبٍ وجَرَّتْ به بردا[۶۸]

بوی جوی مولیان آید همی

بوی یار مهربان آید همی[۶۹]

[۵۳] از این کلمات که سلالهٔ نبوت می‌گوید، بوی نبوت می‌آید: إن الله أسس دینه علیٰ مثال خلقه - دین را بر مثال

---

[۶۸] نسخ م و ق هر دو «ردا» ضبط کرده‌اند. ایضاً نسخهٔ خطی اساس جلالی نائینی ولی او به صورت «بردا» در متن آورده است چنان که ما. ابیات گویا از شاعر عرب، کُثَیِّر عَزَّة است. معنای این ابیات به فارسی چنین است: «دوستان من! خاک پیچ و خم درّه و گیاهانش چون کافور معطر گشته است از آن رو که امیمه سوار بر مرکب، دامن‌کشان از میان آن می‌گذشت». ارایهٔ این ترجمه را مدیون محمد تقی کرمی هستم. همچنین بنگرید به: زمخشری، *ربیع الأبرار و نصوص الأخبار*، ج. ۱. صص. ۲۸۶-۲۸۵، تصحیح عبدالأمیر مهنا (بیروت، ۱۹۹۲/۱۴۱۲). این ابیات را زمخشری چنین نقل کرده است:

لعمرک إن الجزع أمسی ترابه

من الطیب کافوراً وعیدانه رندا

وأصبح ماء الشعب خمراً وأصبحت

جلامیده مسکاً وأوراقه وردا

وما ذاک إلا أن مشت في عراصه

عزیزة في سربٍ و جرّت به بردا

اما جز زمخشری، این ابیات در دیوان کثیر عزة به تصحیح و استخراج احسان عباس چه در قصاید قطعی و چه در بخش قطعات منسوب به شاعر نیامده است. والله اعلم.

[۶۹] بیت از رودکی است.

خلق بنا کرده تا از خلق او دین او می‌بینند. و از دین او وحدانیت او می‌شناسند.[۷۰] همان قاعده و اساس خلق و امر است. امر و دین از یک باب؛ خلق و شریعت از یک باب. فریشتگان، متوسطان خلق؛ پیغامبران، متوسطان دین. امر، مصدرِ خلق. خلق، مظهرِ امر. دین، مصدرِ خلق. خلق، مظهر دین. آیا عقل، خلق است یا امر؟ لابد گویی خلق. پس امر، مصدر عقل و عقل مظهر امر آمد. و عقل هم مخلوق، هم مأمور. لمّا خلقّ الله العقل قال له أقبِل فأقبَل ثم قال له أدبِر فأدبَر[۷۱].

---

[۷۰] از سیاق سخن شهرستانی بر می‌آید که او نسبت روایت را به یک امام شیعی، گویا امام جعفر صادق، می‌رساند و تعبیر «سلالۀ نبوت» را گویا حمل بر اهل بیت پیامبر باید کرد. این روایت، تا جایی که نگارنده جست‌وجو کرده است تنها در منابع اسماعیلی نقل شده است. مشخصاً این روایت، چنان‌که پیش‌تر ذکر شد، به مضمون در *أعلام النبوة* ابوحاتم رازی، و به تصریح و با همین عبارت در *جامع الحکمتین* ناصر خسرو و *روضۀ تسلیم* طوسی آمده است. در *روضه* این روایت به پیامبر نسبت داده شده است (ص. ۱۱۸، بند ۴۱۳).

[۷۱] شهرستانی این روایت را در *مفاتیح* در خلال بحث دربارۀ محقّ و مبطل و ملائکه و ابلیس آورده است: «فأعرض هذا التضاد و التشابه في التضاد على الملائكة والشياطين أو على الملک المطيع الأول وعلى الشيطان الفاسق الأول. إن أخذت في ترتيب الموجودات ووصلت ألى أول ما خلق اللّه تعالى وهو العقل، فاعرف أن أول ما يظهر في مقابلته بالتضاد ويشابهه في الوجود الجهل، وهو ابليسه وشيطانه؛ فيكون للعقل إقبال

چون ایزد تعالی عقل را بیافرید، و در روایتی دیگر اول چیزی که بیافرید عقل بود، خطاب کرد[۷۲]: أقبل، روی بما آر، أدبر، پشت بر ما گردان. هر دو خطاب را فرمان برد. پس عقل هم مخلوق بود هم مأمور.

[۵۴] متکلمان در خلق و امر سه مذهب داشتند. معتزلیان گفتند خلق و امر هر دو یکی است. خلق او مخلوق و امر او مخلوق. و لکن امر او صوتی و حرفی و قایم بدرختی. کرّامیان گفتند: خلق و امر هر دو یکی است. خلق او نه مخلوق، و امر او صوتی و حرفی حادث و لکن قایم بذات او. اشعریان گفتند: خلق او مخلوق قایم نه بذات او. امر او نه مخلوق قایم بذات او.

[۵۵] هیچ کس نه حقیقت خلق دانست نه حقیقت امر. نه نسبت خلق با[۷۳] او که چه نسبت است و نه نسبت امر با او که

وإدبار بالأمر فوقه: «قال له أقبل، فأقبل ثم قال له أدبر، فأدبر». فشابه الجهل في الكون الأول وهو الإقبال بحكم المشابهة لا بحكم الأمر، وباينه في الكون الثاني وهو الإدبار» (*مفاتيح*، ص. ۲۷۸).

[۷۲] ج: کرد (که).

[۷۳] در نسخهٔ م، «با» نیامده است.

چه نسبت است. و قرآن مجید می گوید: أَلَا لَهُ الْخَلْقُ وَالْأَمْرُ (۵۴:۷). اگر هر دو یکی بودی، این دو لفظ مختلف چرا؟[۷٤] اگر یکی قایم بذات او نبودی و یکی باین ذات او[۷٥]، این یک لفظ متحد چرا؟ اگر له ملک راست، امر را صفت چرا گویی؟ اگر له صفت راست، خلق را صفت چرا نگویی؟

[۵۶] نه نه چنین گوی که مرد کتاب و جفت کتاب[۷٦] گفت: له الخلق مِلکا و له الأمر مُلکا. او خداوند مِلک و خداوند

---

[۷٤] این جمله در نسخهٔ م دو بار آمده است.

[۷٥] ج: به امر ذات او.

[۷٦] تعبیر مرد کتاب و جفت کتاب به صراحت دلالتی شیعی دارد. جفت کتاب تعبیری است از حدیث ثقلین که اهل بیت از کتاب اللّه جدا نیستند. این روایت از خلق و امر هم حدیثی از امام جعفر صادق است، که شهرستانی در مفاتیح آن را نقل کرده است (بنگرید به بند ۵ در بالا). همچنین، بنگرید به *مفاتیح*: « وکذلک التالي لکتاب اللّه من یتلوه حق تلاوته وهو یشهد له، ویتلوه شاهد منه، وهو أحد الثقلین وأبوالسبطین. قال – علیه السلام – لمّا بویع بالمدینة: «نمتي بما أقول رهینة وأنا به زعیم». ویجري الکلام إلی أن قال: «حق وباطل ولکل اهل فلئن أمر الباطل فلقدیماً فعل، ولئن قلّ الحق فلربما ولعلّ». فقام إلیه الأحوص بن جوّاب وقال: «یا امیرالمؤمنین! أتری فلاناً وفلاناً کانا علی غیر الحقّ. قال: «إنک امرؤٌ ملبوس علیک اعرف الحقّ تعرف أهله واعرف الباطل تعرف من آثاره»...» (مفاتیح، ص. ۲۷۷). از تصریح شهرستانی این‌جا روشن می‌شود که مرادش از جفت کتاب همانا امام شیعی است (این‌جا امام جعفر صادق).

مُلک: الأرواح مُلکه والاجساد مِلکه فأحلّ مُلکه في مِلکه وله علیهما شرط ولهما عنده وعد. فإن وفوا بشرطه وفي لهم بوعده.[۷۷] جان‌ها مُلک اوست، تن‌ها مِلک او. او مُلک خود را در مِلک خود کشید. او را بر ایشان شرطی و ایشان را بنزدیک او وعدی. اگر ایشان بشرط خود وفا کنند، او نیز بوعد خویش وفا کند. شرط من چیست؟ یا بَنِي آدَمَ إِمَّا يَأْتِيَنَّكُمْ رُسُلٌ مِّنكُمْ يَقُصُّونَ عَلَيْكُمْ آيَاتِي فَمَنِ اتَّقَىٰ وَأَصْلَحَ فَلَا خَوْفٌ عَلَيْهِمْ وَلَا هُمْ يَحْزَنُونَ (۷:۳۵)، وعد.[۷۸] مِلک و مُلک او راست: اللَّـهُمَّ مَالِكَ الْمُلْكِ (۳:۲۶). مُلک آسمانی و زمینی او راست: وَلِلَّـهِ مُلْكُ السَّمَاوَاتِ وَالْأَرْضِ (۳:۱۸۹). لشکر آسمانی و زمینی او راست: وَلِلَّـهِ جُنُودُ السَّمَاوَاتِ وَالْأَرْضِ (۴۸:۴). کلیدهای آسمانی و

---

[۷۷] محمد علی آذرشب در ترجمهٔ عربی خود از *مجلس خوارزم* در ضبط کلمهٔ «ملک» در هر دو مورد به ضم میم آورده است. در نسخهٔ چاپی جلالی نائینی ضبط این روایت به همین شکل است که آورده‌ایم. از سیاق عبارات دیگر مجلس بر می‌آید که احتمالاً ضبط صحیح همان است که جلالی نائینی آورده است. در عبارت «خداوند ملک و خداوند ملک»، بی‌شک نمی‌توان دو کلمه را به یک شکل قرائت کرد. این حدیثی است از امام جعفر صادق به روایت خود شهرستانی در *مفاتیح*.

[۷۸] ج: کلمهٔ وعد به ابتدای جملهٔ بعد رفته است. شرط و وعد هر دو در ضمن آیهٔ مزبور آمده است. بعد از وعد، جملهٔ تازه‌ای آغاز می‌شود.

زمینی او راست: لَهُ مَقَالِيدُ السَّمَاوَاتِ وَالْأَرْضِ (۱۲:۴۲). خزینه‌های آسمانی و زمینی او راست: وَلِلَّـهِ خَزَائِنُ السَّمَاوَاتِ وَالْأَرْضِ (۷:۶۳). مُلک را لشکر. لشکر را خزینه. خزینه را کلید. کلید بدست غیب: وَلِلَّـهِ غَيْبُ السَّمَاوَاتِ وَالْأَرْضِ (۱۲۳:۱۱).

[۵۷] مُلکِ آسمانی عالمِ تقدیر اوست؛ عالمِ اسباب خلقی. ملک زمینی عالمِ تکلیف اوست؛ عالمِ اسباب امری.[۷۹] لشگر آسمانی، فریشتگان و مقربان؛ لشگر زمینی، پیغامبران، و اولو الأمر و خداوندان فرمان[۸۰]. خزینه‌های آسمانی، اسرار تقدیر

---

[۷۹] ج با علامت گذاری‌ها معنای جمله را دگرگون کرده است. این جا تقدیر، اسباب خلقی است و تکلیف اسباب امری. ج چنین آورده است: «ملک آسمانی: عالم تقدیر اوست؛ عالم: اسباب خلقی؛ ملک زمینی: عالم تکلیف اوست؛ عالم: اسباب امری».

[۸۰] این لشگر زمینی و اسباب امری، پیامبران و امامان‌اند. امامان اسباب امری‌اند. این مضمون در *سیر و سلوک* طوسی هم آمده است که امام، مظهر امر پروردگار است. نسبت زمینی به پیامبران و امامان از این روست که صورت و جنبهٔ انسانی و خاکی دارند. به همان قیاس فرشتگان لشگر آسمانی‌اند چون در کسوت جسمانیت نیستند.

او؛ و خزینه‌های زمینی، اسرار تکلیف او[۸۱]. کلید آن خزینه‌ها لا إله إلّا اللّه. کلید این خزینه‌ها، محمّد رسول الله. مفتاح الجنة لا إله إلّا اللّه محمّد رسول الله است؛ بل کلید همهٔ فتح و گشایش. کما لا یلتقی الشفتان بکلمة لا إله إلّا اللّه، کذلک[۸۲] لا یحجب سماء سماء حتی تصل الي ساق العرش فیستغفر لقائلها: چنان‌که در کلمهٔ لا إله إلّا اللّه دو لب بر هم[۸۳] نمی‌آید؛ همچنین هیچ آسمانی حجاب نکند او را تا از آسمان بآسمانی می گذرد تا بساق عرش رسد و آمرزش خواهد گویندهٔ لا إله إلّا اللّه [را]. گویند: تنها آمده‌ای، بازگرد و یار خویش را بیاور تا اجابت یابی. ای[۸۴] کلید گشایش! کلیدبند با خود دار تا[۸۵] گوینده رهایش یابد که کلید گشایش در بهشت لا إله إلّا اللّه

---

[۸۱] دوگانهٔ تقدیر-تکلیف از دوگانه‌های دیگری است که شهرستانی در کنار مفروغ-مستأنف می‌آورد. در جای دیگری از اسرار-آیات یاد می‌کند که اشارتی است به تأویل-تنزیل یا همان کاری که در صورت‌بندی و تبویب تفسیر قرآن‌اش می‌کند.

[۸۲] م:ندارد.

[۸۳] ق: ندارد.

[۸۴] ج: این.

[۸۵] ج و م: که.

است؛ و کلیدبند در دوزخ محمّد رسول الله است. تا در دوزخ بر خود نبندی، در بهشت گشاده نگردد.[۸۶]

---

[۸۶] شهرستانی در الملل در نقل آراء باطنیان تعلیمی به روایت از حسن صباح می‌نویسد: «وجعل الحق والباطل، والتشابه بينهما من وجه، والتمايز بينهما من وجه، والتضاد في الطرفين، الترتب في أحد الطرفين، ميزاناً يزن به جميع ما يتكلم فيه، قال: وإنما. أنشأت هذا الميزان من كلمة الشهادة، وتركيبها من النفي والإثبات، أو النفي والإستثناء. قال: فما هو مستحق النفي باطل، وما هو مستحق الإثبات حق، ووزن بذلک الخير والشر، والصدق والكذب، وسائر المتضادات، ونكتته أن يرجع في كل مقالة وكلمة إلى إثبات المعلم، وأن التوحيد هو التوحيد والنبوة معاً، حتى يكون توحيداً، وأن النبوة هي النبوة والإمامة معاً حتى تكون نبوة» (الملل، ص. ۲۳۴). در آغاز و انجام، طوسی می گوید: «بعضی گفته‌اند کلمهٔ «لا إله إلّا اللّه» میزان است، هر چند فرموده‌اند: «كلمة خفيفة على اللسان ثقيلة في الميزان». اما نسبت با بعضی مردم موزون و میزان هر دو یکی است و علامت آنکه این کلمه میزان است آن است که وجود در یک کفه دارد و عدم در یک کفه و حرف استثناء که روئی با عدم دارد و روئی با وجود به مثابهٔ شاهین است که هر دو کفه به آن ایستاده و قائم است و این کلمه فاصل است میان مسلمان و کافر و بهشتی و دوزخی: من قال لا إله إلّا اللّه دخل الجنة» (آغاز و انجام، ص. ۶۵-۶۴، بند ۵۲). این‌ها را مقایسه کنید با سخنانی که شهرستانی در مفاتیح می گوید: «وعندنا ميزان مستقيم يزن للوازن به العلوم والجهالات والعقائد الصحيحة والفاسدة، وذلک الميزان هو الذي قال اللّه تعالى [عنه]: اللَّـهُ الَّذِي أَنزَلَ الْكِتَابَ بِالْحَقِّ وَالْمِيزَانَ (۱۷:۴۲). وهو ميزان لا إله إلّا اللّه، وذلک الوازن هو النبي، قال اللّه تعالى: وَأَنزَلْنَا إِلَيْكَ الذِّكْرَ لِتُبَيِّنَ لِلنَّاسِ مَا نُزِّلَ إِلَيْهِمْ (۴۴:۱۶). وما قال: ليتبيّن للناس، والنائب من بعده مَن يقيم الوزن بالقسط ولا يخسر الميزان، وكذلک الوارث منه من يثبت الحقّ

[۵۸] مردم بمحمّد رسول الله از دوزخ برهد، و بلا إله إلّا اللّه ببهشت برسد؛[۸۷] دیگر این لا إله إلّا اللّه، محمّد رسول الله گفتن بقول، امروزت گشایش و رهایش[۸۸] دهد؛ خون و مال در عصمت آرد. اما فردات رستگاری آن‌گه دهد که باخلاص دل گفته باشی. پس قائمی[۸۹] بباید تا مؤمن مخلص از منافق مرآئی

لمورثه ولا یبطله علیه، وکذلک التالي لکتاب اللّه من یتلوه حق تلاوته وهو یشهد له، ویتلوه شاهد منه، وهو أحد الثقلین وأبوالسبطین. قال – علیه السلام – لمّا بویع بالمدینة: «ذمتي بما أقول رهینة وأنا به زعیم». ویجري الکلام إلی أن قال: «حق وباطل ولکل اهل فلئن أمر الباطل فلقدیماً فعل، ولئن قلّ الحق فلربما ولعلّ». فقام إلیه الأحوص بن جوّاب وقال: «یا امیرالمؤمنین! أتری فلاناً وفلاناً کانا علی غیر الحقّ. قال: «إنک امرؤٌ ملبوس علیک اعرف الحقّ تعرف أهله واعرف الباطل تعرف من آثاره»...» (مفاتیح، ص. ۲۷۷).

[۸۷] این تعبیر از کلمتین خلاصه وچکیدهٔ اعتقاد تعلیمیان است. در عقاید تعلیمی تنها به تعلیم معلم صادق و یگانه می‌توان به معرفت خدا رسید. فلذا کلمهٔ شهادت بدون اقرار به نبوت محمدی ناقص است. این مضمون را در پاسخ علاء الدین محمد به پرسش‌های شفاهی طوسی می‌توان با همین تعابیر دید. بنگرید به تعلیقات ذیل بند ۷۸ متن حاضر.

[۸۸] تعبیر «گشایش و رهایش» یادآور عنوان کتابی از ناصر خسرو است. اگر ادله‌ای را که دلالت بر اسماعیلی بودن شهرستانی است بپذیریم، بسیار دور از ذهن است که به کار بردن این تعبیر در چنین متنی تصادفی باشد.

[۸۹] این تعبیر قائم تعبیری اختصاصاً اسماعیلی است هر چند مضمون این سخن و احادیث و روایت مشابه آن پیش‌تر نزد عموم شیعیان وجود داشته

جدا باز کند؛ و بهشتی از دوزخی جدا باز کند. امروز، ما کنا نعرف المؤمنین من المنافقین الا بحبّ علیّ وبغضه.[۹۰] سعید مسیب می گوید: ما مؤمن از منافق بدوستی علی و دشمنی با او شناختیمی. و فردا، أنت یا علی قسیم الجنة والنار؛[۹۱] پس بر سر دو راه بنشینی تا می گویی: هذا لي - این مراست و ببهشت می‌فرستی. و آتش می گوید این مراست و بدوزخ می‌اندازد. موحّد از مشرک بلا إله إلّا اللّه با دیدار آمد.[۹۲] مسلمان از کافر بمحمّد رسول الله ظاهر گشتی.[۹۳] مؤمن از منافق بحب علی و بغضه ببهشت و دوزخ رسیده.

[۵۹] ما ملکوت خود بخلیل خود ابراهیم - می‌نماییم: وَكَذَٰلِكَ نُرِي إِبْرَاهِيمَ مَلَكُوتَ السَّمَاوَاتِ وَالْأَرْضِ وَلِيَكُونَ مِنَ

است. اگر متون اسماعیلی بعد از شهرستانی را به دقت بخوانیم و مقایسه کنیم، شباهت این جملات و سیاق آن‌ها نکتهٔ مهمی است.

[۹۰] از جمله بنگرید به: امینی، عبدالحسین، *الغدیر في الکتاب والسنة والأدب*، ج. ۳، ص. ۲۵۷ به بعد. (قم: ۱۴۱۶/۱۹۹۵).

[۹۱] بنگرید به: امینی، عبدالحسین، *الغدیر في الکتاب والسنة والأدب*، ج. ۱، ص. ۳۲۹ (قم: ۱۴۱۶/۱۹۹۵)

[۹۲] ج: آمد(ه).

[۹۳] ج: گشته.

الْمُوقِنِينَ (۶:۷۵). ای گردش شب و روز! زمانی چادری قیرگون بسر موجودات زمینی در کش: فَلَمَّا جَنَّ عَلَيْهِ اللَّيْلُ (۶:۷۶). ای صاحبان مراتب روحانی! شما حجاب ستاره و ماه و آفتاب بر روی خویش فرو گذارید، و هر یک خویشتن بر دیدهٔ پاک خلیلی عرضه کنید و بزبان اعتبار با او بگویید که ماییم مربیان نظرطلبِ تو، تا از مرتبه‌ای بمرتبه‌ای رسانیم تا هر یکی را گوید هَٰذَا رَبِّي (۶:۷۶). و چون از حضور در غیبت می‌افتد، یکی را گوید: لَا أُحِبُّ الْآفِلِينَ (۶:۷۶). یکی دیگر را گوید: لَئِن لَّمْ يَهْدِنِي رَبِّي لَأَكُونَنَّ مِنَ الْقَوْمِ الضَّالِّينَ (۶:۷۷). یکی دیگر را گوید: يَا قَوْمِ إِنِّي بَرِيءٌ مِّمَّا تُشْرِكُونَ (۶:۷۸). سرش بتربیت اصحاب مراتب روحانی[٩٤] فرو نیاید. تو پنداری که او ستاره و ماه و آفتاب را می گفت: هذا ربی، و هذا ربی؛ هر یکی از این سه، روحانیتی است که مدبّر اوست. می‌خواست که دست در

---

[٩٤] در *روضه* تعبیری که برای صاحبان مراتب روحانی می‌آید به ترتیب داعی، حجت و امام است. یعنی ستاره و ماه و آفتاب. در روایت *روضه* آن که در نهایت دستگیر ابراهیم می‌آید، ملک السلام است که قائم زمانهٔ اوست. و این همان است که شهرستانی در اشاره به او می گوید: مربی اول. عبارات مزبور در *روضه* نقل قول است از *علیٰ ذکره السلام* در شرح امامت. بنگرید به *روضه*، ص. ۱۰۵ (بند ۳۵۷).

دست تربیت او نهد تا بمراتبِ معراجِ درجاتِ نبوت خویش برآید. نه ستاره دستگیر او آمد، نه ماه، نه آفتاب؛ نه روحانیت حدود و نفوس و عقولِ ایشان. که من ببالای درجات اختیاری خویش بر می‌آیم و ایشان بپای شیب مراتب قسری خویش فرو می‌شوند. دستگیر من چون شوند؟ مربی مرا چون شایند؟ اگر مربی اول مرا دست نگیرد لَأَكُونَنَّ مِنَ الْقَوْمِ الضَّالِّينَ (۶:۷۷).

[۶۰] ای ابراهیم! ما مربی و معلم تو نیستیم؛ ما هر یکی آیینهٔ زدوده‌ایم تا ملکوت آسمانی که عالم تقدیر است، در ما بینی. مالک الملکوت را در ملکوت بینی گویی هذا ربی. و راست گفته باشی. گفتا که آینه‌ای که فرو شود، مرا نشاید. مرا آینه باید که همواره در طلوع و صعود بود و او را افول و غروب نباشد: إِنِّي وَجَّهْتُ وَجْهِيَ (۶:۷۹) خود روی من آینهٔ روی من است که همواره روی فطرت بفاطر السموات و الارض دارد. کمال آن‌جاست که حنیفیت و اسلام است: والحنیفیة رؤیة الکمال في الرجال – و هر چه جز این است همه شرک و ضلال

بر اوست؛[۹۵] نهایت قدم خلیل را بدایت قدم محمّدی سازند تا در نماز اولین چیزی که خواند وَجَّهْتُ وَجْهِيَ (۶:۷۹) خواند و کانت نهایة اقدام الأنبیاء، بدایة لقَدَمه[۹۶] وعجالة من قَسمه.

[۶۱] ای ابراهیم! تو را غاری. ای محمّد! تو را غاری. یا ابراهیم اخرج من الغار، یا محمّد ادخل في الغار. یا ابراهیم! تحرک وأفتح عینیک تری ملکوت السموات و الارض. یا محمّد! أسکن وغمّض عینیک، تری جبروت السموات والأرض. ای ابراهیم! از غار بیرون آی. ای محمّد! تو در غار شو! ای ابراهیم! تو در حرکت آی. ای محمّد! تو ساکن باش. ای ابراهیم! تو دیده بگشای. ای محمّد! تو دیده بر هم نه. ای ابراهیم! تو در ملکوت آسمانی نظاره کن تا چه بینی. ای محمّد! تو در جبروت زمینی نظاره کن تا چه بینی. ای ابراهیم! تو را سه روحانی در سه صورت جسمانی می‌آید تا تربیت تو کند. ای محمّد! تو را سه کلمه در صورت سه شخص می‌آید تا تربیت تو کند. یکی سکینه در صورت صدیقی جسمانی. یکی تأیید و نصرت در صورت

---

[۹۵] ج: برو است.
[۹۶] م: لقومه.

لشکری روحانی. یکی علوّ کلمه در صورت [کلمه‌ای][۹۷] ربانی: فأنزَلَ اللَّـهُ سَكِينَتَهُ عَلَيْهِ وَأَيَّدَهُ بِجُنُودٍ لَّمْ تَرَوْهَا وَجَعَلَ كَلِمَةَ الَّذِينَ كَفَرُوا السُّفْلَىٰ وَكَلِمَةُ اللَّـهِ هِيَ الْعُلْيَا (۹:۴۰). اول سکینه. آخر کلمه. لشکر میان سکینه و کلمه. ای ابراهیم! تو را ستاره، ما را سکینه. تو را ماه، ما را لشکرگاه. وهذا أکبر ترا آفتاب[۹۸]. ما را کلمهٔ لا إله إلّا اللّه و الله اکبر.

[۶۲] برونـد[۹۹] از این سه اشارت خلیلی، سه فرزند برآرند. یکی اسحاق، یکی یعقوب، یکی یوسف. و آن سه نشانه، اشارهٔ او را. یکی ستاره، یکی ماه، یکی آفتاب. بدر سرای فرزند سیمین برند[۱۰۰] تا همه او را سجده کنند: إِنِّي رَأَيْتُ أَحَدَ عَشَرَ كَوْكَبًا وَالشَّمْسَ وَالْقَمَرَ رَأَيْتُهُمْ لِي سَاجِدِينَ (۱۲:۴). تا مسجود، ساجد گردد. و از آن یک اشارت خلیلی بیک نشانه سینهٔ خویش یک فرزند برآرند و اسماعیل‌اش نام کنند تا حنیفیت در اصلاب

---

[۹۷] ق و م: علوی. ج: غاری. هر دو ضبط مشوش به نظر می‌رسند. ضبط قیاسی کرده‌ایم به اعتبار جملهٔ پایان این بند.

[۹۸] ج: ترا آفتاب وهذا اکبر.

[۹۹] م: بردند. ج و ق: بروند.

[۱۰۰] م: به در سرای فرزندت نمی‌برند.

پاکان بارحام پاکان می‌برد تا بمحمّد مصطفی صلوات الله علیه و آله ظهور کند تا گوید: بعثت بالحنیفیة السهلة السمحة[۱۰۱]، والحنیفیة نیابة[۱۰۲] الرّجال والصّبْوة نیابة الروحانیات.

[۶۳] دو نور از ابراهیم میراث مانده. یکی نوری ظاهر. یکی نوری مستور. رَبَّنَا إِنَّكَ تَعْلَمُ مَا نُخْفِي وَمَا نُعْلِنُ (۳۸:۱۴). ما نخفی من حال اسماعیل و ما نعلن من حال اسحاق.

[۶۴] در نور ظاهر: کمالی بیعقوب و یوسف، کمالی بموسی و هارون، کمالی بداود و سلیمان، کمالی بیحیی و عیسی. در نور[۱۰۳] مستور: یکی کمال مجمع همهٔ کمالات، هر چه یعقوب و یوسف را بود از محنت و نعمت، ما را هست. هر چه موسی و

---

[۱۰۱] بنگرید به: خلیل مأمون شیحا (بیروت: ۲۰۱۳)، *موسوعة المعجم المفهرس لألفاظ النبوي الشريف للكتب الستة*، ج. ۹. ص. ۵۷.

[۱۰۲] در هر دو مورد، ج کلمهٔ «نیابة» را به شکل «نباهة» ضبط کرده است که نادرست است. در نسخه‌ها کلمه نقطه ندارد اما شهرستانی در متن *ملل* عبارتی دارد که گره گشاست: «الآن نزلتم عن نیابة الروحانیات إلی نیابة هیاکلها، وترکتم مذهب الصبوة الصرفة» (ص. ۳۳۶) و همچنین: «اجابت الحنفاء بجوابین. أحدهما: نیابة عن جنس البشر والثاني: نیابة عن الأنبیاء علیهم السلام» (ص. ۳۳۳).

[۱۰۳] نک. به مورد قبلی.

هارون را بود از علم تنزیل و تأویل، ما را هست. هر چه داود و سلیمان را بود از علم کتاب و حکمت، ما را هست. هر چه یحیی و عیسی را بود از قبض و بسط، ما را هست[١٠٤]. هر چه[١٠٥] ما را هست از اسرار و آیات، کس را نیست.[١٠٦]

[۶۵] اوست جوامع الکلم.[١٠٧] اگر جوامع الکلم را تفسیر بقرآن کنی راست، که همهٔ اسرار و آیات در اوست. اگر جوامع

[١٠٤] برگرفته از این حدیث است: «قال: التقي يحيى بن زكريا و عيسى بن مريم، فضحك عيسى في وجه يحيى و صافحه، فقال له يحيى: يا ابن خالتي ما لي أراك ضاحكا كأنك قد أمنت؟ فقال له عيسى: يا ابن خالتي ما لي أراك عابسا كأنك قد يئست، قال: فأوحى اللّه إليهما: إنّ أحبّكما إليّ أبشّكما بصاحبه». بنگرید به: ابن عساکر، *تاریخ مدینة دمشق* (بیروت: ۱۴۱۷)، جز ۴۷، ص. ۴۶۷.

[١٠٥] ج: (و) هر چه.

[١٠٦] در ق به جای «هر چه» همه جا داریم: هرچ.

[١٠٧] بنگرید به: خلیل مأمون شیحا (بیروت: ۲۰۱۳)، *موسوعة المعجم المفهرس لألفاظ النبوي الشريف للكتب الستة*، ج. ۶. ص. ۲۱۸.

الکلم[۱۰۸] را تفسیر بکلمهٔ لا إله إلّا اللّه کنی راست. هر چه در جملهٔ قرآن است، در اوست[۱۰۹].

[۶۶] قرأ القاری: الرَّحْمَـٰنُ عَلَّمَ الْقُرْآنَ (۵۵: ۱-۲).

[۶۷] ما را کارگاهی است، ما را بارگاهی. کار و بار ما راست. کارگاه ما عالم، بارگاه ما آدم. بکارگاه ما در آمدی، ببارگاه ما درآی، و الا از کارگاهت بدر کنیم. ای فریشتگان! بدرگاه ما درآمده‌اید، ببارگاه ما در آیید: اسْجُدُوا لِآدَمَ (۲: ۳۴)! آن کس که در آمد فریشته و آن که در نیامد شیطان!

---

[۱۰۸] در نسخهٔ م در هر سه مورد آمده است: جوامع الکلام. در *روضه* این تعبیر به صورت *جوامع الکلم* آمده است. در حاشیهٔ این نکته باید متذکر شد که چنان‌که از شباهت‌های متعدد ذکر شده در تعلیقات متن حاضر بر می‌آید، تصور ۲۶ *روضهٔ تسلیم* گویی بازنویسی بخش‌های مختلف *مجلس خوارزم* است. در *مفاتیح* هم شهرستانی به همین شکل ضبط کرده است: «کانت حجة نبینا المصطفی - صلوات اللّه علیه وآله - کذلک إلّا أنّها في کلمةٍ سمّاها جوامع الکلم یعني لا إله إلّا اللّه، وقال: «أوتیت جوامع الکلم»...» (ص. ۲۱۵).

[۱۰۹] این دو جمله بر اساس م و ج تصحیح شده است. در ق. به جای این دو جمله تنها داریم: «اگر جوامع الکلام را تفسیر به قرآن کنی راست که هر چه در جملهٔ قرآن است دروست».

[۶۸] بوجهی دیگر، کارگاه ما عالم خلق و خلقیات. بارگاه ما عالم امر و امریات. بارگاه ما عَلَّمَ الْقُرْآنَ (۲:۵۵). کارگاه ما خَلَقَ الْإِنسَانَ (۳:۵۵).

[۶۹] کسی در خالقی منازعت نتواند کرد: وَلَئِن سَأَلْتَهُم مَّنْ خَلَقَهُمْ لَيَقُولُنَّ اللَّـهُ (۸۷:۴۳). اگر دعوی منازعتی کند، در امر و امری کند: مَا عَلِمْتُ لَكُم مِّنْ إِلَـٰهٍ غَيْرِي (۳۸:۲۸). مِن خالق غیری نیست، مِن آمر غیری است. ابلیس در خالقی هیچ خلاف نکرد که خَلَقْتَنِي مِن نَّارٍ وَخَلَقْتَهُ مِن طِينٍ (۱۲:۷). در امر منازعت آورد، و با متوسط امر مخالفت کرد، تا گفتند: مَا مَنَعَكَ أَلَّا تَسْجُدَ إِذْ أَمَرْتُكَ (۱۲:۷). اگر هزار حجّت بیاوری، إِذْ أَمَرْتُكَ (۷:۱۲) را هیچ جواب نیست. حال این تقلید است؛ بصیرت کو؟ این که من می گویم، بصیرت است.

[۷۰] مقدماتی مسلم، نتیجه ضروری. مسلم هست که مرا از آتش آفریده، مسلم هست[۱۱۰] که آدم را از گل آفریده، مسلم هست که آتش شریف‌تر از گل. سجودم او را چرا؟ فضل او بر

[۱۱۰] در هر دو نسخه «نیست» آمده است ولی ج «هست» ضبط کرده است.

من چرا؟ این که گویی: فَاخْرُجْ مِنْهَا فَإِنَّكَ رَجِيمٌ (۳۴:۱۵)، زور کل است. دیگر باره: وَإِنَّ عَلَيْكَ اللَّعْنَةَ إِلَىٰ يَوْمِ الدِّينِ (۳۵:۱۵) جور محض است.

[۷۱] ای لعین! مقدمه و نتیجه می گویی؟ منطقی می کنی؟ آتش را از گِل شریف‌تر می‌دانی، طبیعی می کنی؟ بسیط را از مرکب مقدم‌تر داری، الهی می‌کنی؟ مذهب فلاسفه تقریر می کنی؟ چون مسلم کردی که حاکم منم، حکم مراست، بر من چرا حکم می کنی؟ چون آمر منم، فرمان مراست ، بر من چرا فرمان دهی؟ إِذْ أَمَرْتُكَ (۱۲:۷)، جواب همهٔ شبهات است. قَالَ فَبِمَا أَغْوَيْتَنِي لَأَقْعُدَنَّ لَهُمْ صِرَاطَكَ الْمُسْتَقِيمَ (۱۶:۷). گفتا بسبب آن که تو مرا گمراه کردی، من براه راست تو نشینم. و از پیش و از پس، و راست و چپ درآیم و گمراهشان کنم.

[۷۲] ای لعین! سخن متناقض می‌گویی. اگر گمراهی بمن حواله می‌کنی، تو بر راه چه نشینی؟ و اگر بر راه نشینی تا گمراهشان کنی، گمراهی با من چرا حواله می کنی؟

[۷۳] هم جبر می گویی هم قَدَر. مذهب جبریان از این کلمهٔ أَغْوَيْتَنِي خاست. مذهب قَدَریان از این کلمهٔ لَأَقْعُدَنَّ خاست.

هر دو طایفه [را][۱۱۱] دام در دام ابلیس بندند و بآتش دوزخ اندازند.

[۷۴] از پیش در آمدن معلمی کردن: يُعَلِّمُونَ النَّاسَ السِّحْرَ (۱۰۲:۲). از پس در آمدن متعلمی کردن: فَيَتَعَلَّمُونَ مِنْهُمَا مَا يُفَرِّقُونَ بِهِ بَيْنَ الْمَرْءِ وَزَوْجِهِ (۱۰۲:۲). از راست در آمدن زاهدی و ناموس: وَلَا يَذْكُرُونَ اللَّـهَ إِلَّا قَلِيلًا (۱۴۲:۴). و از چپ در آمدن فاسقی و اِباحت: وَلَا تَجِدُ أَكْثَرَهُمْ شَاكِرِينَ (۱۷:۷).

[۷۵] هر جا که شبهتی است از وساوس شیطان است. و هر جا که وسوسه است، از شبهات آن لعین خاست. شبهاتش یا تشبیه است یا تعطیل. یا جبر است یا قَدَر. یا عقل است یا سمع.

[۷۶] مشبّهه اصل خدای را ذاتی و صورتی گفتند: خلق آدم علی صورة الرحمن، حجّت ایشان. کرّامیان جسمی و جهتی گفتند یا قائم بذاتی. و صفتی قدیم، حجّت ایشان: وَهُوَ الْقَاهِرُ فَوْقَ عِبَادِهِ (۱۸:۶). اشعریان ذاتی و هشت صفت قدیم.[۱۱۲]

---

[۱۱۱] کلمه «را» در هیچ یک از دو نسخه نیست. به اقتفای ج چنین آوردیم.
[۱۱۲] ج: [گفتند] را اضافه دارد.

حجّت ایشان: وَلَا يُحِيطُونَ بِشَيْءٍ مِّنْ عِلْمِهِ إِلَّا بِمَا شَاءَ (۲۵۵:۲). معتزلیان ذاتی و احکام صفاتی.[۱۱۳] حجّت ایشان: الْحَيُّ الْقَيُّومُ (۲۵۵:۲). فلسفیان ذاتی، و صفاتی سلبی و اضافی.[۱۱۴] حجّت ایشان: عقل. و در بن هر مذهبی هم تشبیهی لازم، هم تعطیلی لازم.[۱۱۵]

[۷۷] دیگر باره در خلق و امر، معتزلیان گفتند خلق و امر هر دو یکی و هر دو مخلوق. کرّامیان گفتند خلق و امر هر دو یکی و هر دو حادث در ذات حق جل جلاله. اشعریان هر دو یکی نگفتند. خلق را مخلوق گفتند و امر را قدیم نه مخلوق و لیکن در ذات او جلّ جلاله.

---

[۱۱۳] ج: [گفتند] را اضافه دارد.

[۱۱۴] ج: [گفتند] را اضافه دارد.

[۱۱۵] هم در این‌جا و هم در بندهای بعدی، شهرستانی از متکلمان و فلاسفه آشکار انتقاد می‌کند و سخن آن‌ها را مغایر با کلام خدا می‌شمارد. آن‌چه در خلال این رد و نقد باقی می‌ماند این است که رأی تعلیمیان همان است که خود شهرستانی تقریر می‌کند و در این متن از آن دفاع می‌کند. این‌جا شهرستانی هم معتزله را رد کرده است و هم اشاعره را. در *مفاتیح* هم از امامیه نیز انتقاد کرده است و به این ترتیب جای هیچ شبهتی دربارهٔ اسماعیلی بودن او باقی نمی‌ماند.

[۷۸] و این همه نه زبان قرآن است نه عبارت کتاب و سنت است. ما مردِ «قال اللّه» و «قال رسول اللّه»ایم.[۱۱۶] در کتاب

[۱۱۶] بنگرید به *مفاتیح*: «توحیدهم لله: إلهنا أله محمد، فیکون التوحید مع النبوة توحیداً: نَعْبُدُ إِلَهَكَ وَإِلَهَ آبَائِكَ (۲:۱۳۳) طاعتهم لله طاعة رسول اللّه، کما أمر وهدی لا کما یراه العقل ویهوی، شعارهم في اللّه: لا إله إلّا اللّه محمّد رسول اللّه، قال اللّه، قال رسول اللّه، کتاب اللّه وسنة اللّه» (*مفاتیح*، ص. ۶۵۵)؛ همچنین بنگرید به صص. ۶۴۰-۶۴۱. در بخش محلقات *روضه* سؤال و جوابی میان طوسی و علاء الدین محمّد ثبت شده است در باب اتهام ترک شریعت به اسماعیلیان. پاسخ امام اسماعیلی به این اتهام تکرار نعل بالنعل همین تعابیر شهرستانی است که خلاصهٔ اعتقاد به تعلیم را بازگو می کند: «گفته‌اند که شما محمّد مصطفی را و شریعت او را با کنار نهاده‌اید! این محمّد مصطفی را آن‌کس با کنار نهاده است که فتوی کرده است که خداشناسی به مجّرد نظر است و به محّمد مصطفی و قرآن عظیم که او را داده است حاجت نیست، که اگر او و دیگر پیمبران نیامده بودندی مردم به رأی خود خدا را شناختندی و [به] ابلاغ رسالت ایشان در این معنی اصولاً حاجت نیست.اکنون از دو [حال] بیرون نیست: یا این محمّد مصطفی رسول آن خدایی است که به فرمان او واجب است کلمهٔ لا إله إلّا اللّه و قُل هُوَ اللّه أحد از او قبول کردن و [به] تعلیم او در توحید اقرار دادن و این دین داری‌ست که مذهب کی‌ست؟ یا رسول آن خدایی‌ست که به فتوی ایشان واجب نیست نام او بر زبان گرفتن و بر یگانگی او اقرار دادن و این رسالت از او قبول کردن. و چون چنین است پس او رسول کی‌ست و این رسالت به سوی چیست؟ اکنون بنگرند تا محمّد مصطفی و رسالت او ایشان باز داده‌اند یا این جماعت؟ و دیگر باره در شریعت کلمهٔ شهادت لا إله إلّا اللّه است و ایشان آشکارا می گویند و نشنیدی که چون در توحید گفتن و شنیدن روا دارند به مذهب ایشان اتحاد است. پس این شریعت همه ایشان باز

خلق و امر آمده: له الخلق مِلکا وله الأمر مُلکا. اجساد، خلقی: وَلَقَدْ خَلَقْنَا الْإِنسَانَ (۱۲:۲۳). ارواح، امری: قُلِ الرُّوحُ مِنْ أَمْرِ رَبِّي (۸۵:۱۷).

[۷۹] هر چه خلقیّات است مکانی و زمانی و مادی. هي سلالة من طين، اشارت بمادت. ثُمَّ جَعَلْنَاهُ (۱۳:۲۳)، اشارت بزمان. فِي قَرَارٍ مَّكِينٍ (۱۳:۲۳)، اشارت بمکان. در ابداع ارواح نه زمان، نه مکان، نه مادت: وَمَا أَمْرُنَا إِلَّا وَاحِدَةٌ (۵۰:۵۴) كُن فَيَكُونُ (۱۱۷:۲).[۱۱۷]

[۸۰] اجساد را تربیت بغذای جسمانی: طعام و شراب. ارواح را تربیت بغذای روحانی: تنزیل و تأویل. اجساد را از خاک و آب آفریده، غذای او هم از آن ساخته. ارواح را از امر و کلمه آفریده و غذای او هم از کلمه ساخته.

داده‌اند یا این جماعت؟» (بنگرید به رسالهٔ دکتری ج. بدخشانی، ۱۹۸۹، بندهای ۱۳۸-۱۳۷).

[۱۱۷] این بند را مقایسه کنید با *آغاز و انجام* ص. ۵۰ (بند ۲۳) در باب مبرا بودن آخرت و قیامت از زمان و مکان.

[۸۱]   اگر ده من طعام بخوری، عالم نگردی. اگر[۱۱۸] ده علم بیاموزی، فربه نگردی. پیغامبران را گرسنگی سودمند، سیری[۱۱۹] زیان‌کار. أجوع یوماً وأشبع یوماً،[۱۲۰] زیرا که ایشان جان می‌پرورند، نه تن. دنیاداران را سیری سودمند، گرسنگی[۱۲۱] زیان‌کار. يَأْكُلُونَ كَمَا تَأْكُلُ الْأَنْعَامُ (۱۲:۴۷)، زیرا که ایشان تن می‌پرورند، نه جان. چون اجل فرا رسد[۱۲۲] تن بگور سپاری،[۱۲۳] فربهی چه سود دارد؟ جان بعالم روحانی رود لاغری چه زیان دارد؟ آن‌جا مردِ عالم را لاغری عیب نبود.

[۸۲]   موسی علیه السّلام تا در کنار فرعون بود غذای پادشاهی می‌یافت، فربه می‌شد. گفتند: اگر علم شعیب می‌خواهی قدم در راه نه. در زیر درختی بنشین گرسنه و مانده و می گوی: رَبِّ إِنِّي لِمَا أَنزَلْتَ إِلَيَّ مِنْ خَيْرٍ فَقِيرٌ (۲۴:۲۸). ده سال مزدوری کنی

---

[۱۱۸] ج: (و) اگر.

[۱۱۹] ج: (و) سیری.

[۱۲۰] بنگرید به: خلیل مأمون شیحا (بیروت: ۲۰۱۳)، *موسوعة المعجم المفهرس لألفاظ النبوي الشريف للكتب الستة*، ج. ۱، ص. ۶۴۱.

[۱۲۱] ج: (و) گرسنگی.

[۱۲۲] در هر دو نسخهٔ م و ق آمده است: چون اجل فراز شد.

[۱۲۳] م: گورستانی.

تا ده مسألهٔ علمی بیاموزی. اگر علم خضر علیه السّلام می‌خواهی، یک سال در طلب گِردِ عالمَ می گرد: آتِنَا غَدَاءَنَا لَقَدْ لَقِينَا مِن سَفَرِنَا هَـٰذَا نَصَبًا (۶۲:۱۸). بامدادی ما بیار که در این سفر رنج بسیار دیدیم[۱۲۴]. گفت: ماهی‌ای بیش نداشتیم و آن نیز فراموش کردیم که از دست من با دریا شد و دریا از رفتار او ببست. گفت: اینک یافتیم نشانِ مردِ عالم. برخیز تا با منزل او شویم. تا غذای جسمانی از دست او با دریا نشد، غذای روحانی نیافت: فَوَجَدَا عَبْدًا مِّنْ عِبَادِنَا (۱۸:۶۵). بنده‌ای یافتند از بندگان ما که رحمتی خاص داده بودیمش و علمی خاص آموخته. آن رحمت چه چیز؟ الصّبر علىٰ ما لا يَعْلَم حتىٰ يُعلَّم فيَعْلَم: صبر کردن بر چیزی که نداند تا چون بیاموزندش، بداند. این خاصیت او را بود که موسی را نبود.

[۸۳] موسی می گوید: هَلْ أَتَّبِعُكَ عَلَىٰ أَن تُعَلِّمَنِ مِمَّا عُلِّمْتَ رُشْدًا (۱۸:۶۶). شش ادب در تواضع، پس‌روی و شاگردی بجای آورد. اولاً، هَلْ استفهام است نه جزم را. أَتَّبِعُكَ متابعت را نه

---

[۱۲۴] نسخهٔ م: دیدم.

مصاحبت را. عَلَىٰ أَن تُعَلِّمَنِ، استادی و معلمی تو را نه شاگردی و متعلمی مرا. مِمَّا، تنقیص را، نه تکمیل را. عُلِّمْتَ، از آن‌چه تو را آموخته‌اند نه آن‌چه دانسته‌ای. رُشْدًا، بر قدر و شایستگی قبول من، نه بر قدر قوت و قدرت خویش.

[۸۴] این شش ادب تواضع بجای آورده و جواب درشت یافته: إِنَّكَ لَن تَسْتَطِيعَ مَعِيَ صَبْرًا (۱۸:۶۷): تو هرگز با من صبر نتوانی کرد. وَكَيْفَ تَصْبِرُ عَلَىٰ مَا لَمْ تُحِطْ بِهِ خُبْرًا (۱۸:۶۸): و چگونه صبر کنی بر چیزی که ندانی؟!

[۸۵] دیگر باره با سر تواضع آمده: سَتَجِدُنِي إِن شَاءَ اللَّـهُ صَابِرًا وَلَا أَعْصِي لَكَ أَمْرًا (۱۸:۶۹). ای درشتی موسی! کجا شدی؟ آری آن‌جا که با هارون سخن بایست گفت، من معلم بودم و او متعلم: وَأَخَذَ بِرَأْسِ أَخِيهِ يَجُرُّهُ إِلَيْهِ (۷:۱۵۰). آن[۱۲۵] درشتی می‌کردم و او صبر می‌کرد. این‌جا من متعلم، و خضر معلم. او را درشتی رسد و مرا صبر: سَتَجِدُنِي إِن شَاءَ اللَّـهُ صَابِرًا. ان شاء الله مرا صابر یابی که در هیچ فرمان تو عاصی

---

[۱۲۵] ج: من.

نشوم. گفت: چون متابعت خواهی کرد، در هیچ کار که کنم هیچ[۱۲۶] سؤال مکن تا من خود سرّ آن با تو بگویم، قصه شنوده باشی.

[۸۶] در سه حال، سه کار بکرد: یکی شکستن کشتی مسکینان دریا، بی‌سببی. دیگر کشتن کودک نابالغ، بی جرمی. سدیگر، عمارت دیوار کهنه، بی مزدی.

[۸۷] موسی می‌گوید: شکستن کشتی بی سببی تصرف است در مال غیری بی استحقاقی. و آن بشریعت نشاید. کشتن کودک نابالغ بی جرمی، تصرّف است در خون کسی بی قصاصی. و این در شریعت هم نشاید. عمارتِ دیوارِ شکسته بی مزدی، تصرّف است در نفس خویش ببیهوده کاری. و این نیز در شریعت نشاید.

[۸۸] خضر می‌گوید: چون غاصبی می‌آید[۱۲۷] تا کشتی غصب کند، من عیب‌ناک کردم کشتی را تا غاصب در گذرد. و در شریعت تو رواست که کلی نگاه داری با فساد جزوی –

---

[۱۲۶] م، «هیچ» دوم را ندارد.
[۱۲۷] ج: می‌آمد.

چنان‌که از جهت علت آکله دست ببری تا کل تن بماند - این است جوابِ کشتی شکستن. و اما دیگر حادثه: چون کودک بالغ شود، کفر خواهد آورد و کفر او تعدی خواست کرد بمادر و پدر مؤمن. کودک کشتن رواست تا اصل بهلاک فرع نگاه داری - چون شاخی که خشک شود ببرند تا درخت شاخی دیگر بر کند - و این در عقل و شرع رواست. و اما سه دیگر[۱۲۸] حادثه: صلاح و سود غیری بر رنج و زیان خویش اختیار کردن از مکارم اخلاق است که آن دیوار، نشانِ گنجی بود از جهت دو یتیم. اگر بیفتادی نشان برفتی و گنج ضایع ماندی و دو یتیم محروم و ایشان را پدری نیک‌مرد بود.

[۸۹] موسی گوید: اولین در مال کسی بی دستوری او تصرف کردن است در حال، از جهت غاصبی که خواهد آمدن در ثانی حال.[۱۲۹] تو باری در این حال غاصبی بل ظالم و آن غاصب باشد که آید و باشد که نیاید. و دُوُمین در نفس کسی بی جرمی تصرف کردن است در حال از جهت کفری که خواهد آورد در

---

[۱۲۸] در هر دو نسخهٔ ق و م به شکل «سه دیگر» آمده است.

[۱۲۹] ج: ثانی الحال.

ثانی حال. تو باری در این حال قاتل و ظالمی و آن کفر بود که باشد و بود که نباشد. و سیُمین در نفس خویش تصرف کردن است برنجانیدن و بر سر گرسنگی و ماندگی کار بیهوده کردن و آن دیوار باشد که بیفتد و باشد که نیفتد. تو اگر مزدی ستانی بر این اولیٰ‌تر.

[۹۰] خضر گوید: بوک و بوک تو راست که موسی‌ای که در عالم بوک و مگری در عالم شک و شبهت. و من در عالم یقینم که ذَلِكَ الْكِتَابُ لَا رَيْبَ فِيهِ (۲:۲) - هر چه تو را شک است مرا یقین است. هر چه تو را ممکن است مرا واجب است. تو می‌گویی بوک غاصب نیاید و اگر آید این کشتی نبرد. بوک این کودک بالغ شود کفر نیاورد و اگر آرد بپدر و مادر تعدی نکند. بوک این دیوار نیفتد و اگر اوفتد دیگر عمارت نو کند. و من بیقین می‌دانم که غاصب بیاید و یقین می‌دانم که آن کودک کفر آورد و یقین می‌دانم که آن دیوار بیفتد. حکم من بنا بر یقین است و حکم تو بنا بر شک. تو را توقف باید کرد تا شک بیقین بدل شود و مرا توقف نباید کرد.

[۹۱] موسی گوید: این احکام که[۱۳۰] تو می‌کنی، احکام مستقبل است و من آن حکم که کنم، حکم[۱۳۱] حال است. و حادثهٔ امروزین را حکمِ امروز باید کرد و فردا را حکم فردا. هنوز غاصب نیامده، حکم آمدن چون کنی؟ کودک ببلاغت نارسیده[۱۳۲] و کفر ناآورده حکم کفر چون کنی؟ دیوار ناافتاده حکم افتاده چون کنی؟

[۹۲] خضر گوید: دی و امروز و فردا، زمان است. و تو مرد زمانی – تو را حکم زمانی باید کرد. من مرد زمان نیستم. مرا دی و امروز و فردا همه یکی است. هر چه بخواهد بود، مرا ببوده[۱۳۳] است. و غاصب که بخواهد آمد بنزدیک من آمده است. و کفر کودک که بخواهد بود، مرا بوده است. دیوار که بخواهد افتاد، مرا بیفتاده است. من حکم زمان نمی‌کنم، حکم من فوق‌الزمان است. زیرا که حکم من فوق‌الزمان است. تو را سالی بباید گشت تا مرا بیابی. من بیک لحظه تو را بیابم. بیک لحظه از

---

[۱۳۰] در نسخهٔ م کلمهٔ «که» نیامده است.

[۱۳۱] ج: ندارد.

[۱۳۲] م: نرسیده.

[۱۳۳] م: بوده.

مشرق بمغرب رسم. مکان و زمان تحت من‌اند و من فوق الزمان و فوق المکان‌ام. هر حکم که کنم نه زمانی باشد.

[۹۳] موسی گوید: بلی چنین است و لیکن اسباب کارها از پیش بباید تا احکام بنا[۱۳٤] بر اسباب کنی. سبب در وجود ناآمده، حکم چون رانی؟ هنوز کفر ناآورده، حکم کفر چون کنی؟ و هنوز دیوار نیفتاده، حکم افتاده چون کنی؟ هرگز کسی ندیده است که احکام پیش از اسباب رانند.

[۹۴] خضر گوید: در عالم اسباب، اسباب مقدم دارند بر احکام. در عالم بی سببی، حکم بی سبب رانند. حکم بفرمان رانند. حکم بعلم رانند. حکم بمشیت رانند: هِيَ بِمَشِيَّتِكَ دُونَ

[۱۳٤] م: ندارد.

قَوْلِكَ مُؤْتَمِرَةٌ وَبِإِرَادَتك دون نهيك منزجرة.[۱۳۵] آن‌چه[۱۳۶] معلوم است محکوم است. آن‌چه[۱۳۷] مراد است محتوم.

[۹۵] موسی گوید: پس تکلیف بر چیست؟ فرستادن پیغامبران علیهم السّلام چرا؟ اوامر و نواهی بر کجا؟ شرایع و احکام چون رانم؟! عدل و شریعت کو؟! تو بی سببی مال درویشان تلف می‌کنی! بی موجبی خون ناحق ریزی! بی مزدی کار کسان کنی! و گویی بحکم علم کنم، بحکم ارادت و مشیت کنم: فَأَرَدتُّ أَنْ أَعِيبَهَا (۱۸:۷۹)، أَرَدْنَا أَن يُبْدِلَهُمَا رَبُّهُمَا خَيْرًا مِّنْهُ زَكَاةً (۱۸:۸۱)، فَأَرَادَ رَبُّكَ أَن يَبْلُغَا أَشُدَّهُمَا (۱۸:۸۲). مرا

---

[۱۳۵] عبارتی است از دعای هفتم صحیفهٔ سجادیه. این اشاره خود مبنای تحقیق مفصل‌تری است دربارهٔ جایگاه صحیفهٔ سجادیه نزد اسماعیلیان نزاری. در بخش *تهذیب اخلاق* از *روضه*، نویسنده تقریباً این فصل را به طور کامل اختصاص به نقل فرازهایی از *صحیفهٔ سجادیه* داده است. موارد متعددی از نقل فرازهایی از ادعیهٔ *صحیفه* در *اخلاق محتشمی* نیز موجود است. مجمل کلام این‌که بی‌شک با توجه به کثرت نقل ادعیهٔ *صحیفه* این آثار امام زین العابدین در زمرهٔ منابع مهم اعتقادی و مناسکی نزاریان بوده‌اند. این تعلق خاطر به ادعیهٔ *صحیفه* در سال‌های نخستین دعوت نزاریان به طور مشخص سابقه‌اش در همین اثر حاضر شهرستانی موجود است.

[۱۳۶] ق: آنچ.

[۱۳۷] ق: آنچ.

تکلیف کجا ماند؟ حکم شریعت چون شود؟ کن و مکن بر کجا نشیند؟

[۹۶] خضر گوید: ای موسی! تو را آن‌جا غلط افتاده است که تو یک حکم دانسته‌ای.[۱۳۸] خدای را تعالی در مجاری احکام دو حکم است. یکی حکم مفروغ، یکی مستأنف. یکی پرداخته، یکی می‌پردازد. یکی تقدیر رفته، یکی تکلیف می‌رود. یکی: وَتَمَّتْ كَلِمَتُ رَبِّكَ صِدْقًا وَعَدْلًا لَّا مُبَدِّلَ لِكَلِمَاتِهِ (۶:۱۱۵). یکی وَجَعَلَ كَلِمَةَ الَّذِينَ كَفَرُوا السُّفْلَىٰ وَكَلِمَةُ اللَّـهِ هِيَ الْعُلْيَا (۹:۴۰). یکی مَا يُبَدَّلُ الْقَوْلُ لَدَيَّ (۵۰:۲۹). یکی وَإِذَا بَدَّلْنَا آيَةً مَّكَانَ آيَةٍ (۱۶:۱۰۱). و چنان که دو حکم هست، دو حاکم هست. دو قاضی هست. یکی قاضی که بحکم خویش کار کند. یکی قاضی که بدو مرد گواه و سوگند کار کند.[۱۳۹] یکی قاضی شریعت و یکی قاضی قیامت. حکم قاضی شریعت، عدل در شریعت. حکم قاضی قیامت، عدل در قیامت. عدل شریعت،

---

[۱۳۸] ج: داشته‌ای.

[۱۳۹] ج این عبارت را در قلاب اضافه کرده است: یکی قاضی که به علم خود و مشیت کار کند.

گواه و سوگند. عدل قیامت، علم و مشیّت. تو قاضی شریعتی؛ تا نبینی یا نشنوی، حکم مکن. من نایب قاضی قیامتم؛ چون دانستم حکم کردم. چون خواستم کار کردم. تو را، إعملوا تؤجروا – تا کار نکنی، مزد نیابی. تا مزد نستانی، کار نکنی. من بی مزد کار کنم؛ بی کار مزد ستانم: وکلٌ مُیَسَّرٌ لما خُلِقَ له.[۱۴۰]

[۹۷] موسی گوید: چون حال چنین است، فایدهٔ تکلیف چه؟ چون کارها همه پرداخته‌اند، فایدهٔ پرداختن چه؟ چون مسلمان خود بوده است، فایدهٔ أسْلِم چه؟ چون کافر خود بوده است. فایدهٔ لا تکفر چه؟ چون وَسَوَاءٌ عَلَيْهِمْ أَأَنذَرْتَهُمْ أَمْ لَمْ تُنذِرْهُمْ لَا يُؤْمِنُونَ (۳۶:۱۰) آمده است. فایدهٔ قُمْ فَأَنذِرْ (۷۴:۲) [چه]؟ چون کلمه رفته است، جز از آن نباشد که رفته است؟ این دیگر حکم چه سود دارد؟ اگر این حکم، این حکم را بر نمی‌دارد، پس در تکلیف ظلم لازم می‌آید.

---

[۱۴۰] حدیث نبوی. بنگرید به: خلیل مأمون شیحا (بیروت: ۲۰۱۳)، موسوعة *المعجم المفهرس لألفاظ النبوي الشريف للكتب الستة*، ج. ۱۸، ص. ۱۵۰.

[۹۸] و خضر گوید: تکلیف، مظهر تقدیرست. و تقدیر، مصدر تکلیف. آن‌چه در تقدیرست، ظاهر نگردد الا بتکلیف. و آن‌چه در تکلیف است، موجود نگردد الا بتقدیر. پس فایده با دید آمد: مفروغ در مستأنف پدیدار آمد و مستأنف از مفروغ پدیدار آمد. پس مفروغ و مستأنف هر دو بهم مفروغ است، و مع ذلک مفروغ مفروغ و مستأنف مستأنف. من حاکم مفروغم و تو حاکم مستأنف. من مرد تأویلم و تو مرد تنزیل. من بر باطن حکم کنم، تو بر ظاهر و هر دو حکم بهم حق: و کل مجتهدٍ مصیّب. این‌جا روشن شد که نه حکمِ من حکمِ تو را بردارد، نه حکمِ تو حکمِ مرا بردارد. نه از حکمِ من عجز لازم می‌آید و نه از حکمِ تو ظلم. مَا يُبَدَّلُ الْقَوْلُ لَدَيَّ (۲۹:۵۰)، تا بدانی که عجز نیست. وَمَا أَنَا بِظَلَّامٍ لِّلْعَبِيدِ (۲۹:۵۰)، تا بدانی که ظلم نیست. چون در عالم خیر هست مطلق و شری هست مطلق، و خیری و شری باضافت، آن‌چه خیر مطلق است گوهری است که هرگز بنگردد، و آن‌چه شر مطلق است هم گوهری است که[۱۴۱] بنگردد.

---

[۱۴۱] ج: هرگز را اضافه دارد. م: ندارد.

و آن‌چه خیر و شر باضافت است در او[۱۴۲] گردش در آید. پس از این سبب هر چه نیک است و بنگردد، مفروغ است و هر چه می‌گردد، مستأنف است.

[۹۹] آن دو یتیم که گنج داشتند از حیّزِ خیر مطلق بودند. لاجرم دو شخص بزرگوار را بر ماندگی و گرسنگی کار ایشان بایست کرد تا نشان گنج ایشان پوشیده نگردد. و آن کودک طفل از حیّزِ شرّ مطلق بود: کان الغلام الذي قتله الخضر علیه السّلام مطبوعاً علی الکفر. لاجرم سرش ببریدند در حال طفولیّت. اینک نشانهٔ او بنگر که بر او نوشته است: کافر مطبوع. و آن کشتی مسکینان دریا که غاصب بخواست ستدن بر حد امکان بود از حیّزِ خیر اضافی و شرّ اضافی: وَمَا فَعَلْتُهُ عَنْ أَمْرِي ذَٰلِكَ تَأْوِيلُ مَا لَمْ تَسْطِع عَّلَيْهِ صَبْرًا (۱۸:۸۲).

[۱۰۰] موسی علیه السّلام می‌گوید: این دو حکمی و دو کونی[۱۴۳] که تو می‌گویی درست شد، و این‌جا یک سؤال بمانده

---

[۱۴۲] ج: «او» راندارد. م و ق: درو، که به رسم‌الخط حاضر نوشته‌ایم.

[۱۴۳] اشاره می‌کند به «کون مشابهت» و «کون مباینت» که اصطلاحات جا افتادهٔ اسماعیلی هستند. در بندهای بعدی هم همین تعابیر به کار رفته است.

است و آن که کدام حکم اصل است و کدام فرع و کدام قول متقدم است و کدام متأخر و کدام حکم سر[144] دیگر حکم در آمده است و محیط گشته و کدام حکم محاط است و کدام کلی است و کدام جزوی یا خود هر دو حکم متساوی‌اند؟

[۱۰۱] خضر می‌گوید: سؤال از سؤال در نگسلد هرگز[145] تا مرد کلمة الفصل نشنود. و اگر مرا بمعلمی تسلیم کرده و خود بمتعلمی آمده، بهمه حال تسلیمت باید کرد که من چیزی دانم که تو ندانی و چیزی کنم که تو را خوش نیاید. اگر اعتراضی کنی، آن تسلیم باطل کردی و اگر خاموش باشی از علم آن خبر محروم مانی.[146] والصبر علی ما لم یعلم حتی یعلم سخت کاری است. کارِ مردانِ کار است. این‌جا که خود را متعلم گفتی و مرا بمعلم داشتی بمفروغ و مستأنف بگفتی. که مفروغ کمال است و مستأنف نقصان متوجه بکمال. مفروغ مردِ کاملْ

---

[144] ج: بر.

[145] ج: ندارد.

[146] مقایسه کنید با *مفاتیح* (ص. ۶۴۶): « ومن کان قائلا بالأمر بعد الخلق ومتّبعا لصاحب الأمر حقّ الاتّباع لم یخطر بباله لم وکیف، ومذهب قوم من لم یقل لأستاذه: لم؟ لم یعلم شیئا أبدا، ومذهب قوم من قال لأستاذه: لم؟ لم یفلح أبدا».

خلقت، مستأنف نطفهٔ متوجه بکمال. مفروغ عالم است، مستأنف متعلم. مفروغ پیامبر است، مستأنف امت. عالم محیط، متعلم محاط. پیامبر کل، امت جزو. کل متقدم بر جزو، جزو متأخر از کل.

[۱۰۲] تنزیل و تأویل، و اول و آخر، و ظاهر و باطن بر این میزان می‌دان. و ترتب میان هر یکی می‌شناس تا تو را هیچ اشکالی بنماند در هیچ حال در هیچ مسأله که هر که این دو حکم و دو کونی[۱۴۷] بنشناخت، همواره در ظلمات شبهات مانده باشد[۱۴۸]. گاهی تشبیهش می‌کشد بکون مشابهت. گاهی تعطیلش می‌کشد بکون مباینت[۱۴۹]. گاهی جبرش می‌کشد

[۱۴۷] بنگرید به یادداشت قبلی. این‌جا نیز در نسخه‌ها «دو گونی» آمده است که به شکل «دو کونی» ضبط کردیم به سیاق عبارت قبل و بعد همین متن.

[۱۴۸] بنگرید به *هفت باب* حسن محمود، ص. ۳۲: بندهای ۶۳ و ۶۴.

[۱۴۹] در باب تعابیر «کون مشابهت» و «کون مباینت»، علاوه بر *مفاتیح* شهرستانی، بنگرید به *آغاز و انجام* طوسی، ص. ۵۱ (بند ۲۴): «پس قیامت روز جمع است: يَوْمَ يَجْمَعُكُمْ لِيَوْمِ الْجَمْعِ (۹:۶۴) و به وجهی روز فصل است چه دنیا کون مشابهت است، در وی حق و باطل مشابه نمایند، متخاصمان در مقابل یکدیگر نشسته‌اند. آخرت کون مباینت است: وَيَوْمَ تَقُومُ السَّاعَةُ يَوْمَئِذٍ يَتَفَرَّقُونَ (۱۴:۳۰)، حق از باطل جدا کنند: لِيَمِيزَ اللَّهُ

بکون مفروغ و قَدَرش لازم می‌آید. گاهی قَدَرش می کشد بکون مستأنف و جبرش لازم می‌آید. گاهی سمعش می کشد بنیابت سمع، گاهی عقلش می کشد بنیابت عقل.

[۱۰۳] و شبهات عالمیان خود بیش از این سه مسأله نیست: یا تشبیه یا تعطیل؛ یا جبر یا قدر؛ یا سمع یا عقل. از این سه حادثه همهٔ شبهات برخاست. همهٔ علوم روشن گشت. و هر که یک حکم می کند، یک چشم می‌آید، اعور[۱۵۰]: بأیّ عینیه شاء.

[۱۰۴] چون میان موسی و خضر علیهما السّلام این مناظره با مفصل آمد و از یکدیگر جدا می گشتند، آهوی از بیابان بیامد و میان هر دو بزرگوار بایستاد. یک نیم او پخته و یک نیم خام. پخته روی سوی خضر داشته و خام رو سوی موسی.

الْخَبِيثَ مِنَ الطَّيِّبِ (۳۷:۸)، خصومت متخاصمان فصل کنند و به حقیقت حق و بطلان باطل حکم کنند: لِيَهْلِكَ مَنْ هَلَكَ عَن بَيِّنَةٍ وَيَحْيَىٰ مَنْ حَيَّ عَن بَيِّنَةٍ (۴۲:۸)، لِيُحِقَّ الْحَقَّ وَيُبْطِلَ الْبَاطِلَ (۸:۸). پس قیامت روز فصل استٌ و آن فصل اقتضای جمع می کند که در پیش بیامد: هَٰذَا يَوْمُ الْفَصْلِ جَمَعْنَاكُمْ وَالْأَوَّلِينَ (۳۸:۷۷)» (صص. ۵۱-۵۰).

[۱۵۰] بیتی از ناصر خسرو با همین مضمون داریم: هر که در تنزیل بی تأویل رفت | او به چشم راست در دین اعور است.

[۱۰۵] خضر گفت: ای موسی! اگر می‌خواهی که از گوشت او بخوری، برخیز و آتش بزن و هیزم بیار و آتش برافروز. گوشت خام پخته کن[151] تا بتوانی خوردن. و خضر خود دست کرد و از آن پخته می‌خورد.

[۱۰۶] من از تفسیر آن می‌خواندم بوقت جوانی.[152] می گفتم آیا این چه مثل تواند بود؟ تا چون خبر جبر و قدر بشنودم که میان بوبکر و عمر رفته بود که پیغامبر صلی الله علیه و آله بر ایشان انکار کرد و گفت: أبهذا أمرتم هلا تکلمتم فی ملک خلقه الله تعالی نصفه من النار ونصفه من الثلج. فلا النار یذیب الثلج لا الثلج یطفیء النار تسبیحه سبحان من جمع بین النار والثلج.[153] آن فریشته که یک نیمه از آتش آفریده

[151] هکذا در ق و ج.

[152] در م: من از تفسیر این فرود آمدم به وقت جوانی.

[153] شهرستانی در *مفاتیح* نیز همین حدیث را آورده است در عبارات زیر: «اعلم أنّ المفروغ والمستأنف إنما أُخذ من الشیخین العمرین أبي بکر وعمر – رضوان اللّه علیها – حیث تکلما فی القدر، وارتفعت أصواتهما حتّی بلغ النبيَّ – صلّی اللّه علیه وآله – صوتهما وهو في الحجرة، فخرج إلیهما، ووجنتاه کأنهما رمّانةً شقّت بنصفین؛ فقال – علیه وآله السلام «فیم أنتم؟» قالوا: نتکلّم في القدر. قال: «هلّا تکلمتم في مَلَکٍ خلقه اللّه

است و یک نیمه از برف، همین است یک نیمهٔ پخته و یک نیمهٔ خام.

[۱۰۷] ای موسی! چون تو در عالم اسبابی، نیابت خامی می‌داری، نیابت مستأنف. برخیز و آتش بیار، و گوشت خام پخته کن تا بخوری! و چون من در عالم بی سببی‌ام، نیابت پختگی می‌دارم، نیابت مفروغ، مرا پخته می‌باید خورد. و در عالم من همهٔ کارها پخته است. همهٔ درخت‌ها ببار آمده. همهٔ میوه‌ها برسیده. همهٔ بودنی‌ها ببوده. همهٔ عقل‌ها کامل.[۱۵٤] همهٔ نفس‌ها تمام. همهٔ مزاج‌ها معتدل. اگر کشتی شکنم، درستی را شکنم. و اگر کودک کشم، زندگی را کشم. و اگر دیوار نو کنم، گنج را نو می‌کنم. تو که موسی‌ای همین سه حالت در خود

تعالی نصفه من نار ونصفه من ثلج، فلا النار تذیبُ الثلج، ولا الثلج یطفیء النار، تسبیحُهُ سبحان من جمع بین النار والثلج». فقام إلیه عمر حتّی جلس عنده، وقال: یا رسول اللّه! أنحن في أمر مبتدأ أم نحن في أمرٍ مفروغٍ؟ وفي روایةٍ قال: الأمر أنف؟ فقال – علیه السّلام - «نحن في أمرٍ مفروغٍ عنه». فقالَ عمر: إن کان الأمر قد فُرغ منه ففیمَ العمل إذاً؟ فقالَ – علیهِ وآله السلام - «یا عمر! اعملوا وکلّ میَسّرٌ لما خلق له» (*مفاتیح*، ص. ۵۴).

[۱۵٤] م: تمام.

دیده‌ای. کشتی تو، تن تو بود. الواحِ کشتی، اعضاء تن تو. مسکینان کشتی، معانی که در تن تو است. غاصب، فرعون بود. خضر، جبرییل. که دست تو بآتش برد تا در دهان نهادی زبانت بسوخت. و زبان یک لوح بود از الواح کشتی تا غاصب در گذشت. کشتی بمسکینان بماند. دیگر حادثهٔ کشتن غلام همچون کشتن آن قبطی بود که بی جرمی مشت زدی و بکشتی تا سبب آن شد که بگریختی و بمرتبهٔ نبوت رسیدی. و سه دیگر حادثهٔ دیوار: راهی دراز رفته بودی و مانده و گرسنه بسر چاهی رسیدی که شبانان گوسفندان آب می‌دادند. بر ماندگی و گرسنگی آن دو دختر شعیب را یاری دادی تا گوسفندان ایشان آب خوردند. و مزدی نخواستی. آن چرا بود؟ وَأَبُونَا شَيْخٌ كَبِيرٌ (۲۳:۲۸). همین که من گفتم: و کان ابوهما صالحاً. چون آن حالت بر تو رفته بود، چرا بر من آن حالت انکار کردی؟ و همین سه حالت بر هر کسی می‌گذرد. دل مؤمن شکسته به: أنا عند المنکسرة قلوبهم.[۱۵۵]

---

[۱۵۵] ج: «من اجلی» را اضافه دارد.

[۱۰۸] مراحلی با شیطان در گذرد، دل بساکنان دل بماند. نفس هوای مؤمن کشتنی است که مبادا اگر او قوت گیرد، پدر و مادر عقل و نظر[156] را از راه ببرد و بهوای خود کشد تا بدل نفس هویٰ، ما او را نفس مطمئنه باز دهیم. باز دیوار حول و قوت او کندنی است، و نو کردنی که در زیر آن دیوار گنجی است: لا حول ولا قوة الا باللّه کنز من کنوز الجنة. و آن گنج دو کلمه راست، و هر دو یتیم آن عالم. یکی کلمهٔ توحید، یکی کلمهٔ نبوت. یکی لا إله إلّا اللّه، یکی محمّد رسول الله. و پدر ایشان امر اول و اگر پدر و مادر گویی قلم و لوح که یکی مردی است و دیگر یک قابل. یکی فاعل و دیگر منفعل. دیگر باره گنج پرگوهر، قرآن. دیوار که نشان گنج است، انسان. الرَّحْمَـٰنُ عَلَّمَ الْقُرْآنَ خَلَقَ الْإِنسَانَ (۵۵: ۱-۳). هر گاه دیوار بخواهد افتاد، دو شخص بزرگوار نو کنند. گاهی انسان، نشان قرآن، و قرآن گنج. گاهی قرآن نشان انسان، و انسان گنج. امیر المؤمنین علی علیه السّلام جمع قرآن می کرد که در زیر آن گنجی است از بهر

---

[156] م: «و نظر» را ندارد.

دو یتیم. یعنی حسن و حسین علیهما السّلام. وکان أبوهما صالحاً - وأبوهما خیر منهما. یکی گنج تنزیل، یکی گنج تأویل. یکی گنج ایستاده یکی گنج روان. هما إمامان قاما أو قعدا و صلّی الله علی محمّد و آله الطاهرین.

***

نقل من نسخة منقولة من نسخة منقولة من نسخة بخط الامام تاج‌الدین محمد بن عبدالکریم الشهرستانی و مع هذا کانت النسخة سقیمة وأصلحت ما أمکن إصلاحه عند النقل.[۱۵۷]

---

[۱۵۷] م: نقل من خط مولانا قطب الدین الشیرازی وکتب بخطه نقل من نسخة منقولة من نسخة بخط الامام تاج الدین محمّد بن عبدالکریم الشهرستانی و مع هذا کانت النسخة سقیمة وأصلحت ما أمکن إصلاحه عند النقل. از عبارت موجود در انتهای این نسخه بر می‌آید که قطب‌الدین شیرازی متن را از روی نسخهٔ سوم بازنویسی کرده است. نسخه‌های بعدی این سلسلهٔ استنساخ را نیاورده‌اند. ج: نقل من خط مولانا قطب الدین الشیرازی ومع هذا کانت النسخة سقیمة وأصلحت ما أمکن إصلاحه عند النقل.

نمایه‌ی آیات قرآنی

آتِنَا غَدَاءَنَا لَقَدْ لَقِينَا مِن سَفَرِنَا هَـٰذَا نَصَبًا (۶۲:۱۸)، ۸۲

أَنَّا كُلَّ شَيْءٍ خَلَقْنَاهُ بِقَدَرٍ وَمَا أَمْرُنَا إِلَّا وَاحِدَةٌ كَلَمْحٍ بِالْبَصَرِ (۵۰: ۵۴-۴۹)، ۳

أَرَدْنَا أَن يُبْدِلَهُمَا رَبُّهُمَا خَيْرًا مِّنْهُ زَكَاةً (۸۱:۱۸)، ۹۵

إِنَّ الَّذِينَ قَالُوا رَبُّنَا اللَّـهُ ثُمَّ اسْتَقَامُوا تَتَنَزَّلُ عَلَيْهِمُ الْمَلَائِكَةُ (۴۱:۳۰)، ۳۸

إِنَّ هَـٰذَا لَفِي الصُّحُفِ الْأُولَىٰ صُحُفِ إِبْرَاهِيمَ وَمُوسَىٰ (۸۷: ۱۹-۱۸)، ۸

إِنَّا هَدَيْنَاهُ السَّبِيلَ إِمَّا شَاكِرًا وَإِمَّا كَفُورًا (۷۶:۳)، ۲۲

إِنَّمَا أَمْرُهُ إِذَا أَرَادَ شَيْئًا أَن يَقُولَ لَهُ كُن فَيَكُونُ (۳۶:۸۲)، ۱

إِنِّي رَأَيْتُ أَحَدَ عَشَرَ كَوْكَبًا وَالشَّمْسَ وَالْقَمَرَ رَأَيْتُهُمْ لِي سَاجِدِينَ (۱۲:۴)، ۶۲

ثُمَّ رَدَدْنَاهُ أَسْفَلَ سَافِلِينَ إِلَّا الَّذِينَ آمَنُوا وَعَمِلُوا الصَّالِحَاتِ (۹۵: ۶-۵)، ۴۰

وَسَوَاءٌ عَلَيْهِمْ أَأَنذَرْتَهُمْ أَمْ لَمْ تُنذِرْهُمْ لَا يُؤْمِنُونَ (۳۶:۱۰)، ۹۷

الْحَيُّ الْقَيُّومُ (۲:۲۵۵)، ۷۶

وَإِذَا بَدَّلْنَا آيَةً مَّكَانَ آيَةٍ (١٦:١٠١)، ٩٦
وَتَمَّتْ كَلِمَتُ رَبِّكَ صِدْقًا وَعَدْلًا لَّا مُبَدِّلَ لِكَلِمَاتِهِ (٦:١١٥)، ٩٦
وَجَعَلَ كَلِمَةَ الَّذِينَ كَفَرُوا السُّفْلَىٰ وَكَلِمَةُ اللَّـهِ هِيَ الْعُلْيَا (٩:٤٠)، ٩٦
وَحَيْثُ مَا كُنتُمْ فَوَلُّوا وُجُوهَكُمْ شَطْرَهُ (٢:١٤٤)، ٥١
وَعَلَّمَكَ مَا لَمْ تَكُن تَعْلَمُ (٤:١١٣)، ٤٦
وَكَذَٰلِكَ نُرِي إِبْرَاهِيمَ مَلَكُوتَ السَّمَاوَاتِ وَالْأَرْضِ وَلِيَكُونَ مِنَ الْمُوقِنِينَ (٦:٧٥)، ٥٩
وَلَا يُحِيطُونَ بِشَيْءٍ مِّنْ عِلْمِهِ إِلَّا بِمَا شَاءَ (٢:٢٥٥)، ٧٦
وَلَا يَذْكُرُونَ اللَّـهَ إِلَّا قَلِيلًا (٤:١٤٢)، ٧٤
وَلِلَّـهِ غَيْبُ السَّمَاوَاتِ وَالْأَرْضِ (١١:١٢٣)، ٥٦
وَلِلَّـهِ مُلْكُ السَّمَاوَاتِ وَالْأَرْضِ (٣:١٨٩)، ٥٦
وَلَوْ كُنتُ أَعْلَمُ الْغَيْبَ (٧:١٨٨)، ٤٦
وَمَا فَعَلْتُهُ عَنْ أَمْرِي ذَٰلِكَ تَأْوِيلُ مَا لَمْ تَسْطِع عَّلَيْهِ صَبْرًا (١٨:٨٢)، ٩٩
وَنُنشِئَكُمْ فِي مَا لَا تَعْلَمُونَ وَلَقَدْ عَلِمْتُمُ النَّشْأَةَ الْأُولَىٰ فَلَوْلَا تَذَكَّرُونَ (٥٦: ٦١-٦٢)، ٢٧

وَيَتَفَكَّرُونَ فِي خَلْقِ السَّمَاوَاتِ وَالْأَرْضِ (۳:۱۹۱)، ۱۶
هَلْ أَتَّبِعُكَ عَلَىٰ أَن تُعَلِّمَنِ مِمَّا عُلِّمْتَ رُشْدًا (۱۸:۶۶)، ۸۳
هَلْ أُنَبِّئُكُمْ عَلَىٰ مَن تَنَزَّلُ الشَّيَاطِينُ تَنَزَّلُ عَلَىٰ كُلِّ أَفَّاكٍ أَثِيمٍ (۲۶: ۲۲۲-۲۲۱)، ۳۸
يا بَنِي آدَمَ إِمَّا يَأْتِيَنَّكُمْ رُسُلٌ مِّنكُمْ يَقُصُّونَ عَلَيْكُمْ آيَاتِي فَمَنِ اتَّقَىٰ وَأَصْلَحَ فَلَا خَوْفٌ عَلَيْهِمْ وَلَا هُمْ يَحْزَنُونَ (۷:۳۵)، ۵۶
اسْتَوَىٰ عَلَى الْعَرْشِ يُدَبِّرُ الْأَمْرَ (۳:۱۰)، ۴۳
اسْجُدُوا لِآدَمَ (۲:۳۴)، ۴۲، ۶۷
أَلَا لَهُ الْخَلْقُ وَالْأَمْرُ (۷:۵۴)، ۱، ۵۵
إِلَيْهِ يَصْعَدُ الْكَلِمُ الطَّيِّبُ (۳۵:۱۰)، ۱۶
أَمَّا مَا يَنفَعُ النَّاسَ فَيَمْكُثُ فِي الْأَرْضِ (۱۳:۱۷)، ۱۶
أَمْشَاجٍ نَّبْتَلِيهِ (۲:۷۶)، ۲۲
إِن كُلُّ نَفْسٍ لَّمَّا عَلَيْهَا حَافِظٌ (۴:۸۶)، ۳۶
إِنَّكَ لَن تَسْتَطِيعَ مَعِيَ صَبْرًا (۱۸:۶۷)، ۸۴
إِنَّمَا أَنتَ مُنذِرٌ وَلِكُلِّ قَوْمٍ هَادٍ (۱۳:۷)، ۲۴
إِنِّي وَجَّهْتُ وَجْهِيَ (۶:۷۹)، ۶۰
ثُمَّ جَعَلْنَاهُ (۲۳:۱۳)، ۷۹

خَلَقَ الْإِنسَانَ (٥٥:٣)، ٦٨
خَلْقًا آخَرَ (٢٣:١٤)، ٢٥
خَلَقْتَنِي مِن نَّارٍ وَخَلَقْتَهُ مِن طِينٍ (٧:١٢)، ٦٩
ذَلِكَ الْكِتَابُ لَا رَيْبَ فِيهِ (٢:٢)، ٩٠
الَّذِي أَعْطَىٰ كُلَّ شَيْءٍ خَلْقَهُ ثُمَّ هَدَىٰ (٢٠:٥٠)، ٦، ٧
الَّذِي خَلَقَ فَسَوَّىٰ وَالَّذِي قَدَّرَ فَهَدَىٰ (٨٧: ٢-٣)، ٦، ٧، ٨
الَّذِي خَلَقَكَ فَسَوَّاكَ فَعَدَلَكَ (٨٢:٧)، ٨
الَّذِي خَلَقَنِي فَهُوَ يَهْدِينِ (٢٦:٧٨)، ٦، ٧
رَبِّ إِنِّي لِمَا أَنزَلْتَ إِلَيَّ مِنْ خَيْرٍ فَقِيرٌ (٢٨:٢٤)، ٨٢
رَبَّنَا آمَنَّا بِمَا أَنزَلْتَ وَاتَّبَعْنَا الرَّسُولَ (٣:٥٣)، ١٣
رَبَّنَا إِنَّكَ تَعْلَمُ مَا نُخْفِي وَمَا نُعْلِنُ (١٤:٣٨)، ٦٣
الرَّحْمَٰنُ عَلَّمَ الْقُرْآنَ (٥٥: ١-٢)، ٦٦
الرَّحْمَٰنُ عَلَّمَ الْقُرْآنَ خَلَقَ الْإِنسَانَ (٥٥: ١-٣)، ١٠٨
سَمِعْنَا وَأَطَعْنَا (٥:٧)، ٤٨، ٥٢
شِرْعَةً وَمِنْهَاجًا (٥:٤٨) ، ٢٢
عَلَّمَ الْقُرْآنَ (٥٥:٢)، ٦٨
علىٰ مِّلَّةَ أَبِيكُمْ إِبْرَاهِيمَ (٢٢:٧٨)، ٢٦

اللَّـهُمَّ مَالِكَ الْمُلْكِ (٣:٢٦)، ٥٦
مَا عَلِمْتُ لَكُم مِّنْ إِلَـٰهٍ غَيْرِي (٢٨:٣٨)، ٦٩
مَا مَنَعَكَ أَلَّا تَسْجُدَ إِذْ أَمَرْتُكَ (٧:١٢)، ٦٩
مَا يُبَدَّلُ الْقَوْلُ لَدَيَّ (٥٠:٢٩)، ٩٦، ٩٨
نَاكِسُوا رُؤُوسِهِمْ عِندَ رَبِّهِمْ (٣٢:١٢)، ٣٩
وَالظَّاهِرُ وَالْبَاطِنُ (٥٧:٣)، ٤
وَأَبُونَا شَيْخٌ كَبِيرٌ (٢٨:٢٣)، ١٠٧
وَإِنَّ عَلَيْكَ اللَّعْنَةَ إِلَىٰ يَوْمِ الدِّينِ (١٥:٣٥)، ٧٠
وَإِنَّكَ لَتَهْدِي (٤٢:٥٢)، ٢٢
وُجُوهٌ يَوْمَئِذٍ نَّاضِرَةٌ إِلَىٰ رَبِّهَا نَاظِرَةٌ (٧٥: ٢٢-٢٣)، ٥٠
وَكَيْفَ تَصْبِرُ عَلَىٰ مَا لَمْ تُحِطْ بِهِ خُبْرًا (١٨:٦٨)، ٨٤
وَلَا تَجِدُ أَكْثَرَهُمْ شَاكِرِينَ (٧:١٧)، ٧٤
وَلَئِن سَأَلْتَهُم مَّنْ خَلَقَهُمْ لَيَقُولُنَّ اللَّـهُ (٤٣:٨٧)، ٦٩
وَلَقَدْ خَلَقْنَا الْإِنسَانَ (٢٣:١٢)، ٧٨
وَلِلَّـهِ جُنُودُ السَّمَاوَاتِ وَالْأَرْضِ (٤٨:٤)، ٥٦
وَلِلَّـهِ خَزَائِنُ السَّمَاوَاتِ وَالْأَرْضِ (٦٣:٧)، ٥٦
وَمَا أَمْرُنَا إِلَّا وَاحِدَةٌ (٥٤:٥٠)، ٧٩

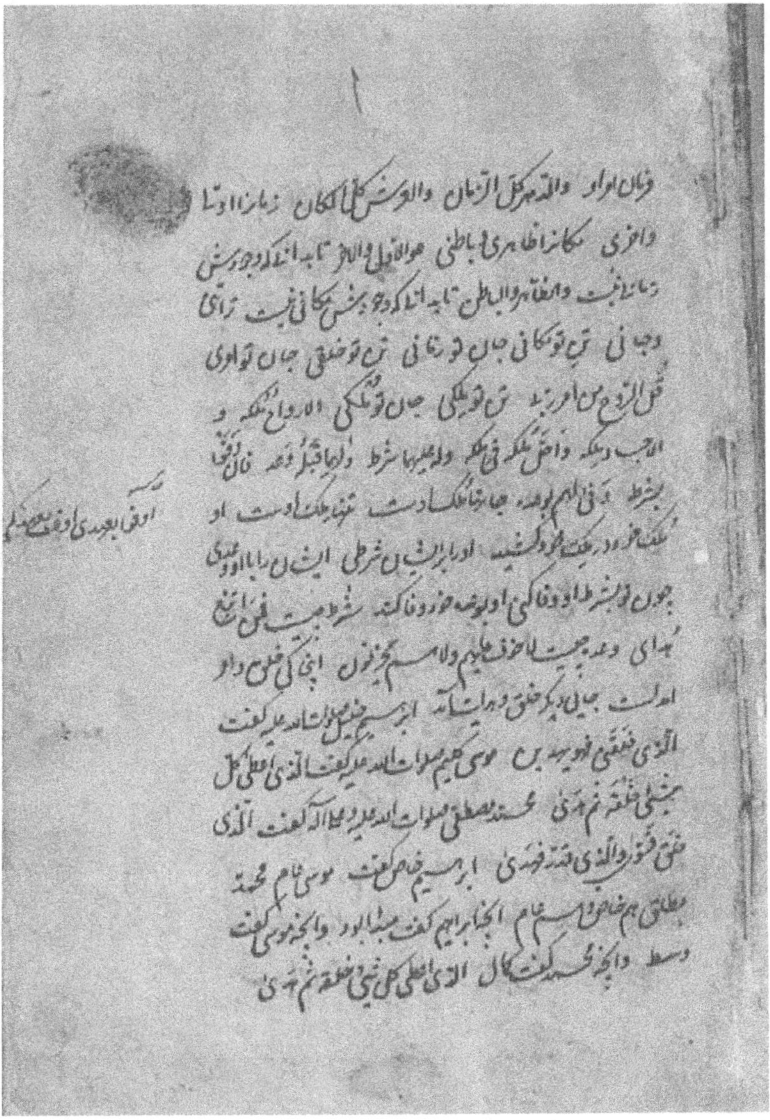

The opening page of a manuscript of the *Majlis-i maktūb*, Ms no. 593, dated 1060/1650, held at the Library of the National Consultative Assembly, Tehran.